Preaching the word of God is essentiall
Mouths and ears are of course involv
is verbal and not visual. But preacl
preacher engaging with the mind of the hearer by way of imparting
information; much less is it the will of the preacher imposing itself on
that of the hearer. It is a real 'heart to heart' - the preacher pours out
the whole of himself along with the content of his message, which is
so phrased and directed that the hearer will take it to himself with
open arms.

Dr Capill's book is a most instructive and stirring study of this kind
of sermonic address which is becoming increasingly rare. Not
surprisingly, he goes back to the 17th century for an example of it and
chooses Richard Baxter who aimed to speak 'as a dying man to dying
men, never sure to preach again'. Capill, however, deals with him in
such a way that it is as if Baxter is speaking today - to preachers and
hearers of the word alike.

A most important book which one hopes will find the place which
it deserves among the (too) many on the subject of Preaching - and
also help produce a new generation of preachers.

Hywel R Jones
Professor of Practical Theology
Westminster Theological Seminary in California

Capill writes out of concern for the church and the pulpit. He sees in
Richard Baxter of the 17th century a model of preaching that still
instructs today. His fine analysis of Baxter is thorough, accurate and
insightful. Capill's many deft quotations from Baxter himself enable
the reader to hear Baxter for themselves. His applications to the
preacher of today are forceful and telling. He is interested not in
preaching that merely entertains or simply informs the mind, but in
preaching that touches the hearts of people to the everlasting benefit
and God's greater glory. As a preacher myself I found in this book
enormous profit and recommend it to readers with enthusiasm.

Graham Cole
Professor of Biblical and Systematic Theology
Trinity Evangelical Divinity School
Former Principle of Ridely College Melbourne

Preaching with Spiritual Vigour

including lessons from the life
and practice of Richard Baxter

Murray A. Capill

Mentor

ISBN 1 85792 857 1

© Murray A. Capill

Published in 2003
by
Christian Focus Publications,
Geanies House, Fearn, Ross-shire,
IV20 1TW, Great Britain.

www.christianfocus.com

Cover design by Alister Macinnes

Printed and bound by
Bell & Bain Ltd, Glasgow

Contents

Acknowledgements

This book really began as a project largely intended for my own benefit. It was a study fueled by my desire to learn more about how to preach and apply God's Word with power, and by the need I felt to be fed and stretched in my own preaching ministry. Having long been drawn to the Puritans and their successors, it seemed best to turn to one of them to learn more about vigourous preaching.

What has unfolded since then has been more rewarding than I could ever have imagined. It has been a great privilege to be able to invest considerable amounts of time studying the writings of Richard Baxter. The opportunity to become familiar with his passion for experimental preaching has been immensely challenging, inspiring and humbling. Now also, the opportunity to share this study with others is most gratifying, and if it can be used to strengthen the ministries of other preachers too, I will be deeply thankful to God.

For the privilege of undertaking this study I am indebted to a number of people. First and foremost, to the elders and congregation at the Reformed Presbyterian Church of Bucklands Beach. They allowed me time and gave me every encouragement to pursue this study, so as to be better equipped to minister God's Word. More than that, throughout my ten years of ministry there, they displayed a love of, and hunger for, the preaching of God's Word that spurred me on and sustained my own love of preaching. To my many precious friends in the congregation, to those who prayed for their preacher, and to those who gave much encouragement, I offer my deepest thanks.

Secondly, I am grateful to the late Tom and Grace Stewart, whose sponsorship enabled me to take up this study at Westminster Theological Seminary in California; to Dr. Joseph Pipa for his personal encouragement and the stimulation of his lectures on the theology of preaching; to Dr. Sally Davey for her detailed and insightful critique of the manuscript; to Dr. Andrew Young, with whom interaction has so often been a source of stimulation; to my brother, Rev. Graham

Capill, not only for his thorough reading of the manuscript but his much-valued friendship; and to my parents who gave helpful comments on the manuscript, and long before that introduced me to the Lord, to Reformed thinking and to the importance of vigourous preaching.

Finally, and most importantly, I wish to acknowledge my deepest gratitude to my wife, Wendy, and our five lovely children. They have selflessly allowed me much time in the study. More than that, apart from the Lord, they are the most constant source of joy in my life.

Introduction

One of the greatest needs of the church today is a multiplication of biblical preaching ministries that are lively, powerful and spiritually vigourous.

In many a church you can find preaching that is topical and contemporary, but light on biblical substance. You can easily find preaching that is personal, but in a largely subjective or emotional way. You may well find preaching that is solidly biblical, yet rather lifeless, even dreary. But to find clear, powerful preaching of the Word that grips your heart and leaves you not so much feeling that you have been in the presence of a great communicator as in the presence of a great God, not so much entertained by a man as enthralled by the truth of God – that, it seems, is all too rare.

The Current Crisis
The reason for this paucity of truly powerful preaching may well stem from preachers having become overly concerned with the wrong thing. Preachers have been grappling with a fundamental crisis in preaching, but it has not been the most fundamental crisis.

The crisis they have centred on has been the seeming out-modedness of preaching in the postmodern world. Faced with congregations conditioned to receiving information in bite-sized quantities, at phenomenally fast rates, and in multimedia formats, a preaching monologue seems rather antiquated. Faced also with congregations that have been conditioned by the relativism, pluralism, secularism and individualism of our times, the authoritative preaching of objective, propositional truth makes the preacher look like something from another planet. Preachers have instinctively felt the need to compensate.

Most preachers have sought to adapt in one of three ways. First, some have sought to modify both the content of their preaching and style of delivery in order to be more 'relevant'. Instead of simply preaching on biblical texts or doctrines, they have felt it better to discuss contemporary needs, problems, and issues in the most approachable manner possible. They seek to address felt needs in a user-friendly way. Their preaching is not 'preachy' but conversational. Extensive use of humour, testimony and illustration help to hold people's attention, and often there is an effective appeal for response. If done well, many will listen.

Unfortunately, this greater hearing is often at the cost of biblical content. This approach makes it almost impossible to feed a congregation meat rather than milk, and does not lend itself to a deepening grasp of God's Word. At worst, it degenerates into the delivery of spiritual candyfloss – sweet and attractive, but quickly melting away and failing to nourish the soul. This approach may account in some measure for the appalling biblical illiteracy and the tragic immaturity and worldliness of many in the church today.

A second approach has been far more radical. Many preachers have questioned the very medium of preaching itself. In view of the seeming irrelevance of an authoritative monologue, they have replaced or at least substantially supplemented it with other forms of communication: dance, drama, music ministry, puppetry, multimedia presentations and the like. The setting itself may be changed as well. Instead of sitting in pews, one can sit around coffee tables in a café-style service, or stand amid the strobe lights in a nightclub setting. The proponents of this approach have redefined 'preaching' so that it is no longer a monologue, no longer an exposition of Scripture, and very definitely no longer 'preachy'.

The great advantage is that it is far more palatable to unbelievers. The concern to communicate the gospel in such a way that the 'unchurched' can also hear and understand is most laudable. The tragedy, however, is that it represents a total loss of confidence in the unique power and authority of *preaching*. It is a denial of the Bible's ceaseless and bold affirmation of the priority of preaching. Throughout the pages of Scripture it is overwhelmingly clear that preaching is sanctioned and commanded by God, no matter how foolish it may seem to the eyes of the world.[1] It is the divinely ordained means of

1. This is particularly clear in 1 Corinthians 1:18–2:5. It is also clear from many other passages in Paul's epistles (e.g., Rom 1:15; 10:13-14; 1 Cor 9:16; 2

advancing the Kingdom, and it was the predominant, if not exclusive, method used by the early church. To change the means of communicating God's truth so radically is to throw the baby out with the bath water.

A third response to the crisis of preaching has been much more conservative. Many preachers have remained committed to the concept of biblical expository preaching. They have retained the conviction that preaching is God-ordained, and that in the foolishness of preaching God is pleased to display his divine power. They have realised, however, the need to upgrade their theological, exegetical and homiletical skills. A rambling homily, a few thoughts scratched together, a simplistic message that wrenches a text from its context will not do. There may have been a time when people believed it because the minister said so, and when the pastor was the most learned in the congregation, but that is no longer the case. Those who preach week by week must at least master both the Scriptures and the act of preaching.

In this regard, plenty of helps have been made available. Theological seminaries offer courses in grammatico-historical exegesis, hermeneutics and biblical theology. Many homiletics texts deal thoroughly with how to approach a text, formulate a proposition, draw applications and illustrate truth. New commentary series are being produced at a great rate, many of which aim at the practical expository preacher who wants biblical content without technical overload. There is also a host of new 'quick-fix' tools for the busy pastor: an endless array of Bible software packages, anthologies of illustrations and quotations, even sermon outlines.

There is again, however, a problem. Preaching can all too easily be spiritually arid even when it is biblically substantial. The opening up of a text in its historical, literary and grammatical context does not

Tim 4:2); from many passages in Acts (e.g., 2:42; 4:8; 13, 31, 33; 6:4, 10; 8:4; 10:42); and from the ministry of Christ (e.g., Matt 4:17; Mark 1:38; 3:14). A useful summary of a biblical-theological perspective on the centrality of the preached word can be found in Graeme Goldsworthy, *Preaching the Whole Bible as Christian Scripture: The Application of Biblical Theology to Expository Preaching* (Grand Rapids: Eerdmans Publishing Co., 2000), 34-45.

necessarily produce a message of life and power. Such 'preaching' can in fact be mere lecturing. Biblical truth is faithfully taught, affirmed, explained and defended, but it is not brought home to the heart. It does not significantly move, change or inspire people. They leave thinking they have heard a 'good sermon' yet knowing that they have not really been spiritually fed. Why? Because there is more to good preaching than accurate exegesis, good structure, able communication, powerful illustration and practical application. Something is still missing.

Something is missing

These three responses to the seeming out-modedness of preaching in the post-modern world all potentially run the same risk: the risk of ignoring a more fundamental crisis. The more fundamental crisis concerns the lack of *spiritual vigour* in much preaching. It is the crisis of preaching that is powerless: preaching that fails to deeply convict sinners, fails to convert the lost, fails to sanctify saints, fails to produce deep and lasting change in people's lives, fails to overwhelm people with sheer majesty, grandeur, excellency and beauty of God, and his only Son, Jesus Christ. It is the crisis of preaching that, for all its relevance, innovation or soundness, is devoid of the power of the Holy Spirit.

We must recognise that there is a dimension to preaching that lies beyond explication and application, beyond illustration and communication. There is a spiritual dimension to preaching, and when that is missing, no skill in communication, no degree of contemporary relevance, no exegetical faithfulness can ever compensate for it.

Preaching, we must remember, is not merely intended to entertain, help or inform. It is intended to produce, by the grace of God, a deep impression on the hearts and souls of the hearers. It is a divinely ordained means of drawing people to God and compelling them to respond to him. It is intended to grip, thrill, move and change lives, well after the excitement of the meeting has worn off. What John Murray says of personal reading and study of Scripture must be true of preaching. He pleads for that study of prolonged thought and meditation by which our hearts and minds may become soaked with the truth of the Bible and by which the deepest springs of thought, feeling and action may be stirred and directed; the study by which the Word of God will grip us, bind us, hold us, pull us, drive us, raise us up from the dunghill, bring us down from our high conceits and make us its bondservants in all of thought, life and conduct.[2]

It is precisely this dimension of preaching, however, that is too often absent. Often among reformed evangelical preachers there is a lack of spiritual vitality. J. I. Packer wrote of orthodox evangelicals:

We can state the gospel clearly, and can smell unsound doctrine a mile away. If anyone asks us how men may know God, we can at once produce the right formulae -- that we come to know God through Jesus Christ the Lord, in virtue of His cross and mediation, on the basis of His word of promise, by the power of the Holy Spirit, via a personal exercise of faith. Yet the gaiety, goodness, and unfetteredness of spirit which are the mark of those who have known God are rare among us – rarer, perhaps, than they are in some other Christian circles where, by comparison, evangelical truth is less clearly and fully known.[3]

Other writers have concurred with this perceived weakness in preaching and appealed for more than an intellectual presentation of biblical truth. Martyn Lloyd-Jones, for example, wrote to preachers: 'You are not simply imparting information, you are dealing with souls, you are dealing with pilgrims on the way to eternity, you are dealing with matters not only of life and death in this world, but with eternal destiny.'[4] He went on to say that the chief end of preaching is to give people a sense of the presence of God: 'I can forgive a man for a bad sermon, I can forgive the preacher almost anything if he gives me a sense of God, if he gives me something for my soul, . . . if he gives me some dim glimpse of the majesty and glory of God, the love

2. John Murray, 'The Study of the Bible,' in *Collected Writings of John Murray,* vol. 1, *The Claims of Truth* (Edinburgh: Banner of Truth Trust, 1976),3.

3. J. I. Packer, *Knowing God* (London: Hodder and Stoughton, 1973), 22.

4. Martyn Lloyd-Jones, *Preaching and Preachers* (Grand Rapids: Zondervan, 1971), 91.

of Christ my Saviour, and the magnificence of the Gospel.'[5]

The problem has not been confined to recent times either. It is interesting that in his own day Jonathan Edwards addressed exactly the same issue:

Clearness of distinction, illustration, and strength of reason, and a good method in the doctrinal handling of the truths of religion, is in many ways needful and profitable, and not to be neglected; yet an increase in speculative knowledge in divinity is not what is so much needed by our people as something else.... Our people do not so much need to have their heads stored, as to have their hearts touched; and they stand in greatest need of that sort of preaching which has the greatest tendency to do this.[6]

This need for preaching that touches hearts cannot be met by merely applying certain techniques or methodologies. It is not simply a matter of improving our communication skills, sermon structure or use of illustration. What is needed is spiritual renewal, beginning in our hearts as preachers, and permeating every facet of the truth we proclaim. Only then will there be spiritual vigour in preaching, resulting in people's hearts being stirred and their souls fed.

Walter Kaiser in his book *Toward an Exegetical Theology* correctly states that 'One of the most depressing spectacles in the Church today is her lack of power.... At the heart of the problem is an impotent pulpit.'[7] In addressing that impotence, he says:

From the beginning of the sermon to its end, the all-engrossing force of the text and the God who speaks through that text must dominate our whole being. With the burning power of that truth on our heart and lips, every thought, emotion, and act of the will must be so captured by that truth that it springs forth with excitement, joy, sincerity, and reality as an evident token that God's Spirit is in

5. Ibid., 98.

6. *The Works of Jonathan Edwards*, Vol. 1, 369, quoted in Martyn Lloyd-Jones, *The Puritans: Their Origins and Successors* (Edinburgh: Banner of Truth Trust, 1987), 369.

7. Walter C. Kaiser, Jr., *Toward an Exegetical Theology: Biblical Exegesis For Preaching and Teaching* (Grand Rapids: Baker Book House, 1981), 235-6.

that word. Away with all the mediocre, lifeless, boring, and lacklustre orations offered as pitiful substitutes for the powerful preaching of the Word of the living Lord. If that Word from God does not thrill the proclaimer..., how shall we ever expect it to have any greater effect on our hearers?[8]

How, then, are we to infuse greater spiritual vitality into our preaching? How can we learn to preach with greater power, spiritual insight and vigour?

Experimental Christianity

A significant part of the answer lies in developing, emphasising and cultivating a more 'experimental' approach to the Christian faith. The word *experimental* is used advisedly, having been used at various times in the history of preaching. A more readily understandable term may be 'experiential', but it has too many overtones of a subjective, experience-based faith. That is not what is meant by the word experimental.

The word 'experiment' has to do with testing something. A scientist conducts experiments to test his hypotheses. Applied to theology, it refers to the work of testing the reality and truth of God's word in the hearts and lives of people. Truth is not left as a mere hypothesis – a detached, intellectual belief. Truth is applied to life; its reality and validity is shown and demonstrated; its presence in our lives is tested and proven.

Experimental Christianity values genuine spiritual experience. It is not content merely to know the truth, but desires to experience, live and feel it. It is not satisfied with affirming the importance of holiness, but gives rise to an earnest pursuit of godliness. It wants not only to make a stand for sound doctrine, but cultivate a burning zeal for the honour of Christ and the glory of his name. It was this that Paul was praying for when he wrote to the Ephesians:

> I keep asking that the God of our Lord Jesus Christ, the glorious Father, may give you the Spirit of wisdom and revelation, so that you may know him better. I pray also that the eyes of your heart may be enlightened in

8. Ibid., 239.

order that you may know the hope to which he has called you, the riches
of his glorious inheritance in the saints, and his incomparably great power
for us who believe (Eph. 1:16-17).

The desire to know God better and know (experimentally) greater
hope, power and love, is at the heart of experimental Christianity.

Such experimentalism leads to a different quality of Christian life.
It breeds a life of godliness, prayer, sanctification, depth, maturity
and reality. It gives rise to genuine piety. Such piety, however, must
not be confused with sentimental and subjective responses to God.
There is the danger that people who desire spiritual experience
become so hungry for it they will take any shortcuts offered. They
make the mistake of pursuing the experience rather than pursuing
God who gives it. They pursue joy, love, power, excitement, the
miraculous or emotion as ends in themselves, forgetting that these
are the by-products of a true relationship with the living God. In their
confusion, they open themselves to mysticism, supposed new
revelations of the Spirit, emotion-based Christianity, subjective
interpretations of the Word and so on. Sadly, such distortions of true
biblical experience abound in contemporary Christianity, but they do
not produce genuine spiritual vigour.

The challenge for preachers is to cultivate in their own lives a
vibrant spirituality, and then, with the enabling of the Spirit, preach in
such a way that true spiritual experience is promoted and inculcated
in other people's lives also. Experimental preaching is therefore
marked by a fourfold concern.

*First, there is a concern to bring the objective truth of God's
Word to bear on people's hearts.* It is not the preaching of someone's
personal experience, but the preaching of biblical truth. The Word of
God is the sole authority for the preacher. Apart from the authoritative
Word, the preacher has no reason to say anything. His personal
opinion is no more valid than anyone else's. The task of the preacher
is to open the truth of God's Word. He is to do so thoroughly and
consistently. He is to preach the whole counsel of God, not holding
back anything that may be beneficial for his hearers. Indeed he is to
preach whether people want to hear it or not, for he is not in the

business of scratching itching ears. Experimental preaching, therefore, depends on sound hermeneutical and exegetical skills.

It does not, however, seek merely to propound truth for truth's sake. Truth is never to be preached in a vacuum. It is to be brought to bear on the hearts and lives of those who hear it. It is to address their whole person – the mind first, and through the mind, the conscience, the affections and the will. Only in so far as the very soul of a person is addressed is truth preached experimentally.

Second, there is a concern to address people's experience of the truth under consideration, whether their experience is right or wrong, healthy or unhealthy, biblical or unbiblical, godly or ungodly. Experimental preaching takes the realities of people's lives seriously. It speaks to their joys, sorrows, hopes, fears, aspirations and disappointments. It strikes a chord with them because it relates to their actual experience. They sense that the Word is relevant and that the preacher understands them. They often leave afterwards feeling that he has spoken to exactly their situation. In fact, they may well wonder how he knew so much about them!

The preacher, however, not only relates the truth he is addressing to their experiences, he also helps them to analyse their experiences in the light of biblical truth. He both describes and prescribes what their experience ought to be. The hearers are challenged to review their experience in the light of God's Word.

Third, there is a concern to lead people to an experience of the transforming power and grace of God in regard to that truth. The aim is not merely to give people a head knowledge of the truth or a greater self-awareness, but to lead them to an encounter with the God of truth himself. People ought to have, as Lloyd-Jones said, a sense of the presence of God and a glimpse of his majesty and glory. Such preaching is theocentric, not anthropocentric. The preacher's desire is that people will be enabled by the Spirit to experience something of the grace, glory and power of God. Preaching ought to uplift, ennoble and inspire them as they are drawn into the presence of God himself.

Such preaching is necessarily Christocentric, because only in Christ can a person have access to God, and only in him can they find grace to help them in their time of need. Such preaching must also be pneumocentric. It is utterly dependent on and deeply conscious of the empowering, transforming, sanctifying work of the Spirit. Without this, there can be no encounter with the living God.

Finally, experimental preaching is marked by a concern to stimulate greater godliness in the hearer. Godliness, in all its fullness, is the end goal of such preaching. It aims to bring people nearer to God, give them a deeper and truer knowledge of him, urge them toward greater conformity to his will, and enable them to serve him more fully and consistently in their daily lives.

In the chapters that follow these ideas will be unfolded much more fully. It should already be apparent, however, that experimental preaching is qualitatively different from much contemporary preaching. Its focus is on objective biblical truth, not subjective personal experiences. Its concern is to address the whole person, not just the mind, or the will, or the emotions alone. It aims at godly change in people's lives, rather than seeking to entertain crowds, or merely impart information. It is not so much concerned with teaching people how to have a happy and successful life, as how to seek first the kingdom of God and his righteousness; how to glorify God and enjoy him forever.

Chapter 1

A Model for Preachers

I was but a Pen in God's hand, and what praise is due to a Pen?[1]

There is an unspeakable difference as to the edification of the
hearers, between a judicious, clear, distinct, and skilful preacher, and
one that is ignorant, confused, general, dry, . . .[2]

I preach'd as never sure to preach again,
And as a dying man, to dying men![3]

Models for ministry and church life abound. Churches, Christian
ministries and individuals who have attained some measure of success
in church growth, pastoral care, youth ministry, outreach programmes
or the like are held before us as useful patterns to follow. Their
strategies, approaches and methodologies are set before us as
providing keys to greater success in our own ministries.

There is great value in this. It is most helpful to learn from those
who have been used by God. Yet for all the models available, few
set before us the principles and patterns of an experimental preaching
ministry. There are perhaps two likely reasons for that. First, few
such ministries exist. Ours is not a great day for experimental
preaching. Second, no quick steps or simple formulas can be
produced for this type of ministry. It requires the cultivation of a
mindset, an orientation, a lifestyle, that cannot be reduced to a few
easy 'keys to experimentalism.'

[1]Quoted in Geoffrey F. Nuttall, *Richard Baxter* (London: Thomas Nelson,
1965), 131, citing W. Bates, *Funeral Sermon for Richard Baxter*, epistle
dedicatory.

[2]Richard Baxter, *A Christian Directory,* in *The Practical Works of Richard
Baxter in Four Volumes* (London: George Virtue, 1846; reprint, Ligonier, PA:
Soli Deo Gloria Publications, 1990), 1:473.

[3]Richard Baxter, *Poetical Fragments* (1681; reprint, Westmead, England:
Gregg International Publishers, 1971), 40.

To find a model of this type of ministry it is most helpful to turn to an earlier age – an age when such preaching was common but quick success formulas were not – and seek to learn how biblical truth can be preached experimentally. Our model will be Rev. Richard Baxter, a Puritan experimental preacher and writer of considerable note.

The Kidderminster ministry

Baxter's main pastoral ministry took place in the town of Kidderminster in seventeenth century England. He ministered there for two years before the civil war (1641-42) and another fourteen years after the war (1647-60). At the time, the Kidderminster parish consisted of a market town and about twenty small villages, comprising in total some 800 households, with an adult population of about 2000. During his ministry the majority of the inhabitants were converted as a great and effective work of God advanced there.

Baxter's preaching, in his own words, 'met with an attentive diligent auditory' and the church grew rapidly:

> The congregation was usually full, so that we were fain to build five galleries after my coming thither, the church itself being very capacious,... Our private meetings also were full. On the Lord's-days there was no disorder to be seen in the streets, but you might hear an hundred families singing psalms and repeating sermons as you passed through the streets. In a word, when I came thither first there was about one family in a street that worshipped God and called on his name, and when I came away there were some streets where there was not passed one family in the side of a street that did not so, and that did not, by professing serious godliness, give us hopes of their sincerity.[4]

[4] *The Autobiography of Richard Baxter (Reliquiae Baxterianae)* (1696), abridged by J. M. Lloyd Thomas (London: Dent, 1925), 79. The practise of 'repeating sermons' mentioned here was a common Puritan practise in which the head of a family would repeat the main points of the sermon with his family afterwards, having taken notes during the sermon, and would seek to make application of it to them.

The lives of hundreds were changed, so that Baxter recalled:

> When I first entered on my labours I took special notice of every one that was humbled, reformed or converted; but when I had laboured long, it pleased God that the converts were so many, that I could not afford time for such particular observations... families and considerable numbers at once... came in and grew up I scarce knew how.[5]

In his autobiography, Baxter reflected on what made Kidderminster an advantageous place to pastor. He cited ten blessings and the first was that his congregation was not 'sermon-proof'![6] One of the things that had drawn Baxter to the congregation when he first went to them in 1641 was that they had never really experienced a vigorous preaching ministry before:

> My mind was much to the place as soon as it was described to me, because it was a full congregation and most convenient temple; an ignorant, rude and revelling people for the greater part, who had need of preaching, and yet had among them a small company of converts, who were humble, godly, and of good conversations, and not much hated by the rest, and therefore the fitter to assist their teacher; but above all, because they had hardly ever had any lively, serious preaching among them.[7]

Baxter had learnt from an earlier experience that it was better to minister to people who had experienced little effective preaching, than to preach to a congregation that had become resistant to powerful preaching:

> I came to a people that never had any awakening ministry before (but a few cold sermons of the curate); for if they had been hardened under a powerful ministry and been sermon-proof I should have expected less.[8]

---

[5] *Reliquiae Baxterianae,* Part 1, 21. Quoted in J. I. Packer's introduction to Richard Baxter, *The Reformed Pastor* (1656, abridged by William Brown, 1829; reprint, Edinburgh: Banner of Truth Trust, 1974), 11-12.

[6] Baxter, *Autobiography,* 79.

[7] Ibid., 24-25. [8] Ibid., 79.

Second, he himself had much vigour in his preaching. He had 'a familiar moving voice' and the seriousness with which 'to preach as a dying man to dying men'.[9] This phrase became a favourite of Baxter's and is found in several places in his writings. It arose from his own chronic ill-health. Even in his early twenties he had been close to death on several occasions. In the years at Kidderminster he was almost constantly unwell, doing all 'under languishing weakness, being seldom an hour free from pain.'[10] His ailments were many:

> Measles, smallpox, catarrh and coughs, indigestion, insomnia, haemorrhages, rheumatism, and fears of a consumption had all left their mark before he was twenty, and he continued all his life to be plagued with tumours, lameness, headaches, and what he called 'vertiginous or stupifying conquests of my Brain.' But he was never melancholy and seems to have hit upon a combination of dieting and exercise which kept him active, if not free from pain, for well over half a century following his youthful fear of death.[11]

Indeed, he regarded his ill-health as a particular blessing because his weakness made him 'live and preach in some continual expectation of death,... And this I found through all my life to be an unvaluable mercy for me, for... it made me study and preach things necessary, and a little stirred up my sluggish heart to speak to sinners with some compassion as a dying man to dying men.'[12]

Third, he had freedom to preach the gospel without interference by others. His ministry, during the Interregnum, was not hampered by demands imposed either from a church hierarchy or the State, and the congregation was free of division and faction. 'Not a Separatist, Anabaptist, Antinomian etc., in the town!'[13] Baxter loved peace, and although often embroiled in controversy, hated time being expended on theological matters that were not of great urgency and importance.

---

[9] Ibid.   [10] Ibid., 76.
[11] Owen C. Watkins, *The Puritan Experience* (London: Routledge, 1972), 127.
[12] Baxter, *Autobiography*, 26.
[13] Ibid., 80.

He loved the freedom to focus on the gospel above all else.

Fourth, his hearers were mostly tradespeople, engaged in the weaving industry of Kidderminster. They therefore had 'time enough to read or talk of holy things.'[14] When people are preoccupied with business affairs, or today, with sport, leisure and entertainment activities, it is hard to make an impression on their hearts. When they have time, however, to speak of spiritual matters, it is a great aid to effective ministry.

Fifth, he mentions his own singleness. Throughout his time in Kidderminster he was a single man, able to devote all his time and energy to the work of ministry. He said it enabled him to 'take my people for my children'[15] – a phrase suggestive of the love and diligence that characterised his ministry. He was accustomed to preach once or twice on a Sunday and once on a Thursday. After the Thursday sermon people would gather at his house to consider the sermon and its implications further. Then, in addition to his preaching ministry, there was his monumental pastoral work. One of the remarkable achievements of the Kidderminster ministry was his commitment to visit all 800 families of the township each year, individually catechising each family. Finally, in addition to preaching and pastoring, there was his writing ministry which he in fact regarded as his 'chiefest daily labour'.[16] Baxter saw his singleness as a blessing, allowing total dedication to the work of ministry.

In the sixth place he mentions a curious advantage: 'the quality of the sinners of the place.'[17] By that he meant the drunkards and madmen of the town who made sin look so stupid that others were more easily won to the gospel! He was thankful for the top-quality sinners God had placed in his vicinity!

[14] Ibid.   [15] Ibid.

[16] Ibid., 78. Baxter wrote voluminously, producing over 140 books, many of which run to several hundred pages. His most well-known works, worthy of perusal or study, are, *The Reformed Pastor, The Saints' Everlasting Rest, A Christian Directory*, and *A Call to the Unconverted*. A complete bibliography of his writings may be found in Nuttall, *Richard Baxter*, 132-6, and, with additional information and secondary sources, in N. H. Keeble, *Richard Baxter: Puritan Man of Letters* (Oxford: Clarendon Press, 1982), 156-84.

[17] Ibid., 81.

Next he identified the blessing of practising church discipline which had 'no small furtherance of the people's good'.[18] Baxter firmly believed that if churches are to be strong and faithful, vibrant and effective, there must be the practice of biblical discipline in which sinners within the church are called to account for their ungodliness, are privately and if necessarily publicly admonished and rebuked, and if stubbornly unrepentant, eventually excommunicated.

In the eighth place he said, 'another advantage which I found to my success was by ordering my doctrine to them in a suitableness to the main end, and yet so as to suit their dispositions and diseases.'[19] In other words, he preached *to* them, not *over* them, and was concerned to bring the truth home to their hearts, not just their minds, and to make it useful to their daily lives. Baxter's great concern was for 'holy, practical Christianity' and the twin emphases of godliness and practical daily obedience colour all his writings.

The ninth advantage was that his people were not rich, and therefore not above being taught and helped. In fact he saw an important part of his ministry being practical help to those in need. He especially loved to give books to his people, but would do anything for them if he could help relieve their poverty. Often he would give some money to his poorer members after he had visited them, and he was also frequently called on to give medical advice, arising from his own experience of health problems.

Finally he identified the length of his ministry as being an advantage, 'for he that removeth oft from place to place may sow good seed in many places, but is not like to see much fruit in any unless some other skilful hand shall follow him to water it.'[20] He would love to have stayed longer in Kidderminster, but the political tide changed, and it was not possible.

These ten 'advantages' may not all be characterised as blessings by many preachers. They are not the commonly identified bases for church growth! But they were the considered opinion of a man who felt that he had been graciously placed by God, and knew that the hand of the Lord had been upon his life work there. Together, they indicate many of the aspects of an effective, vigorous preaching ministry

[18] Ibid.   [19] Ibid., 82.   [20] Ibid., 83-84.

that will be unfolded in the pages that follow. God was pleased to grant and bless these characteristics of the Kidderminster pastorate, and the change that took place in the township amounted to nothing less than a great work of revival in the church and a spiritual awakening of the entire township.

An age of deep spirituality

In that regard, the Kidderminster ministry, while in one sense exceptional, was also representative of the wider work of God in England at that time. Baxter was one of the later Puritans, and Puritanism is best understood as a work of both reformation and revival, beginning in the Church of England and spreading far beyond it. Historically, Puritanism began as a political movement, intent on bringing pressure to bear on Queen Elizabeth I to complete the reformation of the church that had broken from Rome under Henry VIII, been partially reformed under Edward, swung back to blatant Catholicism under Mary, and was now in a state of compromise under the Elizabethan settlement. Elizabeth established a compromise between reformed theology, certain Roman Catholic worship practices and Episcopal church government. The Puritans, dissatisfied with partial reformation, sought, initially by political means, to bring about a total reformation of the church.[21]

From a political point of view Puritanism must be judged a failure. Neither under Elizabeth I, nor James I or Charles I, did they achieve the reforms they desired. For a brief time under Cromwell their reform program was realised with Presbyterianism and Independency replacing Episcopalianism, and the *Westminster Confession of Faith* and *Directory for Public Worship* replacing the *Thirty Nine Articles* and the Anglican *Book of Common Prayer*. But the triumph was short-lived with the Restoration of the monarchy in 1660 bringing their program of church reform to a halt.

---

[21] It should be noted, however, that Puritanism was never a homogenous movement. Some Puritans only desired change to certain worship practices; some desired greater freedom in preaching and prayer; others sought major changes in church government – though they were not united in the exact form of ecclesiastical polity to be employed.

Yet Puritanism itself was no failure. Not only did the movement survive persecution, but it was able to effect genuine spiritual change in the nation as a whole. By means of the power of their spirituality, expressed in their private lives, the pulpit, the press and pastoral ministry, they were enabled by the Holy Spirit to exert an enormous influence on the spirituality and morality of England. Puritanism became a powerful movement of spiritual revival at every level of national life: the home, the church, the workplace, the theatre and the parliament.

The Puritans, though often misrepresented as mean-spirited, austere and legalistic, were men infused with the deepest love of God, his Word, his church and the lost. They were passionate in their concern to see God glorified in their nation. Through the course of almost 150 years they wrote and preached on every facet of public and private life, seeking to bring the truth of God to bear on all human endeavour. In their concern for the pursuit of holiness and godliness, they forged new depths of spirituality. The great significance of the Puritan legacy to us is the depth of spirituality that they cultivated in their own lives, their churches and, to a large extent, their nation. Puritanism was essentially a reform movement. It sought to reform people's hearts, their morals and consciences, their church life and their society. It aimed at nothing less than a society that was thoroughly God-centred.

Theologically, the Puritans were the direct heirs of the early Protestant reformers. The vast majority of them were Calvinists and doctrine was of the utmost importance to them. As Baxter said, 'Sound doctrine makes a sound judgement, a sound heart, a sound conversation [life] and a sound conscience.'[22]

Foremost among their theological convictions was belief in *the absolute authority of Scripture*. The centrality of preaching and the place of the Bible in the lives of individual Christians rested on their conviction that the Bible is God's Word, in which God speaks today and governs and directs perfectly every facet of life. They earnestly believed that 'all Scripture is God-breathed, and useful for

[22] Uncited quotation in Peter Lewis, *The Genius of Puritanism* (Heath, Sussex: Carey Publications, 1979), 12.

teaching, rebuking, correcting, and training in righteousness'.[23] The Bible was to have supreme authority not only in the church, but in personal and daily life. Baxter urged his people to 'love, reverence, read, study, obey and stick close to the Scripture'.[24] In their preaching the Puritans evidenced just such devotion to the Word. Their sermons and treatises are liberally sprinkled with quotations from every portion of the Word. The Bible was no mere theological textbook; it was the rule of faith and life. Biblical principles were applied rigorously to every arena of life. The force and power of Puritan preaching can only be understood in relation to this view of Scripture. Vigour in preaching has its fountainhead here.

Arising out of this high view of Scripture came the Puritan emphasis on *the sovereignty of God*. Again, this was no theoretical belief, but the conviction that God was involved in every event of people's lives. They were concerned to submit their lives to his sovereign hand, live in close relationship with him, and trace in their lives his gracious dealings with them. Many of the Puritans kept spiritual journals,[25] and Baxter himself reflected personally on God's dealings with him in *Reliquiae Baxterianae*, his autobiography. God's sovereignty over the affairs of the nation, the church, the workplace, the family and the individual conscience was a passionately held belief. This, undoubtedly, enabled them to endure the persecutions, disappointments and setbacks they suffered time and again, without losing heart or compromising in any way. They developed a theology of suffering and perseverance that comfortable middle-class Western Christianity knows little of today.

They also believed strongly in God's sovereignty in the work of salvation. They preached uncompromisingly the doctrines of God's sovereign election and Christ's particular redemption. Their

[23] 2 Timothy 3:16.

[24] Richard Baxter, *The Saints' Everlasting Rest*, in *Practical Works*, 2:84.

[25] Owen C. Watkins says that over 200 personal autobiographies of Puritans exist. 'Puritan auto-biographies were the product of a Puritan conviction that the highest art a man could practise was the art of living, that the only masterpiece worthy of the name was to be achieved in the most complex and difficult of all forms of creative endeavour: a human life.' *The Puritan Experience*, 1.

evangelistic preaching is of the utmost significance in reconciling what today is often seen as contradictory: the absolute sovereignty of God's free grace in the salvation of sinners on the one hand, and the urgency of preaching God's law so as to bring men to conviction of sin, humility, repentance and faith, on the other. They preached both aspects unabashedly.

Another great concern of the Puritans was, of course, *the doctrine of the Church*. Puritanism, as a reform movement within the Church of England, sought to rid the church of state intervention, and see her teachings and practices conformed to the rule of Scripture. They were concerned to purge the church of Anglo-Catholic practices and ensure that all church polity and worship was based directly on biblical principle. This led to a simplicity and sincerity in worship in which the preaching of the Word was central, ceremonies were rejected, liturgies and set prayers were largely set aside, buildings were plain (and unnecessary oftentimes when the preachers were evicted from their churches), and music comprised the congregational singing of psalms only. This passionate concern for purity of worship won them their nickname *Puritan*.

Church discipline was also practised in order to preserve the purity of the church. The church itself was no longer deemed to comprise those living in a particular parish, but those saved by the Lord. It was the company of the redeemed, the body of believers.[26] The church was not about cathedrals, popes, bishops and councils, but about the community of saints. According to Baxter, the church is 'a holy Christian society for ordinary holy communion and mutual help in God's public worship and holy living.'[27]

---

[26] The *Westminster Confession of Faith* affirms that, 'The catholick or universal church, which is invisible, consists of the whole number of the elect that have been, are, or shall be gathered into one, under Christ the head thereof;... The visible church, which is also catholick or universal under the gospel,... consists of all those throughout the world that profess the true religion' (Chp XXV. Arts. 1 and 2).

[27] Richard Baxter, *A Christian Directory*. Quoted in Ryken, *Worldly Saints: The Puritans as they Really Were* (Grand Rapids: Zondervan, 1986), 115, citing, Sidney H. Rooy, *The Theology of Missions in the Puritan Tradition* (Grand Rapids: Eerdmans, 1965), 92.

A final doctrinal emphasis that lay at the heart of Puritanism was *the importance of sanctification*. Few things are more characteristic of them than their concern for godliness. They saw no basis for a distinction between sacred and secular activities. All of life was sacred, and therefore a rigorous Christian ethic was applied to the whole of life. They were concerned to bring the love of God and truth to bear upon marriage, family life, education, work, and politics. Every job was a calling; every task a sacred act. All was to be done to the glory of God.

With this view of life, they emphasised personal devotion and developed a distinctive reformed piety, in which they fostered communion with God above all else. They took the fight against sin most seriously, seeking to mortify the flesh and subdue in their hearts, minds, affections, relationships and leisure activities all that was not holy.

These doctrinal emphases were drawn together in a distinctive package. We may speak of a certain ethos, a spirit and attitude that was characteristic of the Puritans. Haller describes Puritanism as a new way of life, 'an attitude of mind, a code of conduct, a psychology, a manner of expression, the vitality of which far outran the particular forms of religious life.'[28] To twenty-first century ways of thinking they were extreme in these matters. There is a tendency to look back at them as legalistic, obsessive, austere and pedantic. But in their extremity they laid bare true spirituality. It is this true spirituality that needs to be recovered if the same measure of power and vigour is to return to the pulpit today.

Baxter's Life

It was into that world that Baxter was born. He was an intriguing man in his own time, and remains so today.[29] Born in Rowton, Shropshire, on the 12 November 1615, he was brought up in relative poverty owing to his father's gambling debts. But about the time of

[28] William Haller, *The Rise of Puritanism* (Columbia: Columbia University Press, 1938; reprint, New York: Harper Torchbooks, 1957), 115.

[29] The main source of information on Baxter's life is his autobiography, *Reliquiae Baxterianae* (1696). The two main biographers of Baxter are Frederick J. Powicke, *A Life of the Reverend Richard Baxter, 1615-1691*

Richard's birth, his father was converted and became a Puritan. He became the first godly influence on young Richard, though, for reasons not entirely clear, Richard was raised by his grandparents for the first ten years of his life. He was a serious lad, and an only child. He excelled in school and under private tuition, though he received no university education. He was never able to trace the exact time of his conversion, citing many significant influences on his early spiritual development: his father, books and friends.[30] In his late teens he undertook a rigorous program of self-study, becoming steeped in the writings of the early Puritans as well as the scholastics.

He was persuaded after his schooling to seek a position at court, and served 'as a kind of apprentice page'[31] at Whitehall. He lasted there only a month, however, being appalled by the ungodliness of court life. He returned home, and remained there from 1634 to 1638. In these years his mother died (1635), his father remarried, and Baxter himself first endured extreme ill-health. It was this that particularly drew him to the work of the ministry. 'My own soul being under the serious apprehension of the matters of another world, I was exceeding desirous to communicate those apprehensions to such ignorant, presumptuous, careless sinners as the world aboundeth with.'[32]

At twenty-two he was ordained as a deacon by the bishop of Worcester and taught in a school in Dudley.[33] While there, he had his first opportunities to preach, and less than a year later had been invited to take up a position as an assistant to the pastor in Bridgnorth. There he had considerable freedom to preach, but 'the people proved

(London: Jonathan Cape Ltd., 1924) and *The Reverend Richard Baxter Under the Cross (1662-1691)* (London: Jonathan Cape Ltd., 1927); and Nuttall, *Richard Baxter* (London: Thomas Nelson, 1965).

[30] One book he notes as being of particular influence on him was Edmund Bunny's abridgement of the Jesuit Robert Parsons's *Book of Resolution*. See *Autobiography*, 7. He read this at about the age of fifteen, and through it 'it pleased God to awaken my soul.'

[31] Hugh Martin, *Puritanism and Richard Baxter* (London: SCM Press, 1954), 36.

[32] *Autobiography*, 15.

[33] This was on 23 December 1638. It was his only ordination recorded, though evidently he must have been ordained to the ministry at some later date.

a very ignorant, dead-hearted people.... Though I was in the fervour of my affections, and never anywhere preached with more vehement desires of men's conversion... yet with the generality an applause of the preacher was most of the success of the sermon'[34] He remained there for two years (1639-40) before being called to Kidderminster in March 1641.

The call to Kidderminster came after the town had lodged a complaint against the incumbent vicar. George Dance, who had been vicar there since 1628, was woefully incompetent and ungodly, frequenting ale-houses and sometimes being found drunk. He only preached once a quarter, and then so pathetically he was the laughing stock of the town. The 1640 Parliament, in an agreement with Charles I, had appointed a committee to investigate complaints against clergy, and the town's complaint was lodged against this man and his two equally incompetent curates. A compromise was reached in which the vicar was allowed to remain but a new curate would be appointed to take over the preaching ministry.[35] It was to this position that Baxter was called, and appointed as 'preacher and lecturer' at the age of twenty-five.

In 1642, however, the bitter struggle between Parliament and the Royalists degenerated into civil war. In royalist Worcestershire, Puritans (who typically sided with Parliament) were treated roughly and it became unsafe for Baxter to remain in Kidderminster. He spent the next two years in Coventry in relative peace, preaching regularly to soldiers and undertaking study and writing. By 1645 the parliamentarians had the upper hand under the command of Oliver Cromwell, but to Baxter's consternation, the standard of conduct among the parliamentarian soldiers, and even the cause of the war itself, had been somewhat corrupted. Baxter therefore felt led to take up an earlier invitation to serve as an army chaplain. He did so under Colonel Whalley, in a regiment in the West Country, but relations between Baxter and Cromwell were cool.[36]

[34] Ibid., 18-19.

[35] Vicar Dance had to allow £60 of his £200 living for Baxter's support.

[36] This was partly due to Baxter declining an earlier offer to be chaplain in Cromwell's own regiment, and more substantially due to their very different

In February 1647, however, Baxter's health collapsed, and he was no longer able to remain in the army. He moved to Worcestershire where, under the care of Sir Thomas and Lady Rous, he rested and began to write his monumental work, *The Saint's Everlasting Rest* – a book written in contemplation of his own seemingly imminent death.

Far from being the end of his life, however, it was in many ways only the start. Later in 1647 he was able to return to his flock at Kidderminster, and from that time on, established the ministry for which he is so well-known. His fruitful ministry continued there until the time of the Restoration.

That was the crisis point for all the Puritan ministers because they were faced with the grim alternatives of compromising their convictions by conforming to the Establishment, or reaping the harsh consequences of nonconformity. Although Baxter had been instrumental in bringing about the Restoration and was immediately appointed as one of Charles II's chaplains and offered the bishopric of Hereford, he was, along with all the Puritans, wary of the terms that would be established for their continued ministry. He declined to accept the bishopric, not relishing the thought of being in a position where he might have to enforce the silencing of fellow Puritans who failed to cooperate with the established church.

Baxter was removed from Kidderminster at this time owing to an agreement under the terms of the restoration that meant positions and property sequestered during the Commonwealth were restored to their former incumbents. His attempts via king, bishop and local vicar, to preach to his own flock again were unsuccessful. Even the *Farewell Sermon* that he wrote for them was never preached in Kidderminster.[37]

perspectives on the war and church polity. Baxter was, at heart, an episcopalian and a royalist, and so his views were in direct conflict with Cromwell's agenda. Baxter was disturbed that so many Separatists and Nonconformists had been appointed to high ranks in the army, and his decision to take up chaplaincy was in no small measure motivated by a desire to counteract that.

[37] This sermon, slightly abridged and with modernised language, is included in the Appendix to this book as an example of his preaching. The original can be found in Baxter, *Practical Works*, 4: 1013-27.

For the next year Baxter preached in and around London, but the political tide was changing rapidly. The new Parliament in 1661 was largely royalist, and the bishops were again in the House of Lords. There followed the legislation the Puritans had feared: the Corporations Act which restricted the holding of public office to Anglicans, and the Act of Uniformity that required the clergy to subscribe to the new Prayer Book. The latter contained a number of extra-biblical ceremonies, that, with their Roman Catholic overtones, had been the focus of Puritan objection for over a century. Conscience prevented them from subscribing, and in 1662 some 2000 of them were ejected from their livings. Some went overseas, some preached out of doors until they were silenced, and some, like Baxter, took what opportunities they could to preach in private gatherings of Independents or Presbyterians, but always under threat of arrest. Many developed writing ministries and no small number spent time behind bars.

Soon after the crisis of 1662 Baxter was blessed with the special friendship and companionship of a wife – Margaret Charlton. Her mother had moved to Kidderminster in 1658, and Margaret had followed soon after. Under Baxter's ministry she had experienced a dramatic conversion from worldliness to godliness. She was also the subject of a day of special prayer and fasting arranged by Baxter in 1659 when she became ill and was close to death.

When Baxter left Kidderminster for London in 1660, Margaret and her mother followed soon after. Her mother died in 1661, but the following year, on 10 September 1662, Richard and Margaret were married. Baxter was aged 46, and his new wife just 25. Freed from pastoral responsibilities, he felt free to marry her, and for nineteen years they enjoyed the closest and happiest of marriages. She allowed him the time he wanted to write, and developed herself a ministry of mercy to the poor and needy. Her presence with him was a great encouragement through some bleak years: persecution from the authorities, the Plague, the Great Fire of London, and continued ill-health. Her death in 1681, when she was only 44, was a cause of great grief to Baxter.

Persecution by the authorities led to Baxter being arrested on four occasions. The first was in 1670 when he was arrested for unlawful gatherings for worship. His resulting imprisonment, however, was no great hardship. He records: 'I had an honest jailer, who showed me all the kindness he could; I had a large room, and the liberty of walking in a fair garden; and my wife was never so cheerful a companion to me as in prison, ... and she had brought so many necessaries that we kept house as contentedly and comfortably as at home.'[38]

His stay in Clerkenwell Prison was short-lived. He was released on a technicality a week later. His second arrest, in 1674, also resulted in a quick release on a technicality. Again, in 1682, he was arrested and fined, but due to severe ill-health permitted to remain at home. His final arrest in 1685, however, was a different story and resulted in a fifteen-month imprisonment as a widower, at the age of 70. He was put on trial for 'scandalous and seditious' writings which were perceived to have been a criticism of the bishops and rulers.

The notorious Judge Jeffreys was not about to show the elderly saint any respect. 'Richard,' he was reported as saying, 'thou art an old fellow, an old knave; thou hast written books enough to load a cart, every one as full of sedition, I might say treason, as an egg is full of meat. Hadst thou been whipped out of thy writing-trade forty years ago, it had been happy.'[39] With a rigged jury he was found guilty, fined and imprisoned till he paid in full. Baxter, however, had no intention of paying the fine. He remained in prison from June 1685 to November 1686, receiving many visitors, including the now well-known bible commentator, Matthew Henry. He would have remained in jail longer had the king not been petitioned to release him without paying the fine.

Such trials, common to many of the Puritans, were received by them as the providence of God. They knew well that 'suffering produces perseverance, perseverance character, and character hope.'[40] Their detention gave them opportunity to write, and we are heirs of some of the marvellous works they may never have produced

---

[38] Baxter, *Autobiography*, 207.

[39] An account of these proceedings is appended to his *Autobiography*, 257-64.

[40] Romans 5:3.

had they been able to continue in pastoral ministry.

The years following his imprisonment were very much twilight years, though to the end he continued to write and to open his home to many who would join him for family worship. Having lived almost constantly at death's door, he finally entered glory on 8 December 1691, aged 75.

Lasting influence

Baxter, while very much a Puritan in spirit, was also something of an enigma. He refused to fit into any of the usual boxes either theologically or politically. One writer summarises the paradoxes neatly as follows:

> None of the usual classifications of opinions or allegiance will apply in his case. We find a man who preached against the Presbyterian Solemn League and Covenant, who refused Engagement to the Commonwealth, and declined the oaths imposed by Restoration legislation; one who denounced Cromwell as a usurper, and who was yet regarded by the restored Court as its greatest adversary; a nonconformist who yet communicated with the parish churches and wrote against separatism. If we look into his books, we find him refusing to choose between positions which his contemporaries habitually regarded as incompatible: he champions faith and works, the operation of the Spirit and the value of 'humane' learning, the enlightenment of faith and the power of man's reason, episcopacy and the independence of parish ministers, a liturgy and extemporary prayer, preaching and catechising, the need for a thorough conversion and the need to grow in grace through education. His contemporaries, we find, prove him Papist, Arminian, Socinian, Presbyterian – what you will.[41]

[41] N. H. Keeble, introduction to *The Autobiography of Richard Baxter,* abridged by J. M. Lloyd Thomas, ed. N. H. Keeble (reprint, London: Dent, 1974), pxiv-xv. The 'Solemn League and Covenant' referred to here was the legislation approved by the English Parliament in 1643, in which the continuance of the Presbyterial Church of Scotland was assured, and a commitment made to reform the churches of England and Ireland, preparing the way for Presbyterianism in England. In return, Parliament secured the assistance of the Scottish army in its war against the Crown. 'Socinianism' was a rationalistic interpretation of Scripture that was the forerunner of Unitarianism.

Baxter himself, while holding these seemingly contradictory positions, and defying simple analysis, prized himself on being 'meerly Christian'. He was not interested in the party spirit of the many groups and sects that emerged at the time. His concern was with the power of the gospel to change hearts and lives, the urgency of saving the lost, and the importance of cultivating a godly and holy life. Though he departed, at points, from mainstream Puritan theology,[42] he was in spirit a Puritan through and through. He may not be remembered as a great theologian, but his reputation as an outstanding pastor and preacher is beyond question. It was his spiritual vigour in these callings that made him a powerful tool in the hand of God.

Although in turning to Baxter we are taken back some three hundred and fifty years to a world in many ways far removed from our own, there are, nonetheless, sufficiently compelling reasons to take him seriously as a model for today. At least three benefits of being acquainted with his ministry stand out.

First, his intense and pure passion for the things of God is infectious. Baxter felt deeply the things of God and communicated them piercingly. He appealed to the heart, the conscience, the mind, the will and the affections. He reasoned rigorously, driving people into a corner until they felt they could not escape the truth he was addressing. His zeal for the gospel, his urgent concern for the lost, his burning passion for the holiness of God are apparent in almost every line he wrote. He had a clear sense of what was important and what was not, and he was not about to waste time on nice uncertainties. Eternity stood before him as an immense reality, and he spoke with the vigour of one who knew spiritual realities intimately. 'Baxter's life was a sermon, demonstrating, explaining, and applying the text, "My soul is athirst for God." '[43]

In other words, the vigour that is needed in preaching today is

---

[42] J. I. Packer describes Baxter's theology as 'an eclectic middle route between the Reformed, Arminian, and Roman doctrines of grace'. Introduction to Baxter, *The Reformed Pastor*, 9. His theology is discussed in more detail in chapter 4 below.

[43] A. R. Ladell, *Richard Baxter: Puritan and Mystic* (London: SPCK, 1925), 121.

marvellously exemplified in his writings. True, it is couched in the language and style of the seventeenth century, and that creates something of a barrier. But if you pry behind the barrier and catch something of his ardour, it cannot but challenge you to greater vigour in your own handling of the truth.

Second, his concern for absolute integrity in the entirety of one's life and ministry is profoundly challenging. Baxter believed passionately in preaching, but he did not depend on preaching to do all. He knew that preaching was most usually impotent if it was not the overflow of a heart that loved God and was truly devoted to spiritual things. In the most convicting terms he challenged the ministers of his day to greater personal spirituality. It is a challenge that rings true in our own day when so many men fade from ministry either from burnout or personal moral failure. The single-mindedness and godliness of the Puritan provides a much needed challenge to us.

Moreover, he knew that if a man was to be a powerful preacher he must also be an effective pastor, a shepherd of souls. He developed in Kidderminster one of the most thorough systems of pastoral care and oversight in the history of the church, and while the model itself may not fit the twenty-first century, the convictions that lay behind it are of enduring value. His challenge to preachers to be pastors cannot be ignored if we would see greater spiritual vigour in our ministries.

Third, his thoroughness and depth is a much needed corrective to the superficial dealing that is common in contemporary Christianity. There is a desire on the part of many today to have our problems remedied by quick and easy success formulas. The Puritans, living long before the 'instant' age, were under no such illusion that true spirituality could be bought cheaply. Sure, their writings are rather laborious to twenty-first century ears, but there was method to what they were doing. Baxter, and fellow-Puritans, sought not only to discover biblical truth, but to apply it consistently and rigorously to the whole of life. To study Baxter is to be challenged to think more deeply about the what, why and how of preaching, and indeed of life itself.

Chapter 2

Preaching to Yourself

Preach to yourselves first, before you preach to the people,
and with greater zeal. O Lord, save thy church from worldly
pastors, that study and learn the art of christianity, and ministry; but
never had the christian, divine nature, nor the vital principle which
must difference them and their services from the dead....
Nothing doth more to make you good preachers, than
that which doth most to make you good Christians.[1]

Nothing is well done by him that beginneth not at home:
as the man is, so is his strength, and work.[2]

When your minds are in a holy, heavenly frame, your people are
likely to partake of the fruits of it. Your prayers, and praises, and
doctrine will be sweet and heavenly to them. They will likely feel
when you have been much with God: that which is most on your
hearts, is like to be most in their ears.[3]

If there is one thing Baxter would impress on us with great urgency it
is this: we must always begin at home. There is much 'heart work' to
be done on ourselves before we can begin to work on the hearts of
others. We cannot suddenly become experimental in our handling of
biblical truth in the pulpit. We must first be experimental in our own
spiritual life.

Baxter was wary of cold professionalism. He feared the mentality
that allows a man to prepare a message without preparing his own
heart; pray for success in ministry but not for personal sanctification;
convict others of sin, but never face squarely his own sins; take an

[1] Baxter, 'A Sermon Preached at the Funeral of Mr. Henry Stubbs' (1678), in
Practical Works, 4:974.

[2] Baxter, *A Christian Directory*, 3.

[3] Richard Baxter, *The Reformed Pastor*, 61.

interest in the study and proclamation of God's Word, but seldom experience its power and influence in his own life. He knew the most basic biblical premise of spiritual leadership to be the integral relationship between a man's personal spiritual life and his public effectiveness as a pastor, preacher and spiritual leader. In order to be useful to the Lord and equipped for ministry, a man must watch over himself spiritually, guarding his own heart, cultivating his relationship with God, and paying careful attention to his spiritual well-being. If he is diligent and serious in these things he will most likely be effective in spiritual leadership. If he is negligent he will find himself ill equipped and ultimately disqualified for public ministry.

In the New Testament, the qualifications for elders and deacons are chiefly matters of personal godliness and spiritual maturity.[4] The call to Timothy as pastor of a church was to 'watch his life and doctrine closely', in that order. He was to 'set an example for the believers in speech, in life, in love, in faith and in purity'. He was to train himself to be godly, knowing that 'physical training is of some value, but godliness has value for all things'.[5] Paul himself, who gave these injunctions, could appeal to the Thessalonians saying, 'You are witnesses, and so is God, of how holy, righteous and blameless we were among those who believed.'[6] To the Corinthians he could write: 'Now this is our boast: Our conscience testifies that we have conducted ourselves in the world, and especially in our relations with you, in the holiness and sincerity that are from God.'[7]

Personal integrity and a vital relationship with the Lord are the imperative prerequisites of a vigorous preaching ministry. Yet failure at this point is all too common. If the truth were known, the crisis in preaching today may be due not so much to where society is at, but to where pastors and preachers are!

---

[4] See 1 Timothy 3:1-7, Titus 1:6-9, 1 Peter 5:1-4.
[5] 1 Timothy 4:16; 4:12; 4:8 (all quotations from NIV).
[6] 1 Thessalonians 2:10
[7] 2 Corinthians 1:12

The need of self-watch

Baxter pulled no punches in addressing such matters. They formed the basis for much of what he wrote in his most potent work, *The Reformed Pastor*. Written to his fellow pastors in the county of Worcestershire (a sermon he was prevented from preaching to them because of ill health), he presented in it a stirring appeal to be reformed in life and practice. By 'reformed' he did not mean theologically reformed. That was taken for granted. He meant spiritually reformed. He was concerned to see a spiritually renewed, revived ministry that would be used of God to bring greater spiritual vigour to the churches. He knew that if revival was to come it must begin in the hearts of preachers and pastors.

He opened at length Paul's words in Acts 20:28: 'Keep watch over yourselves and all the flock of which the Holy Spirit has made you overseers. Be shepherds of the church of God, which he bought with his own blood.' The first words of that exhortation formed the basis for his extended consideration of what it means for a preacher to watch over himself spiritually.

Baxter began with the most basic of all concerns – the need for a preacher to be saved:

> See that the work of saving grace be thoroughly wrought in your own souls. Take heed to yourselves, lest you be void of that saving grace of God which you offer to others, and be strangers to the effectual working of that gospel which you preach.[8]

We must know in our own experience the transforming power of the gospel, the Spirit's work in conviction of sin, the excellency and majesty of Christ, the peace of a cleansed conscience, the joy of sins forgiven, the reality of a renewed heart that desires to please God, and the hope of glory. We should not feel that we are eternally secure simply because we have been called to the work of ministry, but because we know in our own heart the regenerating power of God and the transforming grace of the gospel:

[8] Baxter, *The Reformed Pastor*, 53.

Believe it, brethren, God never saved any man for being a preacher, nor because he was an able preacher; but because he was a justified, sanctified man, and consequently faithful in his Master's work.[9]

There are several devastating consequences for the preacher who is not truly saved. First, he will miss out on the very salvation he offers to others:

O what sadder case can there be in the world, than for a man, who made it his very trade and calling to proclaim salvation, and to help others to heaven, yet after all to be himself shut out! Alas! that we should have so many books in our libraries which tell us the way to heaven; that we should spend so many years in reading these books, and studying the doctrine of eternal life, and after all this to miss it! – that we should study so many sermons of salvation, and yet fall short of it! – that we should preach so many sermons of damnation, and yet fall into it?[10]

Second, he will find himself preaching against himself. 'When you pen your sermons, little do you think that you are drawing up indictments against your own souls!... O miserable life! that a man should study and preach against himself, and spend his days in a course of self-condemning!'[11]

Third, he will find it impossible to preach experimentally. How can a man speak personally, powerfully and passionately of that which he has not known in his own soul? If there is any passion in the delivery of an unsaved man, it can only be phoney. He cannot speak with the voice of experience when he opens up truths concerning victory over sin, the glory of heaven, the comfort of the promises of God's Word, the reality of joy in the midst of sufferings, or the wonder of sins forgiven. He cannot speak with conviction, boldness, power, urgency and seriousness of things that he is not utterly persuaded of in his own heart.

Fourth, he will most likely know little success in ministry. Though it is possible for God to use an unsaved man (and at times he has done so), he nowhere promises to do so. 'Can it be expected that God will bless that man's labours,...who worketh not for God, but

[9] Ibid., 54.   [10] Ibid., 72.   [11] Ibid., 54.

for himself?... None but converted men do make God their chief
end, and do all or any thing heartily for his honour; others make the
ministry but a trade to live by.'[12]

It is, then, a great calamity when men preach God's Word without
first having been truly changed by it. But Baxter also knew that the
experience of salvation was not in itself sufficient to keep a preacher
on fire for the work of ministry. He went on to challenge his fellow
preachers by saying, 'Content not yourselves with being in a state of
grace, but be also careful that your graces are kept in vigorous and
lively exercise.'[13]

All too quickly we can decline in spiritual fervour. One day we
may be alive to spiritual things, the next our heart is cold and dull.
When we prepare a message during the week it may grip our heart,
but by the time we come to preach it to others it has lost its sparkle
and we preach mechanically. We may stand in the pulpit on a Sunday,
moved and stirred by the message God has laid on our heart, yet the
following morning we feel discouraged and find ourselves barely
inclined even to pray. At times the experience of the Ephesian church
may become ours: we have lost our first love (Rev. 2:4).

When coldness creeps into our hearts, it is soon felt in our
preaching. With chilling honesty Baxter wrote:

> I confess I must speak it by lamentable experience, that I publish
> to my flock the distempers of my own soul. When I let my heart
> grow cold, my preaching is cold; and when it is confused, my
> preaching is confused; and so I can oft observe also in the best of
> my hearers, that when I have grown cold in preaching, they have
> grown cold too; and the next prayers which I have heard from
> them have been too like my preaching.[14]

There is often a temptation to remedy such spiritual decline by
seeking a quick fix – be it another book, seminar, conference or
video. The one thing most necessary – a revitalised communion with
the Lord – is the thing most easily neglected. Anything else, however,
is but a short-term remedy. The lasting answer is found in the
development of a close, daily walk with the Lord. The preacher

[12] Ibid., 80.   [13] Ibid., 61.   [14] Ibid.

must, above all else, be a man of God. That is the designation used to describe Timothy[15] and it must be the reality of every preacher's life. The preacher must not only know the Word of God, but the God of the Word. He must not only be familiar with the *work* of Christ, but be vitally related to the *person* of Christ. That must be his highest priority in life.

Baxter repeatedly addressed in his writings the fundamentals of a close fellowship with the Lord. Before considering them, however, it is helpful to listen to his warnings about the obstacles that impede such fellowship. He was not one to gloss over the serious impact of sin in a believer's life, and particularly in a pastor's life.

Sins of the heart

Avoidance of scandal and gross moral failure is not enough for the pastor. Like a violin in a small ensemble, the tuning of his soul must be precise. Often power and vigour in preaching are sacrificed not through heinous sins, but subtle sins of the heart – sins we have come to live with, love, rationalise and justify.

Such sins have a special propensity to rob us of spiritual vigour. They distract us from the things of God. They take our time and focus away from that which is of God and point us to the world and the flesh. They may rob us of focus when preparing, of time for ministry, of joy in the things of God, and of peace in presenting the Word to others.

They also prohibit us from being passionate in speaking against the sins we indulge in, unless we have given in to rank hypocrisy. 'Do you think it is a likely thing, that he will fight against Satan with all his might, who is himself a servant of Satan?'[16] Sin in our heart causes us to blunt the edge of our application to others. We will tone down our application in order to ease our own consciences.

Most seriously of all, sins of the heart grieve the Holy Spirit. This may cause him to withdraw his power from us and, while he will never abandon us entirely, he may leave us to labour and struggle in our own strength, until we yield all to him. As Baxter observes:

[15] See 1 Timothy 6:11; 2 Timothy 3:16.
[16] Baxter, *The Reformed Pastor*, 82.

To his faithful servants he hath promised that he will be with them, that he will put his Spirit upon them, and his word into their mouths, and that Satan shall fall before them as lightning from heaven. But where is there any such promise to ungodly ministers? Nay, do you not, by your hypocrisy and your abuse of God, provoke him to forsake you, and to blast all your endeavours, at least as to yourselves, though he may bless them to his chosen?[17]

In view of these realities, Baxter identified particular sins that may be a snare to preachers. He wanted preachers to take the pains to identify and address specific sins of the heart. He knew only too well that 'it is easier to chide at sin, than to overcome it'.[18] It is far easier to address sin in the lives of others than in oneself. It is easier to disapprove of sins in theory than in practice.

Always close to the top of his list was the sin of *hypocrisy*. 'Take heed to yourselves, lest your example contradict your doctrine,...lest you unsay with your lives, what you say with your tongues; and be the greatest hinderers of the success of your own labours.'[19] Because actions speak louder than words, there is the danger that people cannot hear what we say from the pulpit because they hear all too clearly what we say with our lives:

O what a heinous thing is it in us, to study how to disgrace sin to the utmost, and make it as odious in the eyes of our people as we can, and when we have done, to live in it, and to secretly cherish that which we publicly disgrace! What vile hypocrisy is it, to make it our daily work to cry it down, and yet keep to it; to call it publicly all naught, and privately to make it our bed-fellow and companion; to bind heavy burdens on others, and not touch them ourselves with a finger![20]

As preachers we must realise our particular vulnerability in this regard. Because we have said more about biblical truth and sin in public, we are more readily made hypocrites by our practice in private. We are also more culpable for our fall because we generally have greater knowledge of the truth, and have made a greater stand

[17] Ibid., 86. [18] Ibid., 68.
[19] Ibid., 63. [20] Ibid., 76-77.

against sin than those who do not preach. We must also reckon with the fact that we are not only sinners like every other person in the church, but are the special target of the evil one. Indeed, 'the tempter will more ply you with his temptations than other men'[21] because if he can cause a minister to fall he can do great damage to the church in one blow. Many eyes are on a pastor and preacher, and many will observe his fall. The Apostle Paul therefore testified: 'I beat my body and make it my slave so that after I have preached to others, I myself will not be disqualified for the prize.'[22]

Another sin that was constantly addressed by Baxter was that of *pride*. He describes it as 'one of our most heinous and palpable sins'.[23] It is a sin that may colour far more of our duties than we would care to contemplate. Baxter sobers us with the thought that pride may well determine the company we keep, our bearing and countenance, even our accent. It may form our desires and aspirations, and make us envious of others. It may determine the clothes we wear, even the way we do our hair!

> And I would that this were all, or the worst. But alas! how frequently doth it go with us to our study, and there sit with us and do our work! How oft doth it choose our subjects, and, more frequently still, our words and ornaments! ... And thus doth pride make many a man's sermons; and what pride makes, the devil makes; . . .
>
> And when pride hath made the sermon, it goes with us into the pulpit, it formeth our tone, it animateth us in the delivery, it takes us off from that which may be displeasing, how necessary soever, and setteth us in pursuit of vain applause.[24]

The sin of pride has devastating effects on the spiritual power of a preaching ministry. It makes a man unapproachable and unteachable, artificial and superficial, difficult and divisive. The cutting edge of such a man's ministry is blunted and his spiritual vitality diminished.

[21] Ibid., 74.
[22] 1 Corinthians 9:27.
[23] Baxter, *The Reformed Pastor*, 137.
[24] Ibid., 137-8.

Conscious of this Baxter urged preachers to seek, above all else, to be clothed in humility. 'Humility is not a mere ornament of a Christian, but an essential part of the new creature. It is a contradiction in terms, to be a Christian, and not humble.'[25] Pastors must realise that their manner is as important as their matter. They must work to cultivate a gracious, humble, teachable, approachable spirit:

> We must carry ourselves meekly and condescendingly to all; and so teach others, as to be as ready to learn of any that can teach us, and so both teach and learn at once; not proudly venting our own conceits, and disdaining all that any way contradict them, as if we had attained to the height of knowledge,... Methinks we should remember, at least the title of a *Minister*.[26]

A third sin of which Baxter was painfully aware was that of *worldliness*. It is a sin that may be manifested in many ways. One way is the desire for wealth, material possessions, comfort and ease. It is a travesty for a pastor to be more concerned about worldly advancement than the souls of men; to be taken up with business rather than with the things of God.

Baxter led here by example. After the civil war he refused offers of more lucrative pastorates than Kidderminster. He chose, however, not only to return to his precious flock, but to take a modest salary, live in the upper story of a modest rented house (instead of taking the vicarage), and expend large proportions of his income on caring for the poor.[27] He also received nothing for his writings, 'preferring that they be sold as cheaply as might be in order to reach the widest

[25] Ibid., 143.   [26] Ibid., 116.

[27] Some 256 residents of Kidderminster signed the invitation for him to return, and they desired that he do so as their minister, not just lecturer and preacher. During his absence they had renewed their charges against Vicar Dance and his living had been sequestered. Baxter, however, flatly refused to take the living, questioning the legality of depriving another man of it. Baxter therefore returned in his old capacity, but, unbeknown to him, his parishioners secretly obtained an order for him to be appointed to the living. Baxter did not find out about this until 1651. When he learned what had happened, he was careful not to let it make any difference to his position. The sequestered vicar continued to receive £40 per annum (the legally due amount of a fifth of the

possible audience.'[28] In this way he evidenced the purest of motives in ministry, and impressed the importance of that on others. 'Let me entreat you' he said, 'to abound in works of charity and benevolence.'[29] Rather than being a stumbling block to others by his actions, the preacher should cultivate a life of such love, sacrifice and service that others will be won over to his words by the graciousness of his actions.

Such actions 'unlock' hearts to receive the gospel. Baxter particularly advocated acts of personal generosity to those in need. 'Go to the poor, and see what they want, and show your compassion at once to their soul and body. Buy them a catechism, and other small books that are likely to do them good,... Stretch your purse to the utmost, and do all the good you can.'[30] He urged this because, 'Experience hath fully proved that works of charity do most powerfully remove prejudice, and open hearts to words of piety.'[31]

Worldliness may also be manifest by 'sensuality, and fleshly lusts, and all the baits and temptations' that may draw a person to sin.[32] There are temptations to impure thoughts and fantasies, to pornography and illicit relationships. Sadly, this has been an area of special effectiveness in Satan's attacks in recent years. With the advancing promiscuity of society, pastors have found themselves vulnerable. Today it is easier than ever for a pastor to lead a double life, preaching God's Word on a Sunday, but feeding on Internet pornography in the privacy of his own study during the week.

Already 350 years ago Baxter observed the particular danger of ministers in these regards. The nature of the work gives opportunity to interrupt study with wrongful thoughts and fantasies. Pastors are mostly the masters of their own time and can easily misuse that time. Their labour is not so much physical as mental, and they may have

living), and Baxter lived on £80 to £90 per annum. The details of these arrangements can be found in Nuttall, *Richard Baxter*, 40-41.

[28] Keeble, introduction to *The Autobiography of Richard Baxter*, xix.

[29] Baxter, *The Reformed Pastor*, 66.

[30] Ibid.

[31] Ibid., 152.

[32] Richard Baxter, *Compassionate Counsel To All Young Men,* in *Practical Works*, 4: 25.

energy and inclination to pursue physical pleasures that those wearied by manual labour would not bother with. Then add to those observations the emotional and inter-personal dimensions of a pastor's work, such that relationships are formed at a deeper level than may be the case for others in the church, and it is apparent that a minister is especially prone to great temptation and assault. Such sins have undone many and Baxter's warning remains valid: 'if these [temptations] should prevail, alas! you are undone; they will offend God, expel his grace, either wound or scare your consciences, destroy all spiritual affections and delights, turn down your hearts from heaven and holiness to filth and folly.'[33]

Another area that demands special self-examination on the part of the preacher may be called *the sin of ill-discipline*. Baxter did not use that term, but he did frequently warn his peers against laziness and negligence. To many in ministry today that may sound most unlikely. They know pastoral life to be frantically busy. They are on call round the clock. They juggle a seemingly endless list of appointments and responsibilities. They emerge weary from one Sunday with little chance to catch their breath before launching into another week of preparation, meetings, administrative matters, counselling and unexpected crises. Then to the time pressures may be added the emotional pressures: the pressure of an agonising pastoral situation, a critical leadership decision, a disagreement with another brother that needs to be resolved, an address that has soon to be delivered. To suggest to such pastors that they may be guilty of laziness sounds laughable.

Yet sin, by its very nature, is subtle. Even amid all these demands, we may lack discipline. Frequently the issue is not laziness, *per se*, but gross mismanagement of time. Our priorities become twisted. We have time for committee meetings, but not for personal prayer; we can see those we are counselling repeatedly, but do not have time for pastoral visitation; we can allude in our sermons to the latest films and television programmes, but remain unaware of monumental theological works; we have time to surf the Internet, but complain that we do not have enough time for our family!

[33] Ibid., 26.

To be vigorous in spiritual life we must be rigorous in daily life. 'We must study as hard how to live well, as how to preach well.'[34] 'All the week long is little enough, to study how to speak two hours; and yet one hour seems too much to study how to live all the week.'[35] If we give serious thought to biblical priorities, then prayer will come first, preaching will be next, and pastoral work will fall in closely behind. The preacher-pastor is to be just that – a preacher and a pastor – not a manager and administrator.

In these ways Baxter urged the cultivation of a life that would adorn the gospel. 'Maintain your innocency, and walk without offence. Let your lives condemn sin, and persuade men to duty.'[36] The pastor's manner of conversation ought to be such that exalts the level of conversation in the congregation. His use of time ought to be an inspiration to others to redeem their time also. His careful ordering of his own family life ought to provide a pattern that will help others in their family life. Particularly, a pastor's humility, meekness and self-denial ought to demonstrate that the work of ministry is not for personal gain or prestige, but for the honour of the Lord and the advancement of the church.

Such care in daily living requires effort, but it is well worth it if we value ministerial effectiveness. 'One proud, surly, lordly word, one needless contention, one covetous action, may cut the throat of many a sermon, and blast the fruit of all that you have been doing.'[37] The Christian pastor has no choice but to practise actively and deliberately the denial of self, refusing to give in to those temptations that compromise wholehearted commitment to the cause of Christ. He must have a servant heart, prepared to sacrifice self for the sake of others. He may have to accept a lower standard of living, a lower level of success on the golf course, or a lower standing in the eyes of those who want him to be at every committee meeting and present at every crisis. There will be a cost to such servanthood. But there will be great reward also.

---

[34] Baxter, *The Reformed Pastor*, 64.
[35] Ibid.   [36] Ibid., 65.   [37] Ibid., 63.

Stoking the fire

Not only must we take heed to ourselves in these ways, but we must also feed our souls. Our high calling demands spiritual input. 'Do not reason and conscience tell you, that if you dare venture on so high a work as this, you should spare no pains to be qualified for the performance of it?'[38] Baxter's advice was summarised in one passionate appeal: 'O, therefore, brethren, lose no time! Study, and pray, and confer, and practise; for in these four ways your abilities must be increased.'[39] It is to these chief means of increasing spiritual strength that we now turn.

In the first place, Baxter advocated serious, ongoing study and reading. Without this we will wither intellectually, theologically and spiritually. It is significant that the Puritans were for the most part highly educated men. Many received their eduction at Cambridge University in the early days, then later at Oxford also. Baxter was rare in not having a university education, but he more than made up for it in his own rigorous programme of self-education. It is striking that, in an age when the populace had much less education than the majority of people have today, the pastors were highly educated and were set on communicating that knowledge to the unschooled. Today, when the general standards of education are much higher and information is so readily available, the move is towards pastors with little or no higher education. One would think the need for an educated ministry was greater than ever, but that is not generally the thinking! The downgrading of theological training and ministerial requirements is not likely to increase the spiritual vigour of preaching. It is likely to make it more subjective and sentimental, not more vigorous.[40]

Baxter observed:

> Few men are at the pains that are necessary for the right informing of their understanding, and fitting them for their further work. Some men have no delight in their studies, but take only now and then an

[38] Ibid., 71.   [39] Ibid.

[40] This assumes, however, that the theological training actually kindles the fire of love for God, his Word, and his people. If it is a dry and purely academic training, it may well snuff out the fire. Knowledge of God, and love for him, must go hand in hand.

hour, as an unwelcome task which they are forced to undergo, and are glad when they are from under the yoke.... Many ministers study only to compose their sermons, and very little more, when there are so many books to be read, and so many matters that we should not be unacquainted with.... Certainly, brethren, experience will teach you that men are not made learned or wise without hard study and unwearied labour and experience.[41]

In several places he gave advice regarding suitable reading for pastors. He always advocated the basics first:

Begin then with your catechism and practical divinity, to settle your own souls in safe condition for life or death.... I unfeignedly thank God, that, by sickness and his grace, he called me early to learn how to die,...and thereby drew me to study the sacred Scriptures, and abundance of practical, spiritual English books, till I had somewhat settled the resolution and the peace of my own soul.[42]

He recommended books that 'contain the essentials of religion, plainly, affectionately, and practically delivered, in a manner tending to deep impression, renovation of the soul, and spiritual experience'.[43] This dual emphasis is tremendously helpful: read the basics, rather than theological obscurities and oddities; and read books works that are warm, pastoral, personal and practical, not merely academic or esoteric.

In a similar vein, in *A Christian Directory*, he advised a combination of English catechisms, confessions of all the churches and 'the practical holy writings of our English divines'. He opposed that form of theological education that chiefly studies theoretical and academic works. 'These practical books do commonly themselves contain the principles, and do press them in so warm a working manner as is likest to bring them to the heart; and till they are there, they are not received according to their use, but kept as in the porch.'[44] He counselled pastors to

---

[41] Baxter, *The Reformed Pastor*, 146-7.
[42] Baxter, *Compassionate Counsel*, 27.
[43] Ibid.
[44] Baxter, *A Christian Directory*, 730.

read daily the most spiritual heart-moving treatises, of regeneration, and our covenant with God in Christ, of repentance, faith, love, obedience, hope, and of a heavenly mind and life; as also of prayer and other particular duties, and of temptations and particular sins.[45]

Baxter's concern, as always, was with the heart. Read what most affects your heart and leads it to spiritual vitality. 'It is not the reading of many books which is necessary to make a man wise or good; but the well-reading of a few; could he be sure to have the best.'[46] He went on to compile a list of books that a pastor may build up as a library, distinguishing the absolute basics – 'the poorest library' – through to 'a rich and sumptuous library'.[47] It is in the poorest library that he advocates acquiring 'as many affectionate practical English writers as you can get' and goes on to name such writers as Richard Allen, Gurnall, Preston, Sibbes, Bolton, Perkins, Hooker, Rogers, Rutherford and many others. His fuller library recommendations include histories, commentaries, systematic theologies, classical works, linguistic aids and theological treatises.[48]

Baxter's conviction was that the power of the Spirit came upon the diligent, not the lazy,[49] though he added a valuable counterbalance: 'no minister must be studying, when he should be preaching, praying, catechising, or visiting, or instructing his flock.'[50]

Meditation on the Word

Though Baxter advocated diligent reading, he never allowed human writings to take precedence over the Word of God. 'Let Scripture be first and most in your hearts and hands, and other books be used as subservient to it.'[51] We cannot preach fruitfully year after year if we are barely familiar with the Word and only turn to it in order to fuel our next sermon. The Word must be our daily food and staple diet. We must read it not only to minister to others, but to minister to ourselves. We must love it, be familiar with it, absorb it:

[45] Ibid.   [46] Ibid., 731.   [47] Ibid., 732.
[48] Baxter himself was a voracious reader, and left, at his death, a library of some 1,400 volumes. See Nuttall, *Richard Baxter*, 116.
[49] Baxter, *A Christian Directory*, 725-6.
[50] Ibid., 736.   [51] Ibid., 56.

Let all writers have their due esteem, but compare none of them with the Word of God.... It is the sign of a distempered heart that loseth the relish of Scripture excellency. For there is in a spiritual heart a co-naturality to the Word of God, because this is the seed which did regenerate him. The Word is that seal which made all the holy impressions that are in the hearts of true believers, and stamped the image of God upon them; and, therefore, they must needs be like that Word and highly esteem it as long as they live.[52]

In this regard, the Puritans particularly emphasised the discipline of meditation as an essential element of our communion with God. 'Above all, be much in secret prayer *and meditation*.'[53] Baxter spoke extensively of this discipline in *The Saints' Everlasting Rest*, observing that

It is confessed to be a duty by all, but practically denied by most. Many that make conscience of other duties, easily neglect this; they are troubled if they omit a sermon, a fast, or a prayer in public or private; yet were never troubled that they had omitted meditation perhaps all their life-time.[54]

What is spiritual meditation? It is 'the acting of all the powers of the soul'[55] in which spiritual truth is turned over and digested, so as to be brought home to the heart. 'As digestion turneth food into chyle and blood, for vigorous health; so meditation turns the truth received and remembered into warm affection, firm resolution, and holy conversation.'[56] It is not only the work of understanding the truth intellectually, but absorbing that truth into one's heart and soul, so that it is felt and experienced.[57] In such meditation, one really preaches the truth to one's own heart and life:

[52] Baxter, *The Reformed Pastor*, 120-21.

[53] Ibid., 62 (emphasis mine).

[54] Richard Baxter, *The Saints' Everlasting Rest* (1650; reprint, abridged, London: Religious Tract Society, 19-?), 275.

[55] Ibid., 276. [56] Ibid.

[57] Baxter advocated an approach to meditation that called on all the senses, not just the rational faculties. He emphasised the importance of people using their imaginations to bring before themselves the excellence of the things of God, drawing on faculties more commonly featured in Roman Catholic treatises

By soliloquy, or a pleading the case with thyself, thou must in thy meditation quicken thy own heart. Enter into a serious debate with it. Plead with it in the most moving and affecting language, and urge it with the most powerful and weighty arguments.... It is a preaching to one's self: for as every good master or father of a family is a good preacher to his own family; so every good Christian is a good preacher to his own soul. Therefore the very same method which a minister should use in his preaching to others, every Christian should endeavour after in speaking to himself. Observe the matter and manner of the most heart-affecting minister; let him be as a pattern for your imitation; and the same way that he takes with the heart of his people, do thou also take with thy own heart.[58]

This preaching to one's own heart can be observed in the Psalms. In Psalm 103, for example, the Psalmist stirs himself up to praise the Lord for his mercies to him: 'Praise the LORD, O my soul; All my inmost being, praise his holy name.' Similarly, in Psalm 42, David questions and exhorts himself: 'Why are you downcast, O my soul? Why so disturbed within me? Put your hope in God, for I will yet praise him, my Saviour and my God.'

The purpose of such meditation is not only to awaken our own hearts but to foster and cultivate closeness to the Lord. 'The chief end of this duty is to have acquaintance and fellowship with God.'[59] By this means we draw near to God, and his Word has full access to our hearts. It therefore ought to be practised regularly. In Baxter's case,

on meditation. This point is made both by Keeble in his introduction to *The Autobiography of Richard Baxter,* xix; and by Horton Davies, *Worship and Theology in England,* vol 2: *From Andrewes to Baxter and Fox, 1603-1690* (Princeton: Princeton University Press, 1961-75; combined edition, Grand Rapids: Wm. B. Eerdmans Publishing Co., 1996) 118-20. Davies says of *The Saints Everlasting Rest,* 'It is a treatise of a familiar type in Anglicanism, namely the persuasive to a good life; but within Puritanism..., it is most unusual in that it employed the Catholic techniques of meditation using the Ignatian 'composition' – employing the senses usually regarded as inimical by Protestants to true spirituality, to enable the soul to concentrate more fully on Christ in his sufferings and redemption or on the joys of heaven, and the interior soliloquy as a way of preaching to one's self' (118-19).

[58] Baxter, *The Saint's Everlasting Rest,* 312.
[59] Ibid., 280.

he found the evenings, before he retired to bed, the most opportune time.[60]

Men of prayer

Such meditation is inseparable from prayer. Spiritual vigour is particularly dependent on being 'much in secret prayer and meditation. Thence you must fetch the heavenly fire that must kindle your sacrifices.'[61] Baxter made the significant observation that 'Christians who are much in secret prayer, and in meditation and contemplation, rather than they who are more in hearing, reading and conference, are men of greatest life and joy, because they are nearer the source of the fountain, and have all more immediately from God Himself.'[62] A pastor must constantly turn to that source of life and joy if his preaching is to be marked by life and joy.

Only in earnest prayer to the Father can we express our sense of insufficiency for the task to which we are called. If the Apostle Paul could cry out, 'Who is sufficient for these things?' how much more those of us with lesser stature. In prayer we find a remedy for all our pride and hypocrisy. When we lay our hearts bare before God, the searcher of hearts, we see afresh our utter dependence on his grace – grace that is given freely and abundantly to those who seek.

> Our whole work must be carried on under a deep sense of our own insufficiency, and of our entire dependence on Christ. We must go for light, and life, and strength to him who sends us on the work. And when we feel our faith weak, and our hearts dull, and unsuitable to so great a work as we have to do, we must have recourse to him, and say, 'Lord, wilt thou send me with such an unbelieving heart to persuade others to believe? Must I daily plead with sinners about everlasting life and everlasting death, and have no more belief or feeling of these weighty things myself? O, send me not naked and unprovided to the work; but, as thou commandest me to do it, furnish me with a spirit suitable thereto.'[63]

[60] Ibid., 282.

[61] Baxter, *The Reformed Pastor*, 62.

[62] Taken from an abridgement of *The Saints' Everlasting Rest* in John MacArthur, *The Glory of Heaven* (Wheaton: Crossway Books, 1996), 176.

[63] Baxter, *The Reformed Pastor*, 122.

Not only must we pray for ourselves, but we must also intercede for our people:

> Prayer must carry on our work as well as preaching: he preacheth not heartily to his people, that prayeth not earnestly for them. If we prevail not with God to give them faith and repentance, we shall never prevail with them to believe and repent. When our own hearts are so far out of order, and theirs so far out of order, if we prevail not with God to mend and help them, we are like to make but unsuccessful work.[64]

The example of the apostles is most instructive in this regard. Repeatedly Paul assures the churches of his constant prayers for them. He prayed night and day, ceaselessly giving thanks for them and interceding for their spiritual growth and advancement. In that, he followed the priorities set by the apostles before him when faced with the pressing need of the Grecian and Hebraic widows. They resolved to hand that work over to others in order that they might give themselves to the ministry of prayer and the Word (Acts 6:4). The two went hand in hand. While it may be common for ministers to be ordained to 'the ministry of the Word and sacraments', a more biblical description would be 'the ministry of prayer and the Word'.

Our prayer life ought not to stop with ourselves and our flock, either. If we are truly burdened for the cause of the gospel, our prayers will reflect a deep concern for the lost. In his autobiography Baxter gives an insight into the scope of his prayer-life as he compares his later prayer burdens with his earlier:

> My soul is much more afflicted with the thoughts of the miserable world, and more drawn out in desire of their conversion than heretofore. I was wont to look but little further than England in my prayers, as not considering the state of the rest of the world. Or if I prayed for the conversion of the Jews, that was almost all. But now, as I better understand the case of the world and the method of the Lord's Prayer, so there is nothing in the world that lieth so heavy upon my heart as the thought of the miserable nations of the earth.... No part of my prayers are so deeply serious as that for the

---

[64] Ibid., 122-3.

conversion of the infidel and ungodly world, that God's name may be sanctified and his kingdom come, and his will be done on earth as it is in heaven.[65]

Despite its great importance and the joys and blessings that attend it, earnest prayer remains one of the hardest disciplines for the pastor. Satan will do anything he can to keep a preacher from praying. He will seek to distract his thoughts, make him attend to administrative matters first, settle for brief, superficial prayers, and be content with formal public prayer only. He will do whatever he can to keep a pastor from daily dependence on God's grace. Yet if his prayer-life is dead, his preaching will soon be dead also. Whatever it takes, the pastor must have a disciplined habit of personal prayer, in which he prays for himself, his preparations, his pastoring and his preaching.

The purpose of such prayer, it must be remembered, is not to fulfil a legalistic duty but to draw near to God himself – the source of life and light. Baxter's comments at the funeral of another preacher perhaps sum up well his own emphasis on prayer: 'He prayed as constantly as he preached, and no wonder, then, that his labours had much success....a man of prayer is a man of power with God.'[66]

Godly conversation

Another aid to spiritual vitality is godly conversation. Baxter was convinced of the great need and importance of spiritual fellowship: 'Another help to this heavenly life is to talk seriously of it a good deal, especially with those who can speak from their hearts, and are seasoned themselves with a heavenly nature.'[67] He continued: 'I think we should meet together on purpose to warm our spirits with talking about our rest.'[68]

Baxter regarded it as a spiritual discipline to engage in godly conversation. 'Would that we had the skill and the resolve to turn the

[65] Baxter, *Autobiography*, 117

[66] Baxter, 'Funeral Sermon of Mr Henry Stubbs,' 974. Mr. Stubbs died at the age of 73 after 50 years of preaching.

[67] Richard Baxter, *The Saints' Everlasting Rest*, ed. Christopher Pipe (London: Hodder and Stoughton, 1994), 224.

[68] Ibid.

stream of people's common talk to these more sublime and precious things. When people begin to talk about unprofitable things, would that we could tell how to put in a word for heaven.'[69] Pastors particularly ought to aim at this, endeavouring to bring conversations to matters of faith, godliness, heaven, Christ, Providence – things above rather than things below.

By these means – study, meditation, prayer and spiritual fellowship – Baxter outlined the indispensable spiritual disciplines of a minister. These were to be the foundation on which the fire of the preached Word would be kindled.

Going on to maturity

Any preacher who makes use of these means of grace will grow spiritually. He will see in himself, if he takes the time to examine his own soul, changes and growth in his opinions, emphases and disposition. This aspect of self-watch received some focus in Baxter's autobiography where he responded to those who had urged him to write of his 'soul-experiments' and 'heart-occurrences'.[70] Those phrases are themselves pregnant with meaning, alluding to the spiritual self-awareness that was both the well-spring and overflow of experimental preaching.

Baxter was loath to draw too much attention to himself and his own spiritual experiences, regarding them as essentially the same as all God's dealings with his saints. He would prefer people learn from examining their own soul, not his. But in some fascinating pages he observed the changes that had been manifest in his own heart and mind between his 'unriper times' and his maturer years. He had good reason for going into this, namely, 'that I might take off younger unexperienced Christians from being over-confident in their first apprehensions, or overvaluing their first degrees of grace, or too much applauding and following unfurnished, unexperienced men.'[71]

Baxter recorded no less than forty-one changes in his own experience and perspective. He began by observing a certain

[69] Ibid., 225.
[70] Baxter, *Autobiography*, 103.
[71] Ibid.

mellowing with age: 'The temper of my mind hath somewhat altered with the temper of my body. When I was young I was more vigorous, affectionate and fervent in preaching, conference and prayer, than (ordinarily) I can be now.'[72] He relied, at that time, more on his natural affection and vigour, but presented material that was 'more raw, and had more passages that would not bear the trial of accurate judgements'.[73] At that time his speech may have had greater passion, but it had 'both less substance and less judgement than of late'.

He also observed a change in the area of knowledge, contrasting his earlier years when he had the *faculty* of knowledge with the later in which he had *actual* knowledge. In the earlier years he was quicker intellectually, but knew less because of his inexperience; in later years, while being somewhat slower mentally, his knowledge ran deeper so that his judgement was sounder, having become acquainted with the ways of truth and error. Not that he changed in the substance of his beliefs. He had always been well established in his theological foundations. But on those points that he had studied less carefully as a young man, he found changes in his views and opinions as he studied more.

He noted that in his younger years he was more inclined to controversy and matters of academic interest, whereas later in life he was more interested in the fundamental doctrines of the faith. Part of the reason for this was that he had learned to value things according to their usefulness, and, in his own words, 'I find in the daily practice and experience of my soul that the knowledge of God and Christ, and the Holy Spirit, and the truth of Scripture, and the life to come, and of a holy life, is of more use to me than all the most curious speculations.'[74] He noted too that in his earlier years he was more concerned with his outer failings in thought, word or deed, but later on, was more troubled over inward defects and omissions, and lack of graces in the soul. What he had come to desire above all else was a deep knowledge of God. 'Had I all the riches of the world, how gladly should I give them for a fuller knowledge, belief and love of God and everlasting glory!'[75]

[72] Ibid   [73] Ibid., 104.   [74] Ibid., 108.   [75] Ibid., 112.

Another change was his increased awareness of his own shortcomings. 'Heretofore I knew much less than now, and yet was not half so much acquainted with my ignorance.'[76] Yet with the increased realisation of his own limitations came a greater consciousness of the limitations of others also. He was now less inclined to have a high opinion of learned people and books than in his earlier years, and less likely to buy into one or other side of an argument, but rather to see the merits of each side, and seek a reconciling position wherever possible. He had become 'much less regardful of the approbation of man, and set much lighter by contempt or applause' than he did earlier on. He identified the chief reason for this as being 'the knowledge of man's nothingness and God's transcendent greatness, with whom it is that I have most to do, and the sense of the brevity of human things and the nearness of eternity'.[77] He was therefore more content with a solitary life than a public one, and preferred to spend his time 'with God and conscience and good books'.[78]

His own agonies of body and soul profoundly shaped his approach to ministry. His ill health was a constant aid to vigour and urgency in preaching, making him very conscious of the imminence of eternity. It worked in him an intense seriousness and caused him to write and speak much of heaven and hell, death, the use of time, and preparedness of one's soul for meeting God.

Baxter also experienced agonies of soul. At one time he underwent a crisis in his own faith. His biographer, Frederick J. Powicke, recounts the episode as follows:

His troubles, such as they were, did not all come from without. One of the worst was of a kind he could not speak of. This, to his own surprise, was a lapse into scepticism concerning the very foundations of his faith – viz. – 'the certain Truth of the sacred Scriptures, and also the Life to come and Immortality of the soul'. Hitherto he had taken these for granted, or for such 'Common Reasons' as he had not thought it necessary to test. Now, in this sudden uprisal of doubt, the Common Reasons failed him....

[76] Ibid., 113. [77] Ibid., 123. [78] Ibid., 124.

Formerly, if any least doubt of the sort assailed him he had 'cast it aside as fitter to be abhorred than considered of'. In this crisis, however, it came home to him that the only safety lay in a policy of thorough [sic]. 'I was fain to dig to the very Foundations and seriously to examine the Reasons of Christianity and to give a hearing to all that could be laid against it, that so my faith might be indeed my own.'[79]

Powicke continues: 'His doubts never quite left him but his faith found a rational basis from which it could not be moved.... Hence it was that from this time forward, Baxter felt it to be a duty – which he must not shirk – to write and preach for the rational character and grounds of the Faith.'[80] This most prominent characteristic of his writing and preaching was therefore the outflow of his own bitter experience. True to form, his ministry was the overflow of his own heart. Self-acquaintance and thorough dealing with his own soul was the basis of his ministry to others.

As Baxter mellowed and matured with the passing of the years, so every preacher must be going on to greater maturity. If we are to take others on in the life of holiness we cannot be static ourselves. There must be growth in humility, grace and knowledge. There must also be thorough self-acquaintance. Although Baxter observed that this became less his focus in later years, it is important to note how well he knew his own soul – its struggles and temptations, its changes of temperament, its delights and graces. He had thought deeply about his own spiritual experience. More than that, he had an extensive spiritual experience about which to think deeply. His journey with God had not been slight or superficial, but one that had led him to delight in God, heaven and holiness above all else. That must be the goal and aspiration of every preacher.

[79] Powicke, *A Life of the Rev. Richard Baxter*, 53-4.
[80] Ibid., 54-55.

Chapter 3

Shepherding Souls

If love be the sum and fulfilling of the law,
love must be the sum and fulfilling of our ministry.[1]

It is no small part of a minister's duty to counsel men,
as a wise, skilful, and faithful casuist.[2]

Do you not know, brethren, that it is your own benefit which you
grudge at? The more you do, the more you will receive:
the more you lay out, the more you will have coming in.
If you are strangers to these Christian paradoxes,
you should not have undertaken to teach them to others.[3]

In recent years one of the more dominant models of church leadership
has been the corporate business model. The senior pastor is effectively
the church's CEO. Under him are other professional employees who
oversee multiple ministries, attend to administrative matters, raise
finances and market the church. The senior pastor is the vision caster.
He must keep the big picture before his people and see that it is
realised. He is a leader of leaders. Generally he will be a man of
drive, foresight, motivation and determination. He knows how to
manage human resources, communicate effectively, motivate people
and reach defined goals.

The model is designed for large churches. Only the mega-church
has the resources to make it work. Smaller congregations are
therefore intent on becoming as large as possible. Until that time (if it
ever comes) they are destined to struggle. Often they will virtually

[1] Richard Baxter, 'What Light Must Shine in Our Works' (1674), in *Practical Works*, 4: 909.

[2] Richard Baxter, 'How to do Good to Many' (1682), in *Practical Works*, 4: 937.

[3] Baxter, *The Reformed Pastor*, 222.

strangle their pastor because without the large infrastructure, he is not only the vision caster, but the administrator, the marketer, the counsellor, the youth group leader and, somewhere along the line, the preacher.

As this model is perpetuated, one key question needs to be asked of both the successful large church pastor and the struggling small church pastor. The question is, 'Is the pastor still a pastor?' It seems that by definition, the more 'successful' a church becomes in terms of this model, the more remote the pastor is from his people. He is less and less a pastor, and more and more a CEO. It is increasingly hard for him to know his sheep by name. He is not so much the shepherd of a small flock but the owner of a massive sheep station, with many farmhands under him.

It is interesting to reflect on these dynamics in the light of Baxter's ministry in Kidderminster. In its day Kidderminster was a mega-church with a team ministry under a man who was massively successful and popular. Yet in Baxter's vision, the role of the pastor as pastor was paramount. Free of the big-business models of our own day, he sought to take his cue from the Scriptures and work out in practice a means of faithfully shepherding the flock of Christ. He took seriously the charge of Paul in Acts 20:28: 'Be shepherds of the church of God.' This was his foundational text in *The Reformed Pastor*, in which he not only examined the responsibility of 'self-watch' but also 'flock-watch.'

For Baxter, effective pastoral ministry was foundational to church life and to preaching. He saw the closest of relationships between preaching and pastoring, and questioned the effectiveness of any preacher who did not pastor. He understood preaching to be an extension of pastoring. It is pastoring on a grand scale. It is pastoring many people at once, in a very definitive, authoritative manner. It is pastoring in a most glorious way, which is accompanied by the promise of the Spirit's power. But it is pastoring nonetheless. If the preacher is not naturally a pastor, and does not understand the nature of true pastoring, his preaching will almost inevitably miss the mark:

It is too common for men to think that the work of the ministry is nothing but to preach, and to baptize, and to administer the Lord's supper, and to visit the sick.... It hath oft grieved my heart to observe some eminent able preachers, how little they do for the saving of souls, save only in the pulpit; and to how little purpose much of their labour is, by this neglect. They have hundreds of people that they never spoke a word to personally for their salvation; and if we may judge by their practice, they consider it not as their duty.[4]

Preaching needs a pastoral ministry to undergird it, inform it, shape it and complement it. Preaching cannot do everything in the life of the church. Although it is central, and although it is granted under God's hand the greatest blessing and the highest place, it is unrealistic to expect that preaching alone can grow a church and transform a people. It must go hand in hand with effective pastoring. When the Apostles handed over the task of waiting on tables to other men (Acts 6:1-4), they were not wiping their hands of pastoral responsibility. Rather, they wanted to focus on the ministry of the Word – a ministry that was broader than public preaching alone. Pastoral ministry is a ministry of the Word.

The cure of souls

The Puritan vision of the pastor was most aptly portrayed in the image of a *physician*. The true pastor was a physician of souls. He was entrusted with a certain number of people for whose spiritual health and well-being he was responsible. Like the first priority of a good doctor, the first necessity of a pastor was diagnosing the condition of the souls of his people. He was to be adept at analysing spiritual disease, seeing the root cause of a problem, and being able to describe clearly and accurately the malady of the soul. Any physician who merely treats symptoms without accurate diagnosis ultimately does more harm than good. Similarly, a pastor who fails to really understand the spiritual problems of his people, and proceeds to apply quick-fix remedies, harms their spiritual well-being. The good shepherd will have a deep interest in matters of the soul. He will be concerned to understand people, to probe their hearts and

[4]Ibid., 178-9.

consciences, to uncover deep-seated ills, and to address the greatest
and most urgent needs of their souls.

Next, the physician of the soul had to be able to prescribe biblical
remedies for the ills he had diagnosed. Biblical principles had to be
specifically applied to the needs of the individual. Underlying sins
had to be dealt with, healthy patterns of godly living established,
sound spiritual nutrition built into their lives. Again, this was never by
way of pre-packaged solutions. The pastor's 'cure of souls', as it
was called, was undertaken with individual care and particular
attention to the needs of each person. Baxter was not one to make
generalisations or give simplistic, run of the mill answers. He was a
physician of the soul who took great personal interest in the particulars
of each case.

For effectiveness in this work, Baxter stressed the importance of
knowing individually and personally the people in our congregation.
Expounding Acts 20:28, he explained:

> It is, you see, *all* the flock, or every individual member of our charge.
> To this end it is necessary, that we should know every person that
> belongeth to our charge; for how can we take heed to them, if we
> do not know them? We must labour to be acquainted, not only with
> the persons, but with the state of all our people, with their inclinations
> and conversations; what are the sins of which they are most in
> danger, and what duties they are most apt to neglect, and what
> temptations they are most liable to; for if we know not their
> temperament or disease, we are not likely to prove successful
> physicians.[5]

Baxter reflected on how Christ cared for individuals, not just the
flock as a whole; how the Old Testament prophets were sent to
individuals, not just to the nation as a whole; and how Paul taught not
only publicly but from house to house. To be effective in pastoral
work we must work with individuals as much as possible, and get to
know our people thoroughly.

This personal knowledge of people was to be in the context of
love:

[5] Ibid., 90.

The whole of our ministry must be carried on in tender love to our people. We must let them see that nothing pleaseth us but what proffiteth them; and that what doeth them good doth us good; and that nothing troubleth us more than their hurt. We must feel toward our people, as a father toward his children: yea, the tenderest love of a mother must not surpass ours.[6]

The pastor is to love his people in such a way that they know he cares for them. He is no cold professional, but a warm, affectionate, caring man, ready to spend time with people, sacrifice himself for them, show kindness and generosity to them, and exercise a ministry of encouragement and grace toward them:

I never knew much good done to souls by any pastors but such as preached and lived in the power of love, working by clear convincing light, and both managed by a holy, lively seriousness. You must bring fire if you would kindle fire.... Speak as loud as you will, and make as great a stir as you will, it will be all in vain to win men's love to God and goodness, till their hearts be touched with his love and amiableness; which usually must be done by the instrumentality of the preacher's love.[7]

Baxter's approach in pastoral visitation was shaped by this desire to show love to people. He knew the importance of building healthy relationships with people before seeking to win them to Christ:

If ministers were content to purchase an interest in the affections of their people at the dearest rates to their own flesh, and would condescend to them, and be familiar, and affectionate, and prudent in their carriage, and abound, according to ability, in good works, they might do much more with their people than ordinarily they do.... Labour, therefore, for some competent interest in the estimation and affection of your people, and then you may the better prevail with them.[8]

[6] Ibid., 117.
[7] Baxter, 'What Light Must Shine in Our Works,' 909.
[8] Baxter, *The Reformed Pastor,* 232-3.

In our own situations we will have to discover how best to display practical love. In an area of socio-economic need, financial aid or gifts may be appropriate. In other situations we may communicate love by hospitality, practical help in time of need, a phone-call or informal visit to express personal care, or the giving or lending of books, tapes or videos we feel may be helpful to a particular individual.

So important was this relationship of love between the pastor and his people, Baxter held that in some situations a pastor must leave his charge if he has lost the love of his people and cannot win it again or remove the prejudice against him:

> For an ingenuous man can hardly stay with a people against their wills; and a sincere man can still more hardly, for any benefit of his own, remain in a place where he is like to be unprofitable, and to hinder the good which they might receive from another man, who hath the advantage of a greater interest in their affection and esteem.[9]

It is essential that we focus on building loving relationships within the church. If we are seen to be too busy to see people, too cloistered in our study, or too remote from ordinary people, our ministry, preaching and church will suffer. People everywhere are looking for meaningful, loving, caring relationships. Churches that grow are most usually churches that provide an environment of loving, caring, supportive relationships. Churches that are cold and formal in their interactions between people tend to remain static year after year. As pastors we must reckon with the fact that we do much to set the tone one way or the other.

Love, of course, was not the only characteristic of effective pastoring that Baxter stressed. In describing the manner of pastoral oversight he identified no less than fifteen characteristics that serve to make us effective in pastoral work. He addressed the importance of self-denial and humility; the need for pure motives; the need for diligence and faithfulness in the task. He advised that the work must be done 'prudently and orderly',[10] suiting our approach to the

[9] Ibid., 233. [10] Ibid., 112.

capacities of each individual, and insisting 'chiefly upon the greatest, most certain, most necessary truths'.[11] The pastor's approach is to be reverent, serious and earnest, so that people see that this work is not to be taken lightly. Above all, it is to be undertaken prayerfully and spiritually: 'All our work must be done spiritually, as by men possessed of the Holy Ghost,'[12] and 'our whole work must be carried on under a deep sense of our own insufficiency, and of our entire dependence on Christ'.[13]

Baxter readily acknowledged the many difficulties in undertaking this type of pastoral work. Yet he urged that we must not be overcome by the difficulties, but resolve to be as prepared and diligent as possible. 'The main danger arises from the want either of diligence, or of skill.'[14] He therefore gave strong biblical motives to fortify pastors in their work. In the first place, we are to be motivated by the fact that we have been called to be 'overseers' of the flock. The very office of minister and pastor is that of overseeing the spiritual well-being of the flock. It is an office with great honour. We are ambassadors of Christ. We have the privilege of being maintained by other men's labours so that we may be set aside for this task, and free to study God's Word and minister it to others. 'By your work you are related to Christ, as well as to the flock. You are the stewards of his mysteries, and rulers of his household; and he that entrusted you, will maintain you in his work.'[15]

His second motive concerned the calling of the Holy Spirit. 'It is the Holy Ghost that hath made us overseers of his Church, and, therefore, it behoveth us to take heed to it.'[16] With such a commission from heaven we have an obligation on us to be diligent in the oversight entrusted to us.

He added a third motive in view of 'the dignity of the object which is committed to our charge. It is the *Church of* GOD which we oversee.'[17] We must constantly see our people as the bride of Christ, the household of God, bought with the precious blood of Christ. When energy wanes and zeal flags, this thought must stir us again.

[11] Ibid., 113. [12] Ibid., 120. [13] Ibid., 122. [14] Ibid., 231.
[15] Ibid., 128. [16] Ibid., 129. [17] Ibid., 130 (Baxter's emphasis).

Baxter's final motive was that God had purchased this church with his own blood. 'Oh what an argument is this to quicken the negligent, and to condemn those who will not be quickened to their duty by it!'[18] In summary, he pleaded:

> Oh, then, let us hear these arguments of Christ, whenever we feel ourselves grow dull and careless: 'Did I die for these souls, and wilt not thou look after them? Were they worth my blood, and are they not worth thy labour? Did I come down from heaven to earth, "to seek and to save that which was lost;" and wilt thou not go to the next door, or street, or village, to seek them? How small is thy condescension and labour compared to mine!'[19]

He continued, 'Every time we look upon our congregations, let us believingly remember that they are the purchase of Christ's blood, and therefore should be regarded by us with the deepest interest and the most tender affection.'[20]

This attitude of tender love for and deep interest in our people is to be the spirit of our preaching ministries. When we stand before our congregation to open God's Word, we ought to be standing before people we know and love; people we have spent time with during the week; people whose struggles we have identified with and whose agonies we have shared; people we have prayed with and for, and come to know and care for deeply. We ought to be able to say with the Apostle Paul, 'Who is weak, and I do not feel weak? Who is led into sin, and I do not inwardly burn?'[21] If people sense that, they will listen much more gladly to our preaching of the Word.

Conditions of the soul

In exercising loving pastoral oversight, we soon discover a great variety of spiritual issues in the lives of our people. Each person is an individual, with a particular past shaping a particular current experience. Just as a doctor cannot prescribe the same drug for each patient, neither can the pastor cheer each heart with the same verses, offer the same prayer, and regurgitate the same spiritual

[18] Ibid., 131.   [19] Ibid., 131-2.   [20] Ibid., 132.
[21] 2 Corinthians 11:29.

cliches. The pastor must begin to think in terms of various conditions of soul, and seek to address the particular needs of each person.

The Puritans constantly did this. In their preaching it is not uncommon to find them applying the truth first to one type of person, then to another. Such application, however, was but the overflow of their pastoral work. Baxter identified seven categories of people to be pastored, and he prioritised these categories so that he would give the greatest time and effort where there was the greatest need.

1. The unconverted. Far from separating evangelism from pastoral work, Baxter regarded care of unsaved souls as the highest priority in pastoring. Those both within his church and within his town who knew little of the work of Christ and whose lives were distant from God, were his foremost concern. 'The work of conversion is the first and great thing we must drive at; after this we must labour with all our might.'[22] He explicitly stated that it was a higher priority than helping Christians who had fallen into sin, because their fall was pardonable and would not remove them from God's grace. An unconverted person, however, would be eternally damned:

> It is so sad a case to see men in a state of damnation, wherein, if they should die, they are lost for ever, that methinks we should not be able to let them alone, either in public or private, whatever other work we may have to do. I confess, I am frequently forced to neglect that which should tend to the further increase of knowledge in the godly, because of the lamentable necessity of the unconverted. Who is able to talk of controversies, or of nice unnecessary points, or even of truths of a lower degree of necessity, how excellent soever, while he seeth a company of ignorant, carnal, miserable sinners before his eyes, who must be changed or damned?[23]

It is a challenging perspective. In the reformed evangelical tradition there is a tendency to put pastoral work and evangelism in two different boxes, and then expend the majority of time on the established flock. This was not Baxter's mindset. His highest pastoral priority was the conversion of the lost. To tend to the needs of the

[22] Baxter, *The Reformed Pastor*, 94.
[23] Ibid., 95.

saints and ignore unsaved sinners would be the greatest neglect of his pastoral responsibility. Only if he sought earnestly to win the unsaved, going from house to house as did the Apostle Paul, could he join with him in declaring that he was innocent of the blood of all men (Acts 20:20, 26).

2. Those in need of personal counselling. Baxter's second category concerned the ministry of giving advice to those with 'cases of conscience'. By this he meant answering any concerns that weighed heavily on the hearts or minds of people:

> A minister is not to be merely a public preacher, but to be known as
> a counsellor for their souls, as the physician is for their bodies, and
> the lawyer for their estates: so that each man who is in doubts and
> straits, may bring his case to him for resolution.[24]

The greatest case of conscience he identified was the question, 'What must we do to be saved?' But many other questions may be posed as well. People may bring concerns about some point of truth, the state of their own heart, their lack of assurance, their family duties and responsibilities, their difficulties in witnessing to others, their guilt over past sin, and so on. Cases of conscience were endless, touching every facet of life. In fact, the more vigorous the preaching, the greater the cases of conscience, as people grapple with the implications of God's Word in their lives. Baxter considered it the pastor's task to give time to these particular concerns, helping those with searching questions to reckon seriously with God's Word and will.

3. The converted. Perhaps the most obvious area of pastoral work is among those who belong to the flock of Christ. The pastor's task is to build believers up, strengthening them in the faith, and equipping them for works of service (Eph 4:11-12). Here again Baxter identified various states and conditions of soul. He identified four main categories among believers.

First, he was concerned for the young and the weak spiritually. Even though some may have been long in the faith, they may remain young and weak spiritually.

[24] Ibid., 96.

This, indeed, is the most common condition of the godly. Most of them content themselves with low degrees of grace, and it is no easy matter to get them higher. To bring them to higher and stricter opinions is easy,... but to increase their knowledge and gifts is not easy, and to increase their graces is hardest of all.'[25]

Difficult as it is, it is a most necessary work. Spiritual weakness exposes us to many dangers: it reduces our comfort and delight in God, makes us less serviceable to God and man, makes us more ready to play with Satan's temptations, makes us more readily confuse right and wrong, truth and error, makes us less able to resist and stand in an encounter, makes it easier for us to fall and harder to rise, means we do not know ourselves so well, and causes greater dishonour to the gospel. By contrast 'the strength of Christians is the honour of the Church',[26] because the strong Christian is inflamed with the love of God, has a lively working faith, sets little store by the profits and honours of the world, loves others fervently with a pure heart, can bear and heartily forgive a wrong, will suffer joyfully for the cause of Christ, seeks to do good to others and is ready to be a servant, and is marked by a 'sweet mixture of prudence, humility, zeal and heavenly mindedness'.[27]

A key part of the pastoral task is to take weak Christians on to this kind of spiritual strength. Paul's burden was to 'present everyone perfect in Christ' and it was to this end that he laboured and struggled (Col 1:28-29).

Next, Baxter was pastorally concerned for those who had 'some particular corruption'.[28] In other words, people who have some evident sins and failings that are detrimental both to their own spirituality and to the spirituality of others. Baxter mentioned such sins as pride, worldly-mindedness and sensual desires. Such people must be challenged and helped. Their eyes must be opened to the problem, and the Scriptural remedies opened to them to help them overcome their sin. Baxter again recognised the difficulty of this task, but urged preparedness to address such problems. 'It must, no doubt, be done with much prudence, yet done it must be.'[29]

[25] Ibid., 97. [26] Ibid., 98. [27] Ibid. [28] Ibid. [29] Ibid., 99.

In the third place, he was concerned for backslidden Christians who had lost their first love or fallen into some error or sin. 'As the case of backsliders is very sad, so our diligence must be very great for their recovery.'[30] He focussed on the sadness of such a situation. It is sad for the individual who has lost his or her joy, peace and serviceableness to the Lord. It is sad for us to see them decline when we had held high hopes for them. Above all, it is sad that God should be dishonoured by those for whom he has done so much.

Finally, Baxter's pastoral care among believers extended to the strong in faith, 'for they, also, have need of our assistance: partly to preserve the grace they have; partly to help them in making further progress; and partly to direct them in improving their strength for the service of Christ, and assistance of their brethren; and, also, to encourage them to persevere, that they may receive the crown.'[31] This is a reminder well worth heeding. Often the strongest members of the flock, who make least demands on our time, are the ones most overlooked. The carers are not well-cared for, the hospitable are not invited out, the faithful attenders are not the object of our special interest and attention. If we fail to minister to the strong, they may well decline and become weak, before we pay attention to them.

4. Families. Baxter recognised the importance of the family unit in the purposes of God and identified family ministry as an area of strategic importance. 'If we suffer to neglect this, we shall undo all', because a work begun in a person's heart can easily be undone if they are in a careless, prayerless, worldly family. 'I beseech you, therefore, if you desire the reformation and welfare of your people, do all you can to promote family religion.'[32]

Family visitation was the focus of his personal catechising, and he gave specific advice from his own experience as to how to undertake such visits. First, he advised, find out what you can about a family, so you know how it operates and therefore how you may encourage them to make progress. Then call on them informally and try to speak with the father particularly about his spiritual leadership in the home. Make a particular point of encouraging prayer in the family, and encourage them to read 'some useful moving books, beside the

[30] Ibid.   [31] Ibid., 100.   [32] Ibid., 100.

Bible'.[33] He also encouraged pastors to teach families the right use of the Lord's Day, especially encouraging discussion of the day's preaching with the family.

His conviction was that strong families, headed by strong fathers, would greatly aid the entire work of the church: 'Get masters of families to do their duty, and they will not only spare you a great deal of labour, but will much further the success of your labours.... You are not like to see any general reformation, till you procure family reformation.'[34]

This is an area of particular significance today. With the widespread breakdown of the family unit, and the frequent weakness of men as leaders in the home, there is special need for pastors to minister to families.

5. *The sick.* Those who are sick, weak, elderly or in some other way needy ought to be the special focus of pastoral care. Baxter regarded them as affording a special opportunity for ministry because such people were more likely to speak of spiritual matters. Faced with serious illness or troubles that burden the heart, people are more open to consider God's purposes and take matters of life and death seriously.

6. *Those living offensively or impenitently.* By far the shortest of the sections, Baxter simply noted that before any matter is brought to the church for discipline, it is necessary first to reprove and rebuke privately. We must be careful in this to take note of different people's temperaments and situations, but also be prepared to be plain, so as to shake them from their sin.

7. *Those requiring Christian discipline.* Baxter was a strong advocate of church discipline. In his day it was almost as neglected as in our own. Few churches take seriously the injunctions of Scripture to confront sin by way of admonition and rebuke, let alone excommunicate those who refuse to repent. More commonly, sin and error is simply overlooked, or worse, excused or condoned.

Baxter, in addition to urging serious dealing with the sin of our own souls, urged the importance of the church dealing with the glaring sins of its members. We should not question the effectiveness of

[33] Ibid., 101.   [34] Ibid., 102.

discipline as an ordinance of God, but rather believe that God can render it useful even if we do not see it that way. Baxter regarded discipline as important in publicly shaming and humbling the sinner, and in manifesting the holiness of Christ, his doctrine and the Church. He held that the motive for discipline was not only the well-being of the offender but the honour of the Church. Even when discipline fails to restore the sinner, it deters others, and helps maintain the purity of the church.

Baxter knew church discipline to be hard and unpleasant work. Yet he knew it to be vital for the well-being of the body of Christ. It was for him, as it should be for us, an integral part of the pastoral task.

In identifying these seven categories of pastoral concern, we must not think in terms of 'putting people in boxes'. On the contrary, the burden of Baxter's pastoral approach was to respond to the great variety and complexity of individual cases. This mentality, practised throughout the week in his pastoral dealings with people, accompanied him into the pulpit as well. When he preached to his people, he did so conscious of the variety of conditions of soul represented in the congregation. He was concerned to speak not to all generally, but to many different types of people specifically. He wanted to preach to the lost, to the hardened, to the backsliding, to those in leadership positions, to the depressed, the confused, and so on. His thorough pastoral work was the basis of thorough preaching.

Puritan counselling
One of Baxter's most monumental works was *A Christian Directory* in which he took up the work of 'casuistry'. The Directory, totalling some 900 pages, was divided into four main sections. The first dealt with personal spiritual life, or 'ethics' as he called it. Here he gave dozens of directions to Christians 'for the ordering of the private actions of our hearts and lives, in the work of holy self-government, unto and under God'.[35] His concern was to bring the principles of God's Word to bear in the lives of people so that they conformed to

[35] Baxter, *A Christian Directory*, 7.

God in every detail of their living. He began, as usual, with his highest priority of explaining how those without grace may be saved. Then he proceeded to give directions to those who were weak in the faith. Often his advice was but that of a godly, older man giving sanctified, biblical counsel to the young in faith. Some of his headings indicate this:

> *Direct.* V. Be very thankful for the great mercy of your conversion: but yet overvalue not your first degrees of knowledge or holiness, but remember that you are yet but in your infancy, and must expect your growth and ripeness as the consequent of time and diligence.[36]

> *Direct.* VII. If it be in your power, live under a judicious, faithful, serious, searching, powerful minister; and diligently attend his public teaching, and use his private counsel.[37]

> *Direct.* XVI. Make careful choice of the books which you read. Let the holy Scriptures ever have pre-eminence; and next them, the solid, lively, heavenly treatises, which best expound and apply the Scriptures.[38]

> *Direct.* XIX. Promise not yourselves long life, or prosperity and great matters in the world, lest it entangle your hearts with transitory things, and engage you in ambitious or covetous designs, and steal away your hearts from God, and destroy all your serious apprehensions of eternity.[39]

From there he proceeded to seventeen 'grand directions' for walking with God and leading a life of holiness. He addressed such matters as how to live by faith, how to learn of Christ as our teacher, the nature of Christian warfare, the doctrine of good works and how to be servants of Christ, directions for glorifying God, and so on. This was followed by addressing sins that are contrary to godliness, including unbelief, hardness of heart, pride, covetousness and sensuality. He then moved on to positive direction for the governing of our thoughts, passions, senses, tongue and body.

Repeatedly he advanced his instruction by posing questions. His

[36] Ibid., 41.   [37] Ibid., 44.   [38] Ibid., 56.   [39] Ibid., 60.

concern was to answer the issues that people may grapple with, or suggest to them the spiritual matter they should consider. For example, when dealing with the matter of good works and service to Christ, he posed and answered such questions as these: 'Is doing good, or avoiding sin, to be most looked at in the choice of a calling or employment of life?' 'Is it not every man's duty to obey his conscience?' 'Must I forbear a certain duty...for fear of a small, uncertain sin?'[40] This close dealing with the conscience, and the practical questions of life, was to Baxter what pastoral ministry was all about.

In the second section of the *Directory* he dealt with matters relating to the home and family – what he called 'economics' (used in its most literal sense).[41] Again he addressed many cases of conscience and gave directions on the duty of wives to their husbands, husbands to their wives, leadership in the home, children, masters and servants, and so on.

In the third section he dealt with 174 cases of conscience relating to church life, covering a whole range of practical and theological matters that people may grapple with. He first set out principles relating to worship, Christian ministry, vows and oaths. The many questions he addressed ranged from 'How to know which is the true church' to 'Is a pastor obliged to his flock for life?' to 'How far is tradition and men's words and ministry to be trusted in?' to 'How should the Lord's day be spent?' No stone was left unturned as he brought Scriptural principles to bear in the light of his vast pastoral experience.

The final section of the *Directory* consisted of several hundred cases of conscience in the area of political, economic and societal concerns. Here he addressed the role of civil and church authorities, the responsibilities of lawyers, physicians, schoolmasters, and soldiers. He gave guidance concerning the command to love one's neighbour, and instruction on contracts, borrowing, lending, buying and selling, and the like. No leaf was left unturned. Every part of life had been

[40] Ibid., 114-16.
[41] The word 'economy' stems from the Greek words *oikos,* house, and *nomos,* law, and therefore related to the government and management of a household.

given serious thought in the light of God's sovereign commands.

At least two things are apparent from the work as a whole. First, effective pastoral work often revolves around being able to give clear, practical advice to those who need it. 'One word of seasonable, prudent advice, given by a minister to persons in necessity, may be of more use than many sermons.'[42] Such advice, however, is never to be cheap, simplistic or generalised. Baxter believed in dealing thoroughly, even painstakingly, with people's souls. Keeble explains his approach as follows:

> To be practical, counsel must be realistic: in Baxter, this means never prescribing absolute norms of either behaviour or experience, never offering simplistic answers to moral questions, never generalizing. He is always conscious that no neatly turned theological formulation or ethical direction can do justice to the subtlety, elusiveness, and variety of human nature and experience.[43]

Effective pastoral work requires an understanding of people, their concerns, and particularly their souls:

> To this end it is very necessary that you be well acquainted with practical cases, and especially that you be acquainted with the nature of saving grace, and able to assist them in trying their state, and in resolving the main question that concerns their everlasting life or death.[44]

Baxter's memory of hundreds of cases of conscience is eloquent testimony to his own painstaking pastoral care. Every concern of every individual was taken to heart and dealt with specifically and personally. The cases cited in the *Directory* were 'what my bare memory brought to hand: and cases are so innumerable, that it is far harder, methinks, to remember them, than to answer them.'[45]

It was for this very reason that his practical works and sermons

---

[42] Baxter, *The Reformed Pastor*, 97.

[43] Keeble, *Richard Baxter*, 78.

[44] Baxter, *The Reformed Pastor*, 97.

[45] Baxter, *A Christian Directory*, 3.

swelled to such large proportions. His was no cliché Christianity that could be boiled down to some quick steps or simple solutions. While we will not want to be as exhaustive as he was we will need to be thorough and searching in our consideration of people's problems and needs if we want to be as effective in our pastoral and pulpit work.

The second thing that is apparent from *A Christian Directory* is that to do this, a pastor must have a deep and thorough understanding of the Scriptures and an ability to apply biblical truth to the whole of life. The pastor is to proceed with the conviction that as a 'man of God' thoroughly steeped in the God-breathed Scriptures, he is 'thoroughly equipped for every good work', and able to apply the Scriptures that are most profitable for 'teaching, correcting, rebuking and training in righteousness' (2 Tim. 3:16). From that basis, the pastor is to develop a biblical view of life, including work, home, relationships, church and state, as well as personal spiritual experience. Puritan spirituality was never compartmentalised. Submitting to God and serving him was the business of the whole of life, and the minister was to be one who had a thorough understanding of life from a biblical perspective.

These two perspectives help bring some sanity into the arena of Christian counselling. Baxter was writing well before the advent of modern psychology. When he spoke of 'counselling' he was not thinking in terms of particular theories of human psychology. What he had in view was the need for pastors to be able to respond biblically and pastorally to the questions, concerns and problems people face in their day-to-day personal, spiritual, working and church lives. It is at this level that pastors must be counsellors. We need not be trained psychotherapists. Nor ought we feel that every personal problem is to be referred to some other 'expert' counsellor. Rather, we are to minister God's Word to people, as we spend time with them, encouraging, challenging, advising, admonishing and comforting.

Pastoral strategy

Effective pastoring is dependent on the sort of clear-mindedness indicated above. We need to think in terms of the different categories of people who need our attention. We need to think in terms of the condition of people's souls, seeking to understand, diagnose and assess where people are at spiritually. We need to remember the spiritual task entrusted to us – that of shepherding souls, not mere social visitation. And we need to prioritize our pastoral work, identifying those areas of work that are most necessary. Pastoral strategy is essential.

The strategy Baxter developed for Kidderminster was that of *personal catechising*. His aim was twofold: to visit every family in the parish at least annually, and to use those visits for teaching and instructing them in the faith. 'To upgrade the practice of personal catechizing from a preliminary discipline for children to a permanent ingredient in pastoral care for all ages was Baxter's main contribution to the development of Puritan ideals for the ministry.'[46]

In presenting this model to his fellow ministers he asked them to consider, 'Whether it be not the unquestionable duty of the generality of ministers..., to set themselves presently to the work of catechizing, and instructing individually, all that are committed to their care, who will be persuaded to submit thereunto?'[47] He then reasoned that people must be taught the principles of religion; they must be taught in the most edifying, advantageous way possible; it is beyond dispute that personal conference and examination and instruction has many excellent advantages for their good and is recommended by the Scriptures and by the practice of the saints in all ages. We must, therefore, extend this ministry to those under our care. The work should take up a large part of our time and should be undertaken in an orderly, systematic manner.

To put his strategy into practice Baxter and his assistant arranged to see fourteen families each week. Those in the country would come to visit them; those in the town would be visited by them.[48] The visits

---

[46] Packer, introduction to *The Reformed Pastor*, 13.

[47] Baxter, *The Reformed Pastor*, 42.

[48] Baxter had several assistants during his time at Kidderminster. The first

were arranged by the clerk in advance, and each family was given a copy of the catechism beforehand, to read and study. When they met with the ministers they would be questioned on their understanding of the gospel. Tenderly and diligently the work was advanced, with all 800 households being visited annually.

His time with each family or individual was never merely social. His concern was to minister spiritually to them. First he would seek to build a healthy relationship with each family, showing love to them, persuading them of the importance of such pastoral contact, giving them books that would stimulate them, and acting with gentleness and grace toward all. He would then try to uncover their true spiritual condition. He would seek to ascertain their knowledge of the faith and the state of their heart. Then he would pick up on some point of importance to their spiritual condition. He desired to take them on in their understanding of some truth, or work through some area of need in their life, or, if he felt them to be unconverted, endeavour to lead them to repentance and faith. He would close by pressing on them some practical response, be it a book they were to read, a habit they were to form, a change they were to make. By these means, he ensured that his visits were spiritually focused. He wanted to minister to people's hearts, from the Word of God, in a warm yet direct manner.

His whole approach was uniquely suited to his own situation. He worked in a 'parish' system where the people of the town were his defined mission field and where some connection or affiliation with the established church was important in the eyes of society. Much of his pastoral work was therefore evangelistic. He also ministered at a time when a certain deference was paid to the local minister. The minister was more learned and more revered than most in the town and could command a large measure of respect in the community. Where today people turn to educationalists, psychologists, doctors and other 'experts' for help, then they were more likely to turn to their local pastor.

and main one was Richard Sargeant. Initially they visited together, but in time each undertook their own visits, Sargeant focusing on those who were more retiring. Later assistants were Thomas Baldwin and Joseph Read.

Even with these distinct advantages Baxter felt the inadequacy of his model. He was only seeing his families once a year, and in that brief time endeavouring to discover their needs and meet them. Far from aspiring to a larger church, he longed for a much smaller parish where he could give his people more time.[49]

The benefit of considering Baxter's pastoral ministry in Kidderminster is not in discovering a readily usable model for today, much less in witnessing a perfect model, but rather, in being challenged by the principles and motives that drove it. Baxter's convictions set before us the following issues. First, a significant part of our weekly schedule ought to be invested in time with individuals and families. Amid the flurry of meetings, the demands of administrative matters, the pressure of unexpected crises and the time-consuming work of sermon preparation, we must allot adequate time simply to being pastors.

In this, we ought never to be sole pastors. Our pastoral work should be complemented by the pastoral oversight of an active eldership – a dimension of church leadership conspicuously absent from Baxter's model. Clearly, Paul's conception of the church was of a plurality of elders in each church, with all elders being given to the task of spiritual oversight.[50] As pastors, however, we ought to lead the way in that ministry, and take it on ourselves to equip our fellow elders for their role in this ministry. We must ensure that the whole flock is pastored by the body of elders.

Next, we ought to ensure breadth of pastoral contact. Even if we cannot minister to each person in the congregation, our pastoring

---

[49] He wrote, 'I profess for my own part, I am so far from their boldness that dare venture on the sole government of a county, that I would not, for all England, have undertaken to be one of the two that should do all the pastoral work that God requireth, in the parish where I live, had I not this to satisfy my conscience, that, through the Church's necessities, more cannot be had; and therefore, I must rather do what I can, than leave all undone because I cannot do all. But cases of unavoidable necessity are not to be the ordinary condition of the Church;... O happy Church of Christ, were the labourers but able and faithful, and proportioned in number to the number of souls; so that the pastors were so many, or the particular churches so small, that we might be able to 'take heed to all the flock' (*The Reformed Pastor*, 90).

[50] See, for example, Acts 20:28, Titus 1:5, and 1 Timothy 5:17.

ought to be representative of the many types of people in the church. We need to spend time with the young and the elderly, the spiritually strong and the weak, enquirers and backsliders, those with difficult personal problems, and those blossoming in their faith. Particular note should be taken of Baxter's highest priority: evangelism. If a pastor is not active himself in witnessing to the lost, he is not likely to know how to win them from the pulpit, nor likely to enthuse his people to be active in personal witness. Such variety in pastoral work helps to keep us balanced, forces us to grow, gives us a deeper understanding of people, and better informs our preaching ministry.

Third, we must ensure that pastoral visits are spiritually significant. We must keep before us the clear goals of better understanding the spiritual condition of each person we meet with, and ministering personally and effectively from God's Word to their particular needs. Merely social visitation is inadequate. Our concern must be to turn conversation to matters of eternal significance, seizing every opportunity to address heart issues. Wherever possible we ought to open appropriate Scriptures and lead in meaningful prayer. We must seek to show our deep interest in people's well-being, and seek times of fellowship with them that are spiritually enriching.

Only this type of pastoral focus lays the necessary foundation for an effective experimental ministry of the Word. While it is quite possible to lecture on biblical texts or present contemporary topical messages without this type of pastoral commitment, it is not possible to preach experimentally without this kind of heart for people, or familiarity with their needs. Nor is it possible to secure the degree of sanctification that we should be aiming for in people's lives without diligent pastoral work both undergirding and following-up the preaching ministry. Preachers must reckon with that fact that preaching is not the only ministry of the Word. It is a vital, powerful ministry to be sure, but preaching can never stand alone, and a preacher can never be a preacher alone.

Chapter 4

Preaching Purposefully

He hath appointed the ministerial office, that men might be his
messengers to men, to acquaint them with his grace, and with the
glory which he prepareth for them, that they may truly believe it,
soberly think of it, duly value it, heartily chose it, and diligently seek
it, and live and die in the joyful expectation of it.[1]

He is no true Minister of Christ whose heart is not set on the
winning, and sanctifying, and saving of Souls.[2]

I confess I think NECESSITY should be the great disposer of a
minister's course of study and labour....life is short,
and we are dull, and eternal things are necessary,
and the souls that depend on our teaching are precious.[3]

It is no small matter to remain fresh, focused and faithful in the
preaching ministry. Even when we have the clearest sense of call to
preach, we may find our convictions slowly eroded away by other
forces. The pressure of weekly deadlines, the desire to satisfy people's
varying expectations, the distraction of difficult pastoral situations,
the discouragement of criticism, and the plethora of ideas promoted
regarding contemporary ministry, may combine to distort our view
of what preaching is all about. We may find that slowly, subtly our
confidence in the authority of the Word wanes, our commitment to
preparation diminishes, our convictions about preaching are watered
down, and our goals become blurred.

---

[1] Richard Baxter, 'Reasons For Ministers Using The Greatest Plainness and
Seriousness Possible, in All Their Applications to Their People,' in *Practical
Works*, 4: 1046.

[2] Baxter, *Compassionate Counsel* (1681). Quoted in N. H. Keeble, 'Richard
Baxter's Preaching Ministry: its History and Texts,' *Journal of Ecclesiastical
History*, 35, no. 4 (October 1984): 540.

[3] Baxter, *The Reformed Pastor*, 113.

If we are to withstand such pressures we need to have a very clear-minded view of what preaching is all about. Without a strong theology of preaching driving our ministry forward we will most likely lose heart and lose focus. We will find ourselves merely existing from week to week; opting for what seems to work best, what we have always done, what triggers the greatest response, what feels best or even what is easiest. Eventually we will run dry.

Here, again, the Puritans are most helpful. Their robust preaching was grounded in strong theological convictions. This is clearly evident in Baxter's ministry. Undergirding his entire preaching ministry were three intimately related strands: convictions concerning the Word of God and how it is to be preached; convictions concerning the heart of man and how it is to be addressed; and convictions concerning the essential goals and purposes of preaching.

An expository ministry

All Puritan preaching centred around the exposition of Scripture. The Puritans believed that God's Word is *the* great tool in the preacher's hand. They knew it to be the power of God unto salvation; a double-edged sword that penetrates to the dividing of soul and spirit; God-breathed, and profitable for teaching, rebuking, correcting and training in righteousness; the sword of the Spirit; the bread of life on which man must live; and the truth that sanctifies.[4] They also believed that when the Word is faithfully preached, it is accompanied by the authority and power of the Spirit. They knew that the Spirit had been given for that express purpose, and that in the weakness of preaching God was pleased to manifest his power.[5]

Their conviction, then, was that the Word does the work. Though a preacher must work hard to communicate truth clearly, they knew that it is not the illustrations, the humour, or the eloquence of the preacher that brings change in people's lives, but the power of the Word itself. Consequently, their sermons were utterly soaked in Scripture. The Word was opened, probed, applied, illustrated and

[4] See Romans 1:16, Hebrews 4:12, 2 Timothy 3:16, Ephesians 6:17, Deuteronomy 8:4 and John 17:17.

[5] See Acts 1:8, 1 Corinthians 2:4 and 2 Corinthians 4:7.

enforced. The task of the preacher was to proclaim the Word, teach sound doctrine and drive that truth home to people's minds and hearts.

This was the overwhelming burden of the preacher. He was to preach the Word, in season and out of season. He did so by 'opening' texts – opening up the meaning, purpose, thrust and heart of a passage. The preacher was to exposit, or draw out of a text, the truth that God had put in it.

The Puritan method of expositing a text became known as 'the new reformed method' of preaching and typically consisted of three elements: doctrines, proofs and uses. In the first section the main doctrines, truths or propositions of the text were set out. Here the teaching of the text was distilled and arranged into principles. Then in the second section these doctrines were argued, explained and reasoned from Scripture and from experience. Many other texts were added to give weight and perspective to the doctrine being addressed. Then the third section made 'use' or application of these doctrines to the hearts and lives of the hearers. The intent of the method was to allow Scripture to speak throughout the sermon.

Baxter largely followed this method, though with a considerable degree of flexibility and adaptation. Typically he read his text and then briefly explained any technical difficulties. These exegetical comments were always concise, amounting to little more than a brief introduction to the text. Next he would draw from the text the main 'doctrines' that were to be expounded. These were usually stated propositionally, as central truths or principles that were to be taken to heart. Sometimes he would state just one doctrine that he would then divide into constituent parts and unfold analytically or thematically. Sometimes there would be four, five, six or more doctrines, that were each unfolded one by one, forming the bulk of the sermon. Still other times he would identify several doctrines, but then open them up quite briefly, reserving the bulk of his time for the 'uses'.

Application was the heart of the matter. It was never tacked on to the end of an otherwise theoretical or academic message. The 'uses' were an essential part of the whole. Indeed, they were the main point of preaching. As Haller explains, the Puritan preacher could not entirely avoid getting himself involved in a certain amount of abstract metaphysical and theological argument, but his real concern was to shape and direct feeling and conduct. His doctrine became in fact a theory of human behaviour, a system of psychology.[6]

In some preaching the lion's share of the time is committed to a detailed exegesis of the text. Much time is spent on historical detail, grammatical analysis, controversies surrounding the text and various interpretations that have been put forward. Only late in the sermon does the preacher move from explication to application. For Baxter, this transition was made as early as possible. In his view, making careful and thorough 'use' of the text was the central part of the preacher's work.

It must be said that because of his concern to make 'use' of the text, Baxter's preaching methodology was 'expository' in the very broadest sense of the word. He was committed to open up biblical truth fully, to speak from particular texts, and to assert the absolute authority of Scripture. He was not always concerned, however, to deal with the literary context or biblical theology of a text, sometimes leaning toward a topical discourse on biblical truth rather than a careful exposition of particular texts. In that regard, his preaching is no perfect model of exposition. We should not turn to him to learn the art of biblical-theological preaching. We can learn much, however, from his method of opening up biblical truth.

Sample sermons

Baxter's expository method is best understood by analysing some of his sermons.[7] One significant example of his approach is found in his 'Farewell Sermon' that was intended for his Kidderminster congregation but never actually preached to them because of the

[6] Haller, *The Rise of Puritanism,* 135.

[7] The article by Keeble, 'Richard Baxter's Preaching Ministry,' provides a useful summary of Baxter's printed sermons and their dates. Keeble notes a change both in content and structure after 1662, his sermons becoming more pastoral in focus and less formally structured. He adopted a more expansive approach in such sermons as 'How to do Good to Many,' 'The Cure of Melancholy,' and 'What Light Must Shine in our Works.' See pp. 554-5.

circumstances surrounding the Restoration. He chose as his text John 16:22: 'And ye now, therefore, have sorrow; but I will see you again, and your heart shall rejoice, and your joy no man taketh from you.' Before coming to the text, he spoke at some length of his departure from them, likening it to a death, a funeral. Almost like an essay prefixed to the message proper this introduction amounted to almost 10% of the whole sermon. It was followed by a brief opening of the details and technicalities of the text (only about 3% of the whole).

Then he announced six 'doctrines':

The sense of the text is contained in these six doctrinal propositions:

Doctrine 1. Sorrow goeth before joy with Christ's disciples.

Doctrine 2. Christ's death and departure was the cause of his disciples' sorrows.

Doctrine 3. The sorrows of Christ's disciples are but short. They are but now.

Doctrine 4. Christ will again visit his sorrowful disciples, though at the present he seem to be taken from them.

Doctrine 5. When Christ returneth or appeareth to his disciples, their sorrows will be turned into joy.

Doctrine 6. The joy of Christians in the return or reappearing of their Lord is such as no man shall take from them.[8]

These doctrines formed the main divisions of the sermon and 'uses' were given for all but one of them. Under the first doctrine, for example, he opened up the kinds of sorrows that may precede joy in the Christian life, and gave reasons why God orders it that way. There followed two 'uses', the first highlighting the importance of sorrows in a person's life, the second urging his congregation not to condemn those who were suffering. When dealing with the third doctrine he gave four reasons why a Christian's sorrows are to be seen as only brief. This led to two uses, the first urging his congregation not to stumble or take offence when a few brief sorrows came on them, the second encouraging them to rejoice in their sorrows given that they are so short-lived.

In arguing and reasoning each doctrine he gave numerous Scripture

[8] Richard Baxter, 'Farewell Sermon,' *Practical Works*, 4:1015.

references – some 140 different texts being cited. He appealed to a great diversity of Scriptures: citations from eighteen different psalms, quotations from six different prophets, verses from three other wisdom books, and many New Testament verses, particularly from Hebrews and 1 Peter, both of which are books that deal extensively with the place of suffering in the Christian life. Sometimes the reference was just an allusion to a passage; often verses were quoted in full. Frequently he cited a number of verses from different passages in succession to demonstrate that a particular truth was the emphasis of Scripture as a whole.

Baxter's approach in this sermon is very expansive. He earths the message in the particular circumstances of the disciples' grief and the promise of lasting joy held out to them by Christ, but then opens up the themes of grief, suffering, departures, joy and fellowship with Christ in a full and substantial way, in order to minister to the wounded hearts of his people. This broad, textual-topical approach is typical of his approach to exposition.

It can be seen in a different way in a sermon on Luke 10:22 entitled 'Right Rejoicing': 'Notwithstanding in this rejoice not, that the spirits are subject unto you; but rather rejoice, because your names are written in heaven.' This sermon was not preached to his own congregation but to the Houses of Parliament at the time of the Restoration in 1660. He began by carefully opening up the context, explaining what joy the subjection of the devils might have afforded the disciples, what joy Christ forbade them, and what joy Christ chiefly allowed them. He then adduced just one doctrine:

> The doctrine of the text is contained in this proposition – To have our names written in heaven is the greatest mercy, and first, and chiefly, and only for itself to be rejoiced in; which so puts the estimate on all inferior mercies, that further than they refer to this they are not to be the matter of our joy.[9]

This 'doctrine' distilled the thrust of the text and led him to explain the two aspects of it: what they were not to rejoice in and what they were to rejoice in. This portion of the sermon was textually based

[9] Richard Baxter, 'Right Rejoicing,' (1660), in *Practical Works,* 4: 895.

and together with the opening explication accounted for about 35% of the whole. At that point he moved to application, using two devices we will return to later: the use of tests, and the use of discriminatory application. His dealing with his hearers was thorough and searching, and accounted for over 40% of the whole.

The final section of the sermon became even broader in scope, focusing on the particular occasion they were celebrating, namely the restoration of the monarchy. He stated reasons for which they might rightly rejoice in that occasion, but concluded by stressing that they were inferior mercies to that of having their names in heaven. This final applicatory section accounted for almost 25% of the whole.

A third example of his expository preaching displays another variation on the triple schema of doctrines, proofs and uses. He preached a sermon on Psalm 2:10-12, entitled, 'The Absolute Sovereignty of Christ.' Preached to the Judges of Assize it could scarcely have been a more pointed text: 'Be wise now therefore, O ye kings: be instructed, ye judges of the earth. Serve the Lord with fear, and rejoice with trembling.' After summarising the scope of the Psalm as a whole he observed that his text was the application of the Psalm. He again identified a single doctrine:

> *Doctrine.* No power or privilege can save that man from the fearful, sudden, consuming wrath of God, that doth not unfeignedly love, depend upon, and subject himself unto the Lord Jesus Christ.[10]

The sermon, while heavily weighted toward application, was faithful to the intent of the text and the Christ-centred focus of the Psalm. As usual, he explained his method at the start:

> In handling this point I shall observe this order.
> 1. I will show you what this love, dependence, and subjection are.
> 2. What wrath it is that will thus kindle and consume them.
> 3. Why this kissing the Son is the only way to escape it.
> 4. Why no power or privilege else can procure their escape.
> 5. The application.[11]

[10] Richard Baxter, 'The Absolute Sovereignty of Christ,' (1654), in *Practical Works,* 4: 798.
[11] Ibid.

His opening of the first four points was quite brief, amounting to less than 20% of the whole. The vast bulk of the sermon was the application, which was given as two 'uses'. The first use focused on their spiritual well-being. He urged them to examine their subjection to Christ, their dependence on him, and their love for him. Then he began the second use by saying, 'it is time that I turn my speech to exhortation, and oh that you would encourage me with your resolutions to obey! My business here to-day is, as his herald and ambassador, to proclaim the Lord Jesus your King and Saviour, and to know whether you will heartily acknowledge and take him so to be or not'.[12] At length he pleaded with them and sought to persuade them not to anger God and come under his wrath, but to 'kiss the Son'. These two uses, together with his closing appeals, accounted for 70% of the sermon.

Clearly, his concern in these sermons was not simply to provide a commentary on the text, but to open up broadly and expansively the full implications and applications of it. His focus was on the Word, in all its fullness. He wanted to instil in his people a knowledge of and love for the Scriptures. He maintained that 'it is our very office to teach the people the Scripture' and when we do so 'it will preserve the due esteem and reverence of the holy Scriptures'.[13]

For this reason he was careful to let Scripture speak rather than other authorities. Seldom in his sermons are there references to other commentators or to the original languages. Preaching was not to be scholarly lecturing. It was the plain and forceful opening of Scripture to the hearts of his people. It was the Word that would strengthen, nourish, protect, help and guide his flock.

Preachers who undertake this type of expository preaching ministry need to have a similar commitment to the Word itself as their supreme tool. Having been set aside by a congregation to prepare spiritual food we must spend our week searching the Word, comparing Scripture with Scripture, meditating on the truths to be preached, and praying over the message to be presented. We must labour to have a thorough grasp of the text and study to see how it fits into the

[12] Ibid., 801.
[13] Baxter, *A Christian Directory*, 719.

whole canon of Scripture. Expository preaching demands that we be men of the Word and prayer (Acts 6:4).

This requires discipline and diligence but it also brings freedom. Freedom is found in realising that effectiveness and power in preaching are not dependent on being clever, witty and smart. We do not have to be the world's greatest communicator, the country's finest orator, or the city's foremost comedian to preach a message that has power. What we must do is preach the Word which is itself living and active, sharper than any double edged sword. If the message preached is full of the Word, and opens faithfully the message of Scripture, we may be sure that it will not return to the Lord void.

Accessing the heart via the mind

Although this conviction was fundamental to Baxter's philosophy of preaching, it was inseparable from his convictions concerning the heart of man. His preaching methodology arose not only from his belief that the Word must be brought home to the heart, but from his particular understanding of man's heart. The heart or soul of man, consisting of the faculties of mind, will, conscience and affections, was to be approached in a precise way.

The preacher's first task was to address the mind. Preaching began with the intellect. In Baxter's words, 'the understanding must take in truths, and prepare them for the will, and that for the affections.'[14] He held that '[y]our understandings are the way in to the whole soul.'[15] That is why in Puritan preaching there was such depth and breadth of content. They believed that if there was no true understanding of God and spiritual things, the other faculties of the heart would not respond adequately.

In chapter two we noted that Baxter's own experience led him to place great weight on the importance of a reasoned faith. His season of doubt caused him to investigate thoroughly the bases of his own convictions, and then, in turn, provide for others the most thorough, rational grounds for belief possible. One writer speaks of his 'almost pathetic belief in logic',[16] and it is true that he became virtually

[14] Baxter, *The Saints' Everlasting Rest* (Religious Tract Society), 276.
[15] Baxter, *The Saints' Everlasting Rest*, ed. Pipe, 15.

rationalistic in his theology. Yet it was a case of his strength being his weakness and vice versa. Nothing is more characteristic of Baxter than his ability to appeal to reason:

> His sermons recognise that, as a rational creature, man can adhere steadfastly only to what he rationally accepts, and they therefore seek to arouse more than a merely emotional excitement of necessarily short duration. Rhetoric is the servant of logic, not a substitute for it: 'the work of mans Conversion, and holy Conversation, is...carryed on by Gods exciting of our *Reason*... the misery of the ungodly is, that they have *Reason* in faculty, and not in *use*'.[17]

Behind this emphasis lay the theory that analysis is the key to understanding. This was typical of all the Puritans, and perhaps particularly of Baxter. The theory had been espoused by the sixteenth century French Huguenot educationalist, and martyr, Peter Ramus. Ramus had proposed a teaching method that revolved around dichotomising analysis – breaking a proposition into two constituent parts, and examining each; then breaking each part into two parts, and examining them, and so on.[18] The result was minute and careful analysis by which a person was brought to a thorough understanding of the truth as a whole. The approach accounts for much of the

[16] Hugh Martin, *Puritanism and Richard Baxter*, 139.

[17] N. H. Keeble, 'Richard Baxter's Preaching Ministry,' 553.

[18] Ramus's *Logic* was first translated into English in 1574, but was suppressed by Elizabeth I. However, in 1584 Dudley Fennes published a book in Holland entitled *The Arts of Logike and Rhetoricke Plainely Set Forth in the English Tongue*, and in 1588 Abraham Fraunces addressed Ramus' logic in *The Lawiers Logike*. These works seem to have influenced the early Puritans, and the first clear evidence of that was in William Perkin's *The Art of Prophesying*. Ramus' approach to logic and rhetoric was seen as a useful tool for making searching and far-reaching applications of the biblical text. Leon Howard, in summarising a sermon by the early Puritan Thomas Cartwright, concludes that 'the observable fact is that the Ramean system of logic enabled a representative Puritan to go far beyond the literal meaning of the scriptures without engaging in the Roman practice of allegorizing them' (Leon Howard, *Essays on Puritans and Puritanism*, ed. James Barbour and Thomas Quirk, Albuquerque: University of New Mexico Press, 1986, 155).

detailed division and sub-division of Puritan preaching. It tended toward scholasticism but had the merits of helping people think deeply and carefully about truth. It demanded of preachers logic and careful method, and it enabled hearers to break down and process ideas that may otherwise have remained rather abstract.[19]

Conscience-oriented preaching

This close analysis of truth was never intended merely to satisfy the curiosities of the mind. It was designed as the basis for appeal to the conscience. Baxter maintained that 'the mere explaining of truths and duties is seldom attended with such success, as the lively application of them to the conscience; and especially when a divine blessing is earnestly sought for, to accompany such application'.[20] Such prayerful addressing of the conscience enabled a preacher to make people feel the weight of the truth upon their souls.

The Puritans regarded the conscience as the most critical faculty of man's heart. They saw it as an innate judge of the soul. It is the God-given faculty that deals with questions of right and wrong, truth and error, duty and failure. It is the means by which a man can discern his own actions in the light of his knowledge of God and the law. But the conscience can easily become seared. When its protests are ignored it is increasingly blunted until it is no longer a sharp tool prodding the soul. It becomes less and less useful as a gauge of right and wrong. Baxter therefore commented:

Make not your own judgements or consciences your law,... There is a dangerous error grown too common in the world, that a man is bound to do every thing which his conscience telleth him is the will of God; and that every man must obey his conscience, as if it were the lawgiver of the world; whereas, indeed, it is not ourselves, but God, that is our lawgiver. And conscience is...appointed...only to

[19] Baxter said of his own method in study, 'I never thought I understood any thing till I could anatomise it and see the parts distinctly, and the conjunction of the parts as they make up the whole. Distinction and method seemed to me of that necessity, that without them I could not be said to know...' (*Autobiography*, 10).

[20] Baxter, *The Saints' Everlasting Rest* (Religious Tract Society), 312.

discern the law of God, and call upon us to observe it: and an erring conscience is not to be obeyed, but to be better informed.[21]

That, then, was the preacher's task: to better inform the conscience. The preacher was to make full use of this God-given tool for speaking to the soul. He was to inform it of God's laws and commands so that it was kept sharp and would be a piercing tool in a person's heart. He was to appeal to it, so that people might be pricked in their consciences and cut to the heart. And he was to lead those convicted of sin to Christ, whose blood cleanses us from a guilty conscience.

Conscience-oriented preaching was never vague or general. It was often uncomfortable and searching. Yet in the hands of a skilled preacher it wasn't demoralising or damning. The end goal was spiritual health, and the purpose of preaching to the conscience was to lead people to a fuller experience of Christ's redeeming grace.

'Affective' preaching

Having addressed the mind and pressed the truth against the conscience, the preacher's next task was to appeal to the will and the affections. The will needed to be shaped and changed, so that a person made godly resolves to respond to the truth. Baxter sought to persuade the hearer to embrace, adopt and act on the truth. It should be noted that the will was only persuaded in so far as the mind had been informed and the conscience pricked. Experimental preaching did not coerce people with legalistic demands, but sought to get within a person, and persuade the will by force of reason.

That was usually only possible if the 'affections' were stirred. This word was used by the Puritans to refer to the inner desires and drives of a person. Far from being merely natural instincts, emotions or feelings, affections were the deep heart responses of an informed mind.

In conversion the affections are changed, as Baxter explained in his *Treatise of Conversion*. First, he said, the affections of love and hatred are changed. The natural man does not love spiritual things or

[21] Baxter, *A Christian Directory*, 115-16.

inward holiness or God himself. But in conversion he is drawn to love these things and comes to hate sin and evil. Closely related to these are the affections of desire and aversion. The converted man begins to desire the things of heaven and finds a new aversion to the things of the world. Then he identifies the affections of delight and sorrow. Where once a man delighted in the pleasures of this world, after conversion he comes to delight in the things of God. Similarly, once his greatest sorrows were for his loss of material and physical things, but now it is spiritual failure that causes the greatest sorrow. The next pair of affections are hope and desire, followed by courage and fear. Then comes anger, 'a single passion, and hath no contrary.' Before conversion a man is angry at those who rebuke him or preach the gospel to him; after conversion he is angry at himself for his own sin. The last affections he cites are content and discontent.[22]

A similar list of affections is given in *The Saints' Everlasting Rest*, where he describes the affections that must be stirred in a person when considering the realities of heaven. There he speaks first of love, then desire, hope, courage and joy. He prefaces his description by explaining his method: 'When the judgement hath determined, and faith hath apprehended, the truth of our happiness, then may our meditation proceed to raise our affections. And particularly, – love – desire – hope – courage, or boldness – and joy.'[23] That, for Baxter, was the correct order: rational knowledge, leading to a believing heart, producing changed affections.

It is significant that in both these lists, love is the first affection considered. Baxter saw this, and not fear, as the prime motivating force in a true convert. While fear of God and judgement was a right affection, love for God was a higher one: 'It is love that must be the predominant affection, and therefore it is the discovery of the Amiableness of God...that must be the principal Argument.'[24]

A person must be made to feel the truth. The concern of the preacher was not simply to inform people about the truth of God's

[22] Richard Baxter, *A Treatise of Conversion* in *Practical Works*, 2:418-24.

[23] Baxter, *The Saints' Everlasting Rest* (Religious Tract Society), 296-7.

[24] Baxter, *Treatise of Conversion*, quoted in Keeble, 'Richard Baxter's Preaching Ministry,' 551.

Word, but create a situation in which people were actually drawn in love to Christ, made to feel the horror of sin, and stirred to genuine joy in contemplation of heavenly realities:

> As man is not so prone to live according to the truth he knows except it do deeply affect him, so neither doth his soul enjoy its sweetness, except speculation do pass to affection. The understanding is not the whole soul, and therefore cannot do the whole work.... The understanding must take in truths, and prepare them for the will, and it must receive them and commend them to the affections;... the affections are, as it were, the bottom of the soul.[25]

The saints themselves were to seek this: 'Let all your knowledge turn into feeling and action. Keep open the passage between your heads and your hearts, that every truth may go to the quick.'[26] But they were not left to their own devices. The preacher was to aid them in this, helping them consider biblical truth in such a way that it moved them:

> Consideration, as it were, opens the door between the head and the heart. The understanding having received truths, lays them up in the memory, and consideration conveys them from thence to the affections. What excellency would there be in much learning and knowledge, if the obstructions between the head and heart were but opened, and the affections did but correspond to the understanding! He is usually the best scholar, whose apprehension is quick, clear, and tenacious; but he is usually the best Christian, whose apprehension is the deepest, and most affectionate, and who has the readiest passage, not so much from the ear to the brain, as from that to the heart.[27]

It was this understanding of man that gave rise to a very experimental handling of biblical truth. Baxter was not merely aiming to provide faithful exposition. He sought to handle the truth in such a

[25] Baxter, *The Saints Everlasting Rest* (Westwood, N.J.: Fleming H. Revell, 1962), 142. Quoted in Ryken, *Worldly Saints,* 103.

[26] Baxter, *The Saints' Everlasting Rest,* ed. Pipe, 16.

[27] Baxter, *The Saints' Everlasting Rest* (Religious Tract Society), 293.

way that it penetrated the heart. In one graphic phrase he speaks of the need 'to screw the truth into their minds, and work Christ into their affections'.[28] He wanted his people to know and grasp the truth (with the mind), have it impressed on their hearts (by the conscience), so that they would be inwardly moved by it (with the affections) and resolved to effect change in their lives (by the will).

This was only possible if divine grace was in operation. The fallen condition of man's heart meant that no true change would be effected without the inward regenerating power of the Holy Spirit. Baxter explained in one sermon:

> All men are born with a serpentine malice and enmity against the seed of Christ, which is rooted in their very natures. Custom in sin increaseth this to more malignity; and it is only renewing grace that doth overcome it.[29]

Yet this dependence on the Spirit in no way detracted from the importance of the preacher doing all he could to bring the truth to bear upon the heart so the Spirit may apply it with life-giving force.[30]

This philosophy of preaching, while producing certain characteristics we need to be wary of (such as excessive analysis or a rather introspective probing of the heart) did enable Baxter to avoid some of the devastating failures of contemporary preaching. There

[28] Baxter, *The Reformed Pastor,* 70.

[29] Richard Baxter, 'A Sermon of Repentance' (1660), in *Practical Works,* 4:889.

[30] 'The Puritans inherited without question and almost unchanged the scholastic model of human nature. In relating this to their concept of regeneration they were concerned mainly with the relations between the faculties of the rational soul: the reason, the will and the affections . . . Reason, as the king of the faculties, should be in control, acting with the will to rule the affections; but in fallen man both the will and the affections are in revolt, while reason itself is imperfect. Thus the affections act independently to forestall reason, which itself is misled by the corrupted imagination; and the dominant activity of the will is to command the reason to provide excuses for self-justification and continued rebellion against God.... A harmonious combination of the faculties could be achieved only by a simultaneous seizure of them all by divine grace, accompanied by a rational comprehension of the truth' (Watkins, *The Puritan Experience,* 5-6).

was no place for woolly subjectivism – it was too substantial for that. There was no room for legalistic coercion – it was too reasoned for that. There was no scope for a light playing on the emotions – it was too concerned with deep issues of the soul for that. And there was little risk of false conversion through easy-believism or quick decisionism – it was far too searching for that. When preaching is aimed at the mind alone, it produces intellectualism; when aimed at the conscience alone, manipulation; when aimed at the affections alone, emotionalism; when aimed at the will alone, legalism. Preaching, however, that addresses all these faculties in their right relation to each other, is genuinely persuasive.

Eternal realities

As Baxter sought to 'get within' people in this way, he never lost sight of why he was doing so. The third conviction undergirding his whole approach to preaching was his clear-minded view of its true goals and purposes. Baxter spoke of the sermon as 'a message from the God of heaven, of everlasting moment to the souls of men'.[31] Its significance lay in the fact that it was either to turn people from hell or prepare them for heaven; it was to convert the lost or sanctify the saved; it was to carry out the task of evangelism or of edification. Those were the two great goals of preaching always at the forefront of his mind. He said:

> He hath appointed the ministerial office, that men might be his messengers to men, to acquaint them with his grace, and with the glory which he prepareth for them, that they may truly believe it, soberly think of it, duly value it, heartily choose it, and diligently seek it, and live and die in the joyful expectation of it.[32]

He added:

> We are charged to set before them the great salvation which Christ hath procured, and importunately to beseech them to mind it, believe it, and accept it, that it may be theirs for ever.... We tell them but

[31] Baxter, *The Reformed Pastor*, 70.
[32] Baxter, 'Reasons for Ministers,' 1046.

what God's word, sent from heaven, telleth us and them, that holiness is the love of God and goodness, and the hatred of sin; that the pure in heart are blessed, for they shall see God: but without holiness none can see him. We tell them from God, that heaven is won or lost on earth; and none shall have it but such as hence learn to love a holy and heavenly life; and that the dislike of holiness is the forfeiture of happiness, and the beginning, or forerunner of hell.[33]

One of the most striking features of Baxter's preaching is the frequency with which he spoke of heaven and hell. They were the two great eternal realities he constantly set before people. He was profoundly conscious that in preaching 'we are to God the aroma of Christ among those who are being saved and those who are perishing. To the one we are the smell of death; to the other, the fragrance of life.'[34] He therefore urged pastors to 'speak to your people as to men that must be awakened, either here or in hell'.[35] He believed that 'heaven is such a thing, that if you lose it, nothing can supply the want, or make up the loss; and hell is such a thing, that if you suffer it, nothing can remove your misery, or give you ease and comfort'.[36]

These perspectives drove him to preach passionately both for the sinner's salvation and the saint's edification. It should be noted that these two great goals were not independent of each other, though we will consider them separately here. There is much in evangelistic preaching that edifies the believer, and much in edificational preaching that may move the heart of the unsaved to seek after Christ. While sermons will often have a dominant focus in one direction or the other, frequently they will contain both elements. This is most necessary because believers need to be brought back to the cross of Christ time and again, and unbelievers need to have set before them the great vision of holy living for the glory of God. Besides, it is a great mistake for a preacher to assume that all in his congregation

[33] Ibid.

[34] 2 Corinthians 2:15-16, NIV.

[35] Baxter, *The Reformed Pastor*, 148.

[36] Richard Baxter, *A Call to the Unconverted* (1657; reprint, Grand Rapids: Baker Book House, 1976), 81.

are saved, and therefore need only edificational preaching. It is also a grave mistake to pitch all one's preaching to the unregenerate and never take the saints on to greater maturity.

Evangelistic preaching

Baxter took preaching seriously as the chief evangelistic tool. It was not, for him, the only evangelistic tool. He regarded personal visitation as a tremendous means by which to challenge individuals and families. But in public preaching there was not only a larger audience at one time but the special power and authority of the preached Word.

Baxter knew that a man would not preach fervently to the lost if he did not care deeply for them. He therefore impressed on preachers the great urgency of the work of saving souls. 'The harvest is great, the labourers are few; the loiterers and hinderers are many, the souls of men are precious, the misery of sinners is great,... the joys of heaven are inconceivable.'[37] Such realities were to give preachers a sense of urgency:

> The work of God must needs be done! Souls must not perish, while you mind your worldly business or worldly pleasures, and take your ease, or quarrel with your brethren![38]

He urged:

> O remember, when you are talking with the unconverted, that now you have an opportunity to save a soul, and to rejoice the angels of heaven, and to rejoice Christ himself, to cast Satan out of a sinner, and to increase the family of God![39]

Next to this burden for the lost and urgency of proclamation came a sense of expectancy of God's blessing on the evangelistic preaching of his Word. Baxter believed that a preaching ministry was only likely to be effective in winning souls if that was the goal and aspiration of the preacher:

[37] Baxter, *The Reformed Pastor*, 202.
[38] Ibid., 40. [39] Ibid., 176.

If you would prosper in your work, be sure to keep up earnest desires and expectations of success. If your hearts be not set on the end of your labours, and you long not to see the conversion and edification of your hearers, and do not study and preach in hope, you are not likely to see much success.[40]

The preacher who fails to see much evangelistic fruit from his preaching should not only ask whether he earnestly desires this, but does he truly expect it? Does he pray and preach in faith, with a heart set on seeing people's lives changed by the power of the gospel?

Next, to burden and expectation must be added evangelistic gift and ability. Desire alone will not achieve results. The preacher must become adept at presenting truth to the unsaved mind, and there can be no doubt that Baxter knew how to do this. His chief evangelistic work was a small book entitled *A Call to the Unconverted,* published in 1658. Within a little over a year some 20,000 copies had been printed, and thereafter another 10,000, besides those that were illegally produced. It became instrumental in the conversion of many hundreds, perhaps thousands, of sinners.

Baxter took as his text Ezekiel 33:11: 'Say unto them, As I live, saith the Lord GOD, I have no pleasure in the death of the wicked; but that the wicked may turn from his way and live: turn ye, turn ye from your evil ways; for why will ye die, O house of Israel?' He began by saying how astonishing it seems that only a few will be saved, and asked why this was the case. He argued that it was not adequate to blame Satan, and in the text God cleared himself of the blame. It was therefore the fault of man because he fails to turn and be saved. That led him to deduce seven doctrines from the text:

Doctrine 1: It is the unchangeable law of God, that wicked men must turn or die.

Doctrine 2: It is the promise of God, that the wicked shall live, if they will but turn.

Doctrine 3: God takes pleasure in men's conversion and salvation, but not in their death or damnation: he had rather they would return and live, than go on and die.

[40] Ibid., 121.

Doctrine 4: This is a most certain truth, which because God would not have men to question, he hath confirmed it to them solemnly by his oath.

Doctrine 5: The Lord doth redouble his commands and persuasions to the wicked to turn.

Doctrine 6: The Lord condescendeth to reason the case with them; and asketh why they will die?

Doctrine 7: If after all this the wicked will not turn, it is not the fault of God that they perish.[41]

As Baxter unfolded and applied each of these seven truths he pulled no punches. He made clear from the start that his intention was to confront his readers with issues of life and death. 'If you will believe God, believe this: there is but one of these two ways for every wicked man, either conversion or damnation.'[42] Throughout the discourse he spoke of heaven and hell, salvation and damnation, the godly and the wicked, the way of life and the way of death, depicting the two paths in a manner similar to the way our Lord did in the Sermon on the Mount.

His manner was forthright and his matter full and substantial. It is instructive to note the depth of teaching he gave to unbelievers. Early in the book he unfolded the whole scheme of salvation, explaining man's original state of righteousness, and the fall in which man lost his holy inclination and the love of his soul toward God. He described how man became inclined to love his own flesh and pursue carnal pleasures. He spoke of how this corrupted nature has been passed on to the entire human race so that the sins of our lives spring forth from this nature and we naturally love our present sinful state.

Next he explained that God was not willing that man should perish in his sin. He provided a remedy by sending his own Son to take our nature and act as mediator between God and man. He died for our sins to ransom us from the curse of God. He gave a new law and covenant, 'a law of grace, or a promise of pardon and everlasting life to all that, by true repentance, and by faith in Christ, are converted unto God.'[43]

[41] Baxter, *A Call to the Unconverted,* 9-10.
[42] Ibid., 10. [43] Ibid., 21.

Having spoken of the Father and the Son, he moved on to the role of the Holy Spirit. He explained the necessity of the Spirit's work in view of the spiritual deadness of man's heart. Then he sketched the work of the Spirit in first inspiring the recording of Scripture, then sealing the Scriptures by miracles and wonders, and finally illumining and converting the souls of the elect.

He did not shy away from any doctrine that was a part of the gospel message: original sin, the wrath and justice of God, the substitutionary atonement of Christ, the inner work of the Spirit, election and free will – all were addressed. At one point he posed the objection of those who say, 'We cannot convert ourselves till God converts us; we can do nothing without his grace.'[44] He answered that their lack of ability was because of their unwillingness:

> You could turn if you were but truly willing; and if your wills themselves are so corrupted that nothing but effectual grace will move them, you have the more cause to seek for that grace, and yield to it, and do what you can in the use of means, and not neglect it and set yourself against it. Do what you are able first, and then complain of God for denying you grace, if you have cause.[45]

He then addressed more directly the matter of free will:

> Your will is naturally a free, that is, a self-determining faculty; but it is viciously inclined, and backward to do good; and therefore we see, by sad experience, that it hath not a virtuous moral freedom; but that it is the wickedness of it which procures the punishment.[46]

It is clear that Baxter was not calling people to a decision they did not understand. He laid a theological foundation and answered genuine doctrinal difficulties, so that the response of people to the gospel would be an intelligent one, based on the surety of things hoped for and the certainty of things not seen.

Such doctrinal content is imperative to true evangelism. As preachers, we should not be afraid that it will frighten away unbelievers. Rather, we should be afraid that people may respond to

[44] Ibid., 110. [45] Ibid., 111. [46] Ibid.

the gospel without knowing what it is really about. We ought not to be apologetic for doctrines we suspect will be offensive to our hearers. Our confidence is that true conversion is a work of the Spirit, and the soul that is under the conviction of the Spirit is not repulsed by biblical truth, but drawn to it and compelled by it.

Unfortunately it is rare to hear evangelistic preaching like this today. Too often the gospel is diluted, and then decorated with anecdotes, humour and wit, so that people are charmed into the kingdom. The Christian life is set before people as the answer to all their problems, the new key to success. It is something to try if all else has failed. We should not be surprised then that many so-called 'decisions' for Christ do not stick, and the gospel fails to grip the heart of an unbelieving world. Of course embracing Baxter's approach will not guarantee instant success, and it will not be useable in the same language and manner as he employed. But if today's preachers and evangelists were prepared to be far more direct, more doctrinal, and more intense in their reasoning and persuasion, we would be far closer to an authentic presentation of the gospel that would be owned of God and accompanied by the power of his Spirit.

The pursuit of holiness

While evangelism must be the highest priority in preaching, not every sermon is to be evangelistic. Many sermons, particularly in pastoral ministry, are to be aimed at building up, encouraging and strengthening those who are already saved. The preacher's aim in this regard is to take people on in their love of God and their commitment to the Lord:

> All our sermons must be fitted to change men's hearts, from carnal into spiritual, and to kindle in them the love of God. When this is well done, they have learned what we were sent to teach them; and when this is perfect, they are in heaven.[47]

Our task in edification of the saints is essentially twofold. First, we must *urge holiness of life.* We are to impress truth on people so that it leads to godliness. Our constant concern must be to see growth

[47] Baxter, *Knowledge and Love Compared,* in *Practical Works,* 4: 626.

in grace, increase in holiness, and the pursuit of righteousness. We must stress that without holiness no one will see the Lord:

> Could we make all our hearers never so learned, that will not save their souls; but if we could make them holy, and kindle in them the love of God, and goodness, they should certainly be saved. The holy, practical preacher therefore is the best preacher, because the holy, practical christian is the best and only true christian.[48]

Some in our congregations will hate such preaching. They do not want to be challenged. They want only to be comforted, put at ease, assured. But true saints will love preaching that urges them to press on to greater holiness and that cuts them to the quick. Baxter regarded it as a mark of sincerity of faith to love the closest and most searching preaching of the Word.

In his preaching of holiness a number of themes and emphases returned time and again. They are well summarised in his own words in the 'Farewell Sermon'. In the final pages he gave 'some of my counsels and requests, for the time to come, which I earnestly entreat you not to neglect'. He proferred the following nine exhortations:

1. Spend most of your studies in confirming your belief of the truth of the gospel, the immortality of the soul, and the life to come, and in exercising that belief, and laying up your treasure in heaven. See that you are not merely content with talking of heaven, and speaking for it, but that your hopes, your hearts, and your conversation are there, and that you live for it, as worldlings do for the flesh.

2. Do not flatter yourselves with the hopes of long life on earth, but make it the sum of all your religion, care and business, to be ready for a safe and comfortable death. Until you can fetch comfort from the life to come, you can have no comfort that true reason can justify.

3. Live as in a constant war against all fleshly lusts, and love not the world, as it cherishes those lusts. Take heed of the love of money, as the root of manifold evils. Think of riches with more fear than desire...

[48] Ibid.

4. Be furnished beforehand with expectation and patience, for all
    evils that may befall you. Do not make too much of sufferings,
    especially poverty, or wrong from men. It is sin and folly in poor
    men that they overvalue riches and are not thankful for their peculiar
    blessings.

5. Take heed of self-conceited, unhumbled understanding, and of hasty
    and rash conclusions.... Proud self-conceitedness, and rash, hasty
    conclusions cause most of the mischiefs in the world which might
    be prevented if men had the humility and patience to wait until
    things have been thoroughly weighed and tried. Do not be ashamed
    to profess uncertainty where you are indeed uncertain. Humble
    doubting is much safer than confident erring.

6. Maintain union and communion with all true Christians on earth.
    Hold, then, to catholic principles of mere Christianity, without which
    you will crumble into sects. Love Christians as Christians, but the
    best most. Locally, do not separate from anyone, unless they
    separate from Christ or deny you their communion, unless you sin.

7. Be sure that you maintain due honour and subjection to your
    governors: 'Fear the Lord and the king, and meddle not with them
    that are given to change' (Prov. 24:21).... Obey God with your first
    and absolute obedience, and do not obey man over and against
    him. But obey the just commands of magistrates, out of obedience
    to God, and suffer patiently when you cannot obey.... Trust God
    and keep your innocence, and abhor all thoughts of rebellion or
    revenge.

8. Be sure to keep up family religion, especially in the careful education
    of youth. Keep them from evil company, and from temptations,
    especially of idleness, fullness, and baits of lust. Read the Scripture
    and good books, and call upon God, and sing his praise. Recreate
    youth with reading the history of the church, and the lives of holy
    men and martyrs. Instruct them in catechisms and fundamentals.

9. Above all, live in love to God and man. Do not let selfishness and
    worldliness prevail against it. Think of God's goodness as equal to
    his greatness and wisdom. Take yourselves as members of the
    same body with all true Christians. Blessed are they that faithfully
    practise those three grand principles which all profess, viz., 1. To
    love God as God above all (and so to obey him.) 2. To love our
    neighbours as ourselves. 3. And to do as we would be done by.[49]

Such emphases are typical of Baxter and indicate the type of godliness to which he called his people time and again.

Ennobling the saints

To urge holiness of life, however, was not enough. Too easily it can cause discouragement and degenerate into moralism. Our second great task in edificational preaching, therefore, is to *bring before people the joys and beauty of God and of heaven.* We are to help the saints delight in God and in the things of eternity. Preaching ought to inspire, uplift and motivate. It ought to have the effect of ennobling people, so that they go away with higher and holier thoughts, greater desires and aspirations, and a more heavenly mindset. It ought especially to set before them the excellencies of Christ whose grace is all-sufficient, and the beauty of heaven for which we are striving.

In his autobiography Baxter noted a change in himself in this regard. In his earlier years he had been more inclined to self-examination and introspection. In later years he found his focus to be less inward (to himself) and more upward (to God). His reflections are worth pondering:

> My judgement is much more for frequent and serious meditation on the heavenly blessedness than it was heretofore in my younger days. I then thought that a sermon of the attributes of God and the joys of heaven were not the most excellent, and was wont to say, 'Everybody knoweth this, that God is great and good, and that heaven is a blessed place; I had rather hear how I may attain it.' And nothing pleased me so well as the doctrine of regeneration and the marks of sincerity, which was because it was suitable to me in that state; but now I had rather read, hear or meditate on God and heaven than on any other subject; for I perceive that it is the object that altereth and elevateth the mind.... And that it is not only useful to our comfort to be much in heaven in our believing thoughts, but that it must animate all our other duties and fortify us against every temptation and sin....a man is no more a Christian indeed than he is heavenly.[50]

[49] Baxter, 'Farewell Sermon,' 1026-27 (language modernised).
[50] Baxter, *Autobiography,* 112-13.

He continued:

> I was once wont to meditate on my own heart, and to dwell all at
> home, and to look little higher; I was still poring either on my sins or
> wants, or examining my sincerity; but now, though I am greatly
> convinced of the need of heart-acquaintance and imployment, yet
> I see more need of a higher work, and that I should look often upon
> Christ, and God, and heaven, than upon my own heart. At home I
> can find distempers to trouble me, and some evidences of my peace;
> but it is above that I must find matter of delight and joy and love
> and peace itself. Therefore I would have one thought at home
> upon myself and sins, and many thoughts above upon the high and
> amiable and beatifying objects.[51]

Puritanism has often been criticised for its tendency to introspection
and excessive self-analysis. Baxter himself saw this danger and sought
to cultivate experimental preaching that was searching but not self-
focused. Meditation on God himself and the things of heaven
'elevateth the mind' and that is the effect true preaching ought to
have. The best preaching does not stop at the point of probing the
heart and conscience. It lifts a person above himself, filling his soul
with the beauty of God, lifting his thoughts to things higher, holier and
more glorious than anything this world can offer. It pulls a person
above that which is mundane, worldly and petty, and gives a glimpse
of something majestic and eternal. Preaching ought to be chiefly
positive not negative, uplifting not damning, thrilling not exasperating.

The result of such preaching is to be the expression of greater
love for God on the part of those who hear the Word. It is striking to
hear the almost mystical strain of Baxter, 'the rationalist,' as he
expresses his own love for the Lord – a love he so wanted to
engender in others also:

> I feel that Thou has made my mind to know Thee, and I feel that
> Thou hast made my heart to love Thee, my tongue to praise Thee,
> and all that I have and am to serve Thee; and even in the panting,
> languishing desires and motions of my soul I find that Thou and

---

[51] Ibid., 113.

only Thou art its resting place; and though love do now but search and prate and cry and weep, and is reaching upwards but cannot reach the glorious light, the blessed knowledge, the perfect love for which it longeth; yet by its eye, its aim, its motions, its moans, its groans, I know its meaning, where it would be, and I know its end. My displaced soul will never be well till it come near to Thee, till it know Thee better, till it love Thee more.... Wert Thou to be found in the most solitary desert, it would seek Thee; or in the uttermost parts of the earth, it would make after Thee. Thy presence makes a crowd, a Church; Thy converse makes a closet or solitary wood or field, to be kin to the angelic choir.[52]

The ultimate purpose in preaching God's Word and applying it to men's hearts, in calling them from sin and urging them to godliness is found here. Preaching should draw people to God, causing them to glorify him and *enjoy him* forever.

[52] Baxter, *Reasons for the Christian Religion* (1667), 458. Quoted in Martin, *Puritanism and Richard Baxter*, 137. In his book *Richard Baxter: Puritan and Mystic*, Ladell argues that Baxter was a genuine mystic, and it is this that accounts for his zeal, fervour, seemingly contradictory positions, emphasis on meditation, depth of devotional life, departure from some aspects of Calvinism, his concerns for unity, etc. (pp. 124ff).

Chapter 5

Speaking to the Heart

Oh how many thousands of souls in heaven will forever
rejoice in the effects of the labours of faithful ministers,
and bless God for them! And what an honour, what a comfort
is it to have a hand in such a work![1]

Do not spend the majority of your zeal on external things
and opinions, and the smaller things of religion. Let most
of your daily work be on your hearts.[2]

Keep open the passage between your heads and your hearts,
that every truth may go to the quick.[3]

It is the supreme and irresistible work of the Holy Spirit to open
people's hearts to the truth of God's Word. He alone can break and
remake a sinful heart. Yet in his work he uses means, and preaching
is one of his chief ones. It is the preacher's privilege and responsibility
to co-operate with the Spirit in speaking to the heart.

No one can afford to conclude that because heart-application is
the work of the Spirit, preachers do not have to work hard at it also.
The very opposite is the case. Because it is the Spirit's divine intention
to address the very souls of men and women, we must do all we can
to advance and promote his work. We must ensure that the subject
matter of our preaching is such that will feed and stir the soul (the
focus of this chapter); and we must endeavour to drive that truth
home to the heart as forcefully as we know how (the concern of
chapter 6).

---

[1] Richard Baxter, *Compassionate Counsel*, 23.
[2] Baxter, *The Saints' Everlasting Rest,* ed. Pipe, 23.
[3] Ibid., 16.

The glory of God

The immediate tendency when we think about preaching to the heart is to begin with man – his needs, state and condition. A more direct and biblical route to the heart, however, is to begin with God himself. Baxter, as we noted in the last chapter, had come to appreciate the excellence of focusing on God and the blessedness of heaven above all else because this 'altereth and elevateth the mind' the most.[4]

This concern to ennoble and uplift people by drawing their focus to God is of supreme importance. We minister to people who spend much of their time immersed in the things of the world. They rush from one task to another, amid constant noise and stress. To give them more of the same – noise and stress – when they come to worship God is completely counter-productive. They need to be lifted above the level on which they usually live. They need to have their minds filled with something glorious, beautiful, majestic. They need to be re-focused. They need to be captivated by something beyond themselves and the demands of life. They need to meet God!

The preacher's task is to lead people into another world – a world of peace, joy, hope, love, light, grace and power. That world is not found within, but found in God. It is in preaching him, his attributes, works, plans and purposes, that we uplift people's souls. They are drawn to worship God because of the preached Word. Preaching *is* worship.

The aim of such preaching is to help people rejoice in God. Baxter wrote:

> Let your joyful part of religion be most of your meditations: the infinite goodness of God, who is love; the wonder of man's redemption; the freeness and fullness of the promise; and the certainty and glory of our future state: these are the chief part of our religion, and of chiefest use; which must resolve us, fix us, quicken us, and help us to live in thankfulness and joy.[5]

For preaching to uplift the soul in this way it must centre on great biblical truths. The best preachers usually make you feel that they

[4] Baxter, *Autobiography,* 113.
[5] Baxter, 'Funeral Sermon of Mr Henry Stubbs,' 974.

are dealing with something of immense importance, and that the text they are about to open is of massive significance to you. They are not preaching on mere technicalities, abstract theological niceties, or even down-to-earth practicalities. They preach God: his sovereign grace, power, election, glory and attributes. They preach Christ: his nature, offices, atonement and heavenly intercession. They preach the doctrines of heaven and holiness, regeneration, justification, sanctification and glorification. Great doctrines make for great preaching:

> As the stock of the tree affordeth timber to build houses and cities, when the small though higher multifarious branches are but to make a crow's nest or a blaze, so the knowledge of God and of Jesus Christ, of heaven and holiness, doth build up the soul to endless blessedness, and affordeth it solid peace and comfort when a multitude of school niceties serve but for vain janglings and hurtful diversions and contentions.... study and live upon the essential doctrines of Christianity and godliness incomparably above them all.[6]

Baxter knew the danger of focusing on obscure theological points and engaging in needless controversy from the pulpit. He believed that preaching should focus chiefly on the fundamental doctrines of the faith. 'If that knowledge that kindleth in us the love of God, be the only saving knowledge, then this is it that ministers must principally preach up and promote.'[7] The older he grew, the more convinced he became of that. In his autobiography, he wrote:

> It is the fundamental doctrines of the Catechism which I highliest value and daily think of, and find most useful to myself and others. The Creed, the Lord's Prayer and the Ten Commandments do find me now the most acceptable and plentiful matter for all my meditations. They are to me as my daily bread and drink. And as I can speak and write of them over and over again, so I had rather read or hear of them than of any of the school niceties which once so much pleased me.[8]

[6] Baxter, *Autobiography,* 109.
[7] Baxter, *Knowledge and Love Compared,* 626.
[8] Baxter, *Autobiography,* 107-8.

For Baxter, then, great preaching was doctrinal preaching that focused on the fundamental truths of God and the gospel. The very name that the Puritans used for the points of their sermons – doctrines – highlighted their understanding of the content of preaching. Every sermon was to unfold biblical truth in a manner that was clear, biblical, powerful and substantial.

This necessitated that the preacher be a theologian. He was to be sound in his grasp of biblical and systematic theology. He was to be familiar with the things of God, steeped in biblical doctrine and the Word. He was to be capable of probing the depths of a passage, not merely skimming over the surface. He was to teach his congregation the great truths of the faith.

Such doctrinal preaching has become increasingly rare. In many churches preachers are not expected to be theologians. They may receive little in-depth theological training and have only a slight grasp on the doctrines of the Word. Congregations don't expect to hear doctrinal teaching. They dismiss it as dry, boring, irrelevant, difficult and divisive. The general preference is for a subjective rather than an objective message, one oriented toward feeling rather than fact, personal experience rather than revealed truth. But in this, much contemporary preaching short-changes itself. In an undue pandering to short attention spans, a hunger for entertainment, and the desire for something 'personal', there is a loss of that which is most distinctive and glorious about preaching and worship – the glory of God! The result is a Christian community that is often slight in its knowledge of God, superficial in its worship, and open to every wind of doctrine.

The sufficiency of Christ

'If we can but teach Christ to our people, we shall teach them all.'[9] With this statement Baxter affirmed one special dimension of doctrinal preaching. The centrality of Christ was a hallmark of Puritan gospel preaching. They preached his nature, offices and works. They preached his humiliation and his exalted lordship. They preached his atonement and the merits of his righteousness. They preached his promises, his beauty and his excellence. They also preached the law.

[9] Baxter, *The Reformed Pastor,* 113.

To preach Christ was to preach our need of Christ, and the law as a schoolmaster to lead us to him. Further, they preached the doctrine of the church, understanding the church to be the body of Christ which is to be reformed and purified for the day when she will be presented to him as a spotless bride.

Preaching Christ, then, was in a sense the whole of preaching. Yet this was only true for Baxter in a somewhat deficient way. He certainly held to the belief that Christ was all-sufficient and that to teach Christ was to teach all. He spoke frequently of Christ, and exalted him, calling for trust in him and total allegiance to him. Yet the dominant note of his preaching was the lordship of Christ rather than his atonement. He opened Christ's sovereignty more than his suffering servanthood, his requirements of people more than his redemption of them, the need of love for Christ more than the wonderful love of Christ.

Even in his greatest presentation of the gospel, *A Call to the Unconverted,* his preaching of Christ occupied surprisingly little space. He did say that, 'God, not willing that man should perish in his sin, provided a remedy, by causing his Son to take our nature, and being, in one person, God and man, to become a mediator between God and man; and by dying for our sins on the cross, to ransom us from the curse of God and the power of the devil. And having thus redeemed us, the Father hath delivered us into his hands as his own.'[10] Yet this was about the extent of his treatment of the atonement. He did not explain more fully the suffering of Christ, the nature of the atonement, or the fullness of redemption achieved in the cross.

Why was his preaching of the cross so slight? The answer is found in the deficiencies of his theology. Baxter deviated from orthodox Puritan theology, holding to a position known as Amyraldianism – a halfway house between Arminianism and Calvinism. Most Puritans were Calvinists, holding to God's sovereignty in election, Christ's particular atonement for the elect, and the irresistible and lasting work of the Spirit in the hearts of the elect. Amyraldianism 'retains the Calvinistic belief in election, effectual calling, and final preservation'

[10] Baxter, *A Call to the Unconverted,* 21.

but adopts an Arminian view of the covenant of grace and universal redemption.[11] In regard to the latter, it meant a belief that Christ had potentially died for all men, and therefore the accent fell not so much on the finished work of Christ as on the need to persuade men to respond to his work. In regard to the covenant of grace, it meant a belief that the covenant established a new law – the law of faith – by which we are saved. The accent, therefore, is on our commitment to Christ – evangelical obedience – rather than his finished work for us.

This 'new law' concept was known as 'neonomianism' and was so associated with Baxter that in the 1690s it also became known as 'Baxterianism'. Packer further explains his theology:

> Our salvation requires a double righteousness: Christ's which led to the enacting of God's new law; and our own, in obeying that new law by genuine faith and repentance. Faith is imputed for righteousness because it is real obedience to the gospel, which is God's new law. Faith, however, involves a commitment to keep the moral law, which was God's original code, and every believer, though righteous in terms of the new law, needs pardon every moment for his shortcomings in relation to the old law.[12]

[11] Packer, *A Quest For Godliness: The Puritan Vision of the Christian Life* (Wheaton: Crossway Books, 1990), 157.

[12] Ibid., 158. Baxter's theology was in large measure a reaction against the antinomians of his day who overstressed the grace of God and downplayed the response of man. They were effectively hyper-Calvinists, who positioned justification prior to faith in the *ordo salutis*. Baxter went to the opposite extreme, however, teaching that no one was justified until they were actually righteous. In his scheme, Christ's righteousness was not imputed to the believer. Rather, the atonement only rendered satisfaction to the Lawgiver, not to the law. This left the responsibility on man to fulfil the conditions of the law and thereby contribute to his own salvation. He taught, therefore a two-fold righteousness: Christ's legal righteousness and man's evangelical righteousness.

The subtleties of his theology have been the focus of intense scholarship in recent years, beginning with J.I. Packer's unpublished doctoral dissertation (*The Redemption and Restoration of Man in the Thought of Richard Baxter*, Univ. of Oxford, 1954). Since then many books and theses have been written, exploring aspects of his theology and arriving at varying opinions as to his orthodoxy or otherwise. One of the most thorough and recent studies is the dissertation by Hans Boersma, *A Hot Pepper Corn: Richard Baxter's Doctrine*

This language is often found in Baxter's presentation of the gospel, though his arguing of the case is confined to his more theological and polemical writings. In *A Call to the Unconverted,* he states:

> The Father and the Mediator do make a new law and covenant for man, not like the first, which gave life to none but the perfectly obedient, and condemned man for every sin; but Christ hath made a law of grace, or a promise of pardon and everlasting life to all that, by true repentance, and by faith in Christ, are converted unto God; like an act of oblivion, which is made by a prince to a company of rebels, on condition they will lay down their arms and come in and be loyal subjects for the time to come.[13]

The impact of this theology on his preaching was to lessen the focus on Christ's substitutionary atonement, and heighten his emphasis on man's need to exercise true repentance and faith. He over-estimated man's ability, and underplayed the all-sufficiency of Christ's redemption. It tended toward moralism because sin was regarded chiefly in its external aspect as an act of disobedience to the moral law rather than in terms of indwelling corruption. It also produced legalism because the ground of justification became faith and repentance rather than the atoning work of Christ.

The results were not as devastating as they might have been, chiefly because 'in his own teaching, steeped as it was in the older affectionate 'practical' Puritan tradition, these seeds lay largely dormant'.[14] There was enough true gospel in his preaching for it still to be used of God in winning many to Christ.

His success despite weakness, however, ought not to excuse similar failings in our own preaching. The glory of the gospel is the finished work of Christ for sinners, in which his righteousness is credited to

of Justification in its Seventeenth-Century Context of Controversy (Zoetermeer, Netherlands: Uitgeverij Boekencentrum, 1993). His first chapter gives a thorough review of current Baxter scholarship. Boersma himself concludes, after exploring Baxter's theology in minute detail, that he 'remains firmly entrenched within the Reformed tradition' (p. 330) despite his defective views on justification.

[13] Baxter, *A Call to the Unconverted,* 21.
[14] Packer, *A Quest For Godliness,* 160.

us by the instrumentality of faith alone. It is a righteousness that cannot be added to or taken from, and it is the sole basis of our new standing with God and our response of gratitude by way of obedience to the law. To preach Christ is to preach this. We do well to take our cue at this point not from Baxter, but from those he himself was indebted to for his own salvation – the early Calvinistic Puritans.

Heart issues

In preaching the glory of God and the sufficiency of Christ, we are always to bear in mind the great needs of the human heart. Doctrine is never to be preached in a vacuum. The doctrinal teaching of Scripture is mostly presented in response to real life situations – the problems of churches, the needs of individuals, the attacks of the evil one, the mysterious providences of God. Preachers are not merely verbal textbooks of theology, but heralds of God proclaiming much-needed truth to needy souls.

Recognising this, much contemporary preaching addresses itself to people's 'felt' needs. It focuses on external behaviour and issues of practical interest and concern. It offers 'keys' to success in personal life, relationships, marriage, family life and business. It unveils 'secrets' of happiness and fulfilment. It prescribes 'steps' to growth and change in various areas of life. It is interested in the 'how to' of daily life from a Christian perspective. Such preaching seeks to get down to the level of where people are at, addressing issues of contemporary relevance. It speaks to issues of social justice, AIDS, sex, singleness, money, depression and so on.

Experimental preaching heads down another path. It seeks to address the more fundamental issues of the soul. It is more drawn to focus on aspects of inner spiritual life and what may in fact be the 'unfelt' needs of the soul. It is interested in our relationship with God ahead of our relationships with people; dealing with our own souls before dealing with our daily activities; holiness ahead of happiness. It is not that it is disinterested in practical matters, but it views them as the overflow of spiritual issues. It is more concerned with spiritual relevance than contemporary relevance.

Such preaching shies away from any hint of a quick fix, or easy steps to victory. The experimental preacher is all too aware that the waters of the heart are deep, and it is no small thing to probe their depths and bring to the surface those issues that need to be addressed. Yet that is the preacher's task. His concern in preaching great doctrine is to bring to light the spiritual issues the hearers need to face.

Baxter's preaching was powerfully shaped by this concern. He was concerned to move to 'heart matters' as swiftly and pointedly as possible. He wrote, 'The understanding and memory are but the passage to the heart, and the practice is but the expression of the heart: therefore how to work upon the heart is the principal business.'[15]

When preaching his 'Sermon of Repentance' before the House of Commons in 1660, he said, 'I have purposely chosen a text that needs no long explication, that in obedience to the foreseen straits of time I may be excused from that part, and be more on the more necessary.'[16] The necessary, in his opinion, was that which spoke to the heart.

Even on occasions of great public significance this concern for issues of the heart was to the fore. His sermon entitled 'Right Rejoicing' was preached to the Houses of Parliament at the time of the Restoration on 'a day of solemn thanksgiving for God's raising up and succeeding his Excellency, and other instruments, in order to his Majesty's restoration'.[17] His choice of text? Luke 10:20 – *'Notwithstanding in this rejoice not, that the spirits are subject unto you; but rather rejoice, because your names are written in heaven.'* Baxter sensed that some may struggle with this choice, so he began, 'If any of you say, upon the hearing of my text, that I have chosen a subject unsuitable to the occasion, and that a "rejoice not" is out of season on a day of such rejoicing, they may, I hope, be well satisfied by that time they have considered the reasons of these words, as used by Christ to his disciples, and the greater joy that is here commanded, and so the reason of my choice.'[18]

He reasoned from the greater to the lesser: if the disciples were

---

[15] Baxter, *A Christian Directory*, 475.
[16] Baxter, 'A Sermon of Repentance,' 883.
[17] Baxter, 'Right Rejoicing,' 893.
[18] Ibid., 894.

not chiefly to rejoice in their victory over infernal powers, much less should his hearers chiefly rejoice in their victory over mortal men. His concern was that 'he that is feasting in purple and fine linen to-day, may be to-morrow in remediless torments, . . . He that is to-day triumphing over mortal enemies, may to-morrow be led in triumph to hell-fire, and lie in chains of deepest darkness.'[19] Only after he had spoken at length both to unbelievers and believers in the gathering did he come to speak of the specific joys of the day. Again he justified his course of delivery:

> But you think, perhaps, that I have all this while forgotten the duty proper to the day. No; but I was not fit to speak for it, nor you fit to hear and practise it, till the impediment of carnal rejoicing was removed, and till we had begun with heavenly joy. It is heaven that must animate all our comforts. They are so far sweet as heaven is in them, and no further. Now, therefore, if you first rejoice for your heavenly interest, I dare safely then persuade you to rejoice in the mercies which we are to be thankful for this day.[20]

This was characteristically his concern: to set priorities right before God ahead of anything else, and to set people on rejoicing in things eternal rather than anything temporal. In sermon after sermon he settled on texts that would enable him to pursue such priorities.

This demanded the ability to distil the spiritual essence of a text. We have already noted that he did not like to spend long on technicalities, but would, as early as possible, state the spiritual import of his text. In 'Making Light of Christ,' a sermon on Matthew 22:5, for example, he briefly unfolded the parable of the wedding banquet, albeit in a somewhat allegorical fashion, then quickly moved to the one point he identified as the main thrust of parable:

> *Doct.* For all the wonderful love and mercy that God hath manifested in the giving of his Son to be the Redeemer of the world, and which the Son hath manifested in redeeming them by his blood; for all his full preparation by being a sufficient sacrifice for the sins of all; for all his personal excellencies, and that full and glorious salvation

---

[19] Ibid., 896. [20] Ibid., 902.

that he hath procured; and for all his free offers of these, and frequent and earnest invitation of sinners; yet many do make light of all this, and prefer their worldly enjoyments before it.[21]

His 'doctrine' was experimental, making clear that he intended to challenge his hearers' response to the wonderful love and mercy of God.

It is significant that in one who was incredibly verbose there was such an ability to move swiftly and incisively to the spiritual essence of a text. The reason was simple: that was what preaching was all about. His verbosity was actually an extension of the same concern: once the truth was stated, he wanted to open it up as thoroughly as he could. In a telling sentence in one sermon he said, 'I must be plain with you, gentlemen, or I shall be unfaithful; and I must deal closely with you, or I cannot deal honestly and truly with you.'[22] That was at the heart of his experimental preaching: close, plain dealing with real issues of the soul. His doctrinal preaching was always to that end, and the result was tremendous spiritual vigour. The formula of great doctrines preached with spiritual incisiveness and directness is most compelling.

Spiritual realities

In addressing heart issues it is most helpful to give some description of spiritual experience. We may describe spiritual experience as people know it, analyse wrong and ungodly experiences, and depict true biblical experience.

First, we may open up and describe realities of the Christian life as people know them. In the first doctrine of his 'Farewell Sermon', Baxter opened the truth that 'sorrow goes before joy for Christ's disciples'. Baxter wanted his people to understand the realities of sorrow in the Christian life but he was not content merely to say they would experience sorrows. He described seven types of sorrow that may come to them.

First, 'there is a sorrow that is positively sinful. It should not go

[21] Richard Baxter, 'Making Light of Christ and Salvation, ' (1655), in *Practical Works*, 4: 809.
[22] Baxter, 'Sermon of Repentance,' 888.

before our joy, though in fact it does. Although this is not the direct meaning of the text, it all too commonly precedes our comforts.'[23] Next he says, 'we have our sorrows in which, because of our sinful weakness and imperfection, and the languishing feebleness of our souls, we are overly troubled by what we may legitimately sorrow for with moderation. Impatience causes us to make a greater issue of our afflictions than we ought. If God tests us with wants or crosses; if we lose our friends, or if they prove unkind, we double the weight of the cross by our impatience.'[24]

A third sorrow 'is a mere natural suffering or sorrow, which is neither morally good or bad. Like when we are weary with our labour, or be pained with our diseases; or when we feel hunger and thirst, cold and heat'.[25] Then come 'castigatory sorrows from the hand of God, which are intended to cure us if we use them according to his appointment.... He wounds the body to heal the soul, he lances the sore to let out the corruption, he lets blood to cure our inflammations and apostemated parts. He chastens all that he loves and receives (Heb. 12:1-14) and we must be subject to a chastening Father if we will live, for he does it for our profit, "that we may be partakers of his holiness."'[26]

Then he mentions 'honourable and profitable sufferings that come from blind malicious wicked men. They are for the cause of Christ and righteousness, as the gospel frequently warns believers to expect. These sorrows have the promises of fullest joy.' There are also 'penitential and medicinal sufferings, for the killing of sin and assisting the work of grace. These sufferings are our duty. In the former sorrows mentioned we are to be but submissive patients, but in these we must be obedient agents, and must inflict them on ourselves.' Finally he identifies what he calls 'charitable sorrows' in which we sorrow 'for the dishonour of God, and for the sin, hurt, and miseries of others.'[27]

After identifying these seven types of sorrow he gave several reasons why the Lord may allow such sorrows, and then, only after

---

[23] Baxter, 'Farewell Sermon,' 1015. The language in all the quotations from this sermon has been modernised.

[24] Ibid. [25] Ibid. [26] Ibid., 1015-16. [27] Ibid., 1016.

that, came to two practical applications, namely, 'If sorrow before joy is God's ordinary method of dealing with his most beloved servants, learn to understand, then, the importance of your sorrows!'[28] And second, 'If this is God's method, do not condemn the generation of the righteous simply because you see them undermost in the world and suffering more than other men. Do not consider it a dishonour to them to be in poverty, prisons, banishment, or reproach, unless it be for a truly dishonourable cause. Do not call men miserable for that which God makes the token of his love, and the basis of their joy.'[29]

Such a thorough description of the realities, causes and purposes of suffering is genuinely experimental. It is no mere theory. It is no abstract doctrine. It is the truth of Scripture demonstrated and expounded in the actual experiences of God's people.

A second way in which we may address spiritual realities is to open up unspiritual responses to the truth being preached. In 'Making Light of Christ' Baxter gave ten reasons why people made light of Christ. He was not content to note in passing that it was common for men to make light of the gospel, but wanted his hearers to reckon with the reasons why such a response to Christ was so common and may even be found in their own hearts.[30] He dealt with such realities as man's hardness of heart, and the spiritual deadness of sinful human nature, yet man's failure to reckon with this and take seriously the consequences of such sin. He dealt with people's preoccupation with the things of this world and their tendency to ignore those things which are out of sight, in the world to come. He spoke of men's presumption that God would either save them anyway, or that they would have plenty of time in the future to consider these things.

Another example is found in 'The Fool's Prosperity,' a sermon preached at Covent Garden in 1660. He opened first a number of Scriptures that speak of the difficulty of the rich entering the kingdom of heaven, but then moved on by saying, 'To make you more apprehensive of it, I shall adjoin the testimony of experience: and tell me whether prosperity be not the destruction of fools, when you have noted the fruits of it in these few observations.'[31] He proceeded

---

[28] Ibid., 1017. [29] Ibid., 1018. [30] Baxter, 'Making Light of Christ,' 810-12.

[31] Richard Baxter, 'The Fool's Prosperity,' (1660), in *Practical Works,* 4: 517.

to make eight observations that described the spiritual bankruptcy of the majority of the rich and prosperous in his own society. He noted such things as the predominant disinterest in spiritual things among the wealthy; the poor ordering of their families; their pre-occupation with entertainment, leisure activities and pleasure seeking rather than with godly conversation. He also spoke of their dislike of serious preaching. 'Plain dealing preachers, which honest humble souls delight in, do seem intolerable saucy fellows to these sons of pride.'[32] He observed:

> They must have heart-searching and heart-breaking truths, in a searching, awakening manner, brought home to them, if ever they will be saved by them; but they cannot endure it. The surgeon is intolerable that would search their sores; and yet there is no other way to heal them. Alas! the heart of man is so hard, that all the skill and industry of the preacher can scarce sufficiently sharpen and set home the truth that it may enter; but nothing that is sharp can be endured by these tender souls.[33]

In making these observations he would no doubt have struck a chord with many of his hearers – be they the rich who felt the sting of his attack, or the poor who knew the sickening reality he was describing. Either way, he was interacting not only with biblical texts (which was his first priority) but with contemporary spiritual realities. Both means brought home his point. In the process, he also managed to work in some significant observations about the nature of 'plain-dealing' preaching, which was his chief business.

A third aspect of preaching spiritual realities is to describe and set before our hearers a picture of true spiritual experience. We need to set before them an ideal and hold up a godly model for them to aspire to. An example of this is afforded by a sermon Baxter preached at the funeral of a Mrs Mary Coxe in 1679. After spending some time opening his text, Psalm 119:111 (*Thy testimonies have I taken as an heritage for ever: for they are the rejoicing of my heart*), he made 'use' of the text by telling 'what use she made of such

---

[32] Ibid., 518.
[33] Ibid., 519.

doctrine'. He opened up no less than twenty aspects of her character that were exemplary in displaying what it is to make the things of the Lord our heritage forever. He noted such things as her 'constant, serious, diligent use of the Word of God, by hearing, reading, conference, and meditation'. He spoke of her responsiveness to the preached Word, and her desire to hear the Word from any true minister, not just those of certain parties. He noted that she was 'not of a censorious, backbiting temper' but desired to do good to all, was humble, prudent, and gentle. She enjoyed 'a constant peace of conscience, bewailing her imperfections, but not living in melancholy, despair, hard thoughts of God, or an uncomfortable sort of religion'. In these ways she 'daily learned to die,' and 'as she lived holily and in peace with God and man, so she died with ease and little likelihood of the ordinary miseries of fear and pain'.[34]

In her life Baxter found occasion to set before his hearers a positive description of the life of godliness that would challenge, inspire and move them to greater interest in the things of God. The use of a particular person's life – indeed one just deceased – no doubt made the picture all the more vivid and moving.

Later in the sermon Baxter described spiritual experience from another angle: his own experience of the grace of the gospel. Quite characteristically, Baxter illustrated truth by reference to his own experience:

> And I must second the testimony of our deceased friend, in professing for your encouragement my own experience: I have taken God's testimonies for my own heritage, and they have been these fifty years, or near, the pleasure of my life, and sweeter than honey, and preciouser than thousands of gold or silver.... I take it my duty to add herein my own experience, if it may contribute to the determining of your choice.[35]

[34] Richard Baxter, 'A True Believer's Choice and Pleasure,' (1679), in *Practical Works*, 4: 982-3.

[35] Ibid., 986. Keeble comments on the frequency with which Baxter appealed to his own experience: 'Personal recollections may illustrate a general proposition,... They may support a direction,... They may enforce a point,... Or they may illustrate it,... That we should learn incidentally as we read that

In giving his own testimony he spoke of the realities of his own sinful fears of pain and death, and yet testified to his delight in God's heritage such that by 'this means my life hath been almost a constant pleasure', which had aided him in his work, freed him from sinful snares, given him great thankfulness to God, cured him of weeping too much over his sin, and given him a truer sense of priorities. 'Oh that I had more faith and love, that I might have more of this delight!'[36]

Preachers will often find that when they second the truth of Scripture from their own experience or from the lives of other saints they gain more instant access to the hearts of his hearers. Even when this is not appropriate, drawing pictures of godly response to the Word will help bring biblical truth home to human hearts.

Pastoral preaching
In bringing God's Word to a congregation, a preacher does so as their pastor. Arguably, the best person to preach to a congregation is their own minister rather than some itinerant who does not sustain a pastoral relationship with them. It is the pastor who knows them by name, loves them, lives with them and cares for them. It is he who is accountable to them, and who will live with them through times of trial. He is to feed them by way of expository doctrinal preaching, but he is to do more than that. He is to protect, encourage, watch over, help, assist, spur on, refresh and care for his flock. He is to bind up the wounded, deal tenderly with the young, reprove the belligerent and rescue the straying.

Much of this pastoral work can and should be done from the pulpit. The minister is not two people: sometimes a preacher and sometimes a pastor. He is one: a pastor-preacher, who complements his preaching with diligent pastoring, and who pastors faithfully from the pulpit. To do that he must 'correct, rebuke and encourage, with

Baxter practised medicine, that he was a vegetarian, that he admired Thomas Foley's industry, that as a boy he loved to climb the Wrekin, that he writes with his pockets filled with letters, so personalizes the author that the reader, far from receiving unsympathetic and dogmatic directions, hears reasonable advice from one who is himself a man in the world.' *Richard Baxter: Puritan Man of Letters*, 85.
[36] Baxter, 'A True Believer's Choice,' 987.

great patience and careful instruction' (2 Tim. 4:2). He must make practical application of the Word to the hearts and lives of believers. He must interact in preaching with the specific pastoral issues that his flock faces. He must counsel his people from the pulpit.

This brings an immensely practical dimension into the content of preaching. If the preaching of God and Christ demands that we preach as theologians, and if preaching to spiritual issues of the heart demands that we preach as experienced saints, then preaching pastorally demands that we preach as counsellors and comforters. Baxter very much assumed this role in his preaching. One notable example may be taken from his later years of ministry when his pastoral heart was especially apparent. Circumstances had changed and Baxter faced the need to encourage and strengthen his nonconformist hearers.

In 1682 he preached a sermon entitled, 'The Cure of Melancholy and Overmuch Sorrow, by Faith.' Baxter set about answering the question, 'What are the best preservatives against melancholy and overmuch sorrow?' He took as his text 1 Corinthians 2:7 – *'Lest perhaps such a one should be swallowed up with overmuch sorrow'* – and without taking any time to open the context, went straight to three doctrines:

1. That sorrow, even for sin, may be overmuch.

2. That overmuch sorrow swalloweth one up.

3. Therefore it must be resisted and assuaged by necessary comfort, both by others, and by ourselves.

He then proposed the manner in which he would handle these doctrines: '1. I shall show you when sorrow is overmuch. 2. How overmuch sorrow doth swallow a man up. 3. What are the causes of it. 4. What is the cure.'[37]

It is apparent from these divisions that Baxter abandoned a 'doctrine, proofs, uses' approach in favour of a topical sermon on depression and melancholy. He still desired to establish his teaching in Scripture, but his concern was not so much with careful exposition as with pastoral care and counselling.

Under his first heading Baxter identified two main situations in

[37] Richard Baxter, 'The Cure of Melancholy and Overmuch Sorrow, by Faith,' (1683), in *Practical Works*, 4: 920.

which sorrow may be too great. First, when it is fed by a mistaken cause. That is, when there is no real basis for being sorrowful, such as when a person is sorrowful for neglecting a duty that is really no obligation at all. Second, when it hurts and overwhelms a person, harming them physically and mentally.

Under the second heading he identified some of the ways in which sorrow may swallow a man up. A person may lose sense and reason. He is no longer able to govern his own thoughts. Faith itself is affected, hope is extinguished, and the person begins to lose confidence in the promises of God's Word. In such great sorrow a person may also lose the comfort of knowing God's goodness and love, and is therefore hindered from loving God with all his soul. The person begins to judge the works of God incorrectly and is no longer thankful as he ought to be. This, he points out, is contrary to the joy of the Holy Spirit and the peace in which God's kingdom consists. Such sorrow is a disease that is contrary to the whole tenor of the gospel. It indeed 'swalloweth a man up' when in fact 'Christ came as a deliverer of the captives, a Saviour to reconcile us to God, and bring us glad tidings of pardon and everlasting joy'.[38]

Baxter therefore moved to his third head in order to explain the causes of such melancholy. First he spoke of natural and physical causes of depression: 'distemper, weakness, and diseasedness of the body.'[39] He spoke of such difficulties as violent pain, a natural temper of troubling, sorrow, fear and displeasedness, and melancholy itself. Melancholy was described by him as a 'crazedness' of the mind, giving rise to constant trouble and disquietedness of the mind so that people can see nothing but fear and trouble. They become utterly depressed spiritually, and they live in almost constant despair. They may think they hear other voices telling them to do this or that, and are prone to thinking they have received revelations or prophecies from God. This may lead either to heresy or to feeling they are possessed by the devil.

His second category of causes concerned 'sinful impatience, discontents, and cares, proceeding from a sinful love of some bodily interest, and from a want of sufficient submission to the will of God,

[38] Ibid., 922. [39] Ibid.

and trust in him, and taking heaven for a satisfying portion'.[40] He proceeded to establish a carefully constructed analysis of the connection between these various sins. Impatience leads to a settled discontent and unquietness of spirit; that leads to grief and continual worldly cares; that lays bare the secret root cause of all: too much love of the body and this world. That reveals a further link in the chain – wills that are too selfish and not submitted to God, arising from a lack of humility for sin and distrust of God. Finally, there lies a failure to accept God's love as a sufficient portion.

His third set of causes for overmuch sorrow related to guilt over some great or wilful sin. A person's conscience may be awakened, but their soul not yet converted, and so the wrath of God terrifies them. Or a person may be converted, but their sins plunge them into a great depth of sorrow.

In the fourth place he identified ignorance as a cause of sorrow – ignorance of the gospel and the covenant of grace; ignorance of how to make proper use of sorrow over sin; ignorance of themselves and the state of their own heart; ignorance of the means of gaining comfort from probabilities when they cannot attain certainties; ignorance of the weaknesses and struggles of other men, feeling that they alone have difficulties; and finally ignorance because of unskilled teachers who cause discouragement rather than comfort.

In the final section of the sermon he moved to the cure of melancholy which, he observed, is more easily told than done. He addressed both the 'patient' and his 'friends and teachers'. He began with general advice such as keeping their sin in correct perspective, going back to the basics of the gospel, studying the importance of the submission of their wills to God, and avoiding further sinful pleasure. Next he spoke of cures for those whose depression arose from 'perplexities of mind' concerning doctrine. He outlined how to distinguish true from false in religion. He also addressed those whose trouble was not over doctrine but over their own sins and want of grace. He unfolded no less than thirty-one gospel truths to help them address their sins and want of grace. 'Digest these truths, and they will cure you.'[41]

[40] Ibid., 925. [41] Ibid., 932.

Realising, however, that the disease may be more deeply-rooted, he continued with further advice for those not helped by that counsel. He proffered such pastoral advice as: don't think too long and deep; don't be alone too much; think about the infinite goodness of God, the unmovable love of Christ, the free offer of grace, the glory and joy of those now with Christ; don't give in to 'complaining talk' but rather spend most of your prayer time in thanks and praise; keep busy.

Having given both practical and spiritual advice, he recognised some may still be unchanged from their melancholy. It was in this context that he addressed those who cared for such people – their husbands and wives especially. He advised them to try to please them as best they could; to divert them from their thoughts, encourage them with the gospel, and seek out a good minister for them – 'one that is skilled in such cases.' He also advised that they impress on them the need to be thankful, take them into the company of strangers, get them involved in helping others, and take them to a physician. He noted that 'Medicinal remedies and theological used not to be given together by the same hand; but in this case of perfect complication of the maladies of mind and body, I think it not unfit, if I do it not unskilfully. My advice is, that they that can have an ancient, skilful, experienced, honest, careful, cautelous physician, neglect not to use him.'[42]

This set Baxter himself on the task of proffering medical advice. Having suffered physically for years, and having seen numerous doctors, he felt himself in a position to give some advice regarding cures and potions. In great detail he outlines what he believed would help, not hesitating even to give out recipes for some of his cures!

This 'sermon' displays graphically the immensely practical, pastoral dimension of preaching that Baxter deemed appropriate in caring for souls. He used the pulpit to counsel disturbed souls, helping them deal spiritually and practically with their trials and difficulties. The message was certainly not textual, yet it still upheld his basic convictions regarding preaching: it sought to bring counsel from the Word, it sought to exalt God and stimulate a response of praise and joy to the gospel, and it sought to address real issues of the soul in a

[42] Ibid., 934.

practical and experimental manner. This was biblical counselling from the pulpit.

We may not choose to delve into such a complex subject from the pulpit, nor preach this topically, but we must at least ask whether our preaching is pastorally helpful. Does it address the spiritual issues people struggle with day by day? Does it aid and ultimately diminish the counselling needed among our people? Does it demonstrate a deep awareness of maladies of the soul? Do we patiently instruct, comfort, counsel and assist our people from the pulpit? Such pastoral preaching is a true part of our calling to be shepherds of the flock and an essential element of speaking to the heart.

Things that matter

It is very easy to fill our sermons with things that do not really matter. The more intellectual preacher may be tempted to spend too much time addressing obscure points of theology or technical exegetical details; the more formal, traditional man may be tempted to focus too much on matters of tradition and religious order and practice; the more socially aware preacher may spend disproportionate amounts of time addressing the evils of the day and issues of social justice; the down-to-earth, practical pastor may be tempted to speak chiefly to the more immediate, superficial concerns of life.

At the heart of experimental preaching is the recognition that the deep issues of the heart and soul, man's relationship with God, and the realities of eternity, are the matters of greatest importance:

> Throughout the whole course of our ministry, we must insist chiefly upon the greatest, most certain, and most necessary truths, and be more seldom and sparing upon the rest.[43]

Baxter's ministry was driven by a sense of 'necessity':

> We must, therefore, ever have our people's necessities before our eyes. To remember 'the one thing needful' will take us off gauds and needless ornaments, and unprofitable controversies. Many other things are desirable to be known; but this must be known, or else

[43] Baxter, *The Reformed Pastor,* 113.

our people are undone for ever. I confess I think NECESSITY should be the great disposer of a minister's course of study and labour.[44]

He deliberately avoided matters of less eternal significance, no matter how interesting they might be:

Men's souls may be saved without knowing whether God did predetermine the creature in all its acts; whether the understanding necessarily determines the will; whether God works grace in a physical or in a moral way of causation; what freewill is; whether God have *scientiam mediam* [mediate knowledge] or positive decrees concerning the blame for evil deeds; and a hundred similar questions, which are probably things you would be studying when you should be saving souls. Get well to heaven, and help your people thither, and you shall know all these things in a moment, and a thousand more, which now, by all your studies, you can never know; and is this not the most expeditious and certain way to knowledge?[45]

As we speak to the heart in these ways, we open the way for the Holy Spirit to apply his Word with divine power and force. If this is our focus and concern, we may be expectant of his regenerating and sanctifying work in the lives of those who listen.

[44] Ibid.
[45] Ibid., 213-14.

Chapter 6

Driving the Message Home

Hear the most practical preachers you can well get. Not those that
have the finest notions, or the clearest style, or neatest words; but
those that are still urging you to holiness of heart and life, and
driving home every truth to practice.[1]

God hath shined into our minds with the heavenly, convincing light.
He hath given us the first-fruits and pledge of glory. . . . and what
should we persuade our neighbours to choose, but that which God
hath taught us to choose ourselves.[2]

We must study how to convince and get within men, and how to
bring each truth to the quick, and not leave all this to our
extemporary promptitude, unless in cases of necessity.[3]

Preaching that not only speaks to issues of the heart, but actually
drives the message home with clarity and power, demands great skill
on the part of the preacher:

What skill is necessary to make the truth plain; to convince the
hearers, to let irresistible light in to their consciences, and to keep it
there, and drive all home; to screw the truth into their minds, and
work Christ into their affections; to meet every objection, and clearly
to resolve it; to drive sinners to a stand, and make them see that
there is no hope, but that they must unavoidably either be converted
or condemned – and to do all this, as regards language and manner,
as beseems our work, and yet as is most suitable to the capacities
of our hearers. This, and a great deal more that should be done in
every sermon, must surely require a great deal of holy skill.[4]

[1] Baxter, *A Christian Directory,* 476.
[2] Baxter, 'Reasons For Ministers,' 1047
[3] Baxter, *The Reformed Pastor,* 147.
[4] Ibid., 70.

It is to this holy skill that we now turn. In Baxter's sermons we discover a number of means he repeatedly used to drive the message home. Some of his approaches require adaptation, others are of immediate relevance to contemporary preachers. All help us to preach with greater spiritual vigour.

Rational appeal

We have already observed Baxter's predominantly rationalistic approach to the Christian faith. While the excesses of such rationalism must be avoided, there is much we can learn from his commitment to making a passionate, compelling and persuasive case for the truth.

His reasoned approach led him in the first place to a sermon structure that was always tight and logical. He never offered a rambling discourse or disjointed thoughts. At the start of a sermon he would state his case, and the main sub-divisions of his argument, and then progress logically from point to point. Every point fitted logically within its section and contained sub-points that opened it up further. There was always a sense of progression. The hearer's mind was engaged and taken along with him as he opened thoroughly all the implications of a passage.

Baxter wanted his people to learn. He wanted them to remember the Word. He wanted families to go home and review the sermon. He wanted the text to be etched on their memories. The best way to achieve these ends was, according to Baxter, to use a very clear, logical, structured approach. While some preachers despise announcing points in advance or drawing too much attention to the structure of a sermon, for Baxter it was an integral part of his method. He followed the advice he gave to others:

> Ministers must not only be methodical, and avoid prolix, confused, and involved discourses, and that malicious pride of hiding their method, but must be as oft in the use of the same method, as the subject will bear, and choose that method which is most easy to the hearers to understand and remember, and labour to make them perceive your tract.[5]

---

[5] Baxter, *A Christian Directory*, 474.

He extolled the merits of numbering points and perhaps even choosing words that started with the same letter, as an aid to the memory of the hearer, though this device was seldom practised by Baxter.

This tight structuring of a sermon was often taken to extremes. Baxter was not only exhaustive, but exhausting in his thoroughness! 'To omit one warning, argument, reason, incentive, or illustration, or to neglect to counter a single error, temptation or misunderstanding was to run too grave a risk of failing the reader on the very point where he might need guidance.'[6] Yet, excesses aside, his commitment to absolute clarity, a tight coherent structure and logical progression of thought, was one that will also aid our preaching. We must learn to be teachers. Not lecturers, but clear, incisive, logical, compelling teachers. If people cannot follow the drift of a message, cannot see how the flow of the message has unfolded, and cannot have some retention of the main points, we have failed.

Next to orderly, logical structure was his habit of asking his hearers to 'consider' certain reasons for a particular doctrine or exhortation. Typical of his approach is one passage in *A Call to the Unconverted*:

> Reason the case a little with me, your fellow creature, which is far easier than to reason the case with God; tell me, man, here before the Lord, as if thou wert to die this hour, why shouldest thou not resolve to turn this day, before thou stir from the place thou standest in; what reason hast thou to deny or to delay?'[7]

He then proceeded to name and answer twelve possible objections his hearers may have had to the call to repentance. He took up, for example, the concern that if as few were to be saved as Baxter was implying, heaven would be almost empty; the objection that those who profess the faith are often no better than the unconverted; and the retort that the world was a better place when men made less fuss about religion – surely it is enough just to do your best.

In another sermon he called people to reason with him in this way:

[6] Keeble, *Richard Baxter*, 65.
[7] Baxter, *A Call to the Unconverted,* 83.

I will here back these exhortations with some persuading considerations. Think of what I say, and weigh it as we go. If I speak not truth and reason, then reject it with disdain, and spare not; but if it be, and thy conscience tell thee so, take heed then how thou dost neglect or reject it, lest thou be found a fighter against the Spirit, and lest the curse of God do seize upon that heart that would not yield to truth and reason.[8]

Not only would he commonly present several reasons for a doctrine or duty, but he would give motives for performing a particular duty or responding to an exhortation. *The Reformed Pastor* affords many examples of this approach. After opening the nature of the oversight of ourselves he gave eight motives to such careful self-watch. Following his exposition of the nature of oversight of the flock he gave four motives to it. Following his plea for personal catechising, he presented twenty-two motives to the work – those arising from the benefits, difficulties and necessity of it. Much of the message is presented in terms of these rational motivations to take up the charge he was laying down. He wanted an intelligent response to the Word, and took time to give the basis for this.

To take up this device, we may ask a simple question of any exhortation we give: *why* should my people respond to this? If I am exhorting them to praise and worship, why should they praise? What motives to praise can I give them? If I am urging them to greater prayerfulness, what reasons can I give to persuade them of the importance of prayer? What motives to faithful prayer will encourage them? Thinking this way will prevent us from making cold, simplistic moralistic demands, and force us to reason with our people on the basis of the Word. Biblical preaching is not coercive, but persuasive. It does not force duty on people, but seeks to unfold to them biblical motives for God-honouring living.

We should also ask ourselves, What questions may arise in my hearer's minds? What are they likely to object to, or struggle with? We must learn to anticipate and answer people's concerns in advance.

In this rigorous manner Baxter constantly demanded an intelligent

[8] Baxter, 'The Absolute Sovereignty of Christ,' 802.

response from his people. If they were to reject the gospel, they had better know what they were rejecting and why! If they were to respond to it, they had better understand it, and make an intelligent response to it.

Pressing the conscience

In Baxter's philosophy of preaching, the mind was enlightened in order to awaken the conscience. At the end of 'Making Light of Christ,' Baxter said,

> Oh that I could make every man's conscience a preacher to himself,...: that the next time you go prayerless to bed, or about your business, conscience might cry out, Dost thou set no more by Christ and thy salvation? That the next time you are tempted to think hardly of a holy and diligent life,... conscience might cry out to thee, Dost thou set so light by Christ and thy salvation? That the next time you are ready to rush upon known sin,... conscience might cry out, Is Christ and salvation no more worth, than to cast them away, or venture them for thy lusts?... In a word, that in all your neglects of duty,... yea, in all your cold and lazy prayers and performances, conscience might tell you how unsuitable such endeavours are to the reward; and that Christ and salvation should not be so slighted.[9]

Baxter had several ways of addressing the conscience. One way was simply to inform it. He would impress on people God's laws, commands and requirements. He never hesitated to preach duties and responsibilities, though always in the reasoned, persuasive manner mentioned above. By doing this he kept the conscience true to the Word and will of God. The person who had heard God's law preached would have greater difficulty sinning against it because of his informed conscience.

He also appealed to the conscience as judge of the soul, and asked questions of people in the light of what their conscience told them. Or he would appeal to their experience and to what their own judgement was in the case. In the 'Farewell Sermon,' for example,

[9] Baxter, 'Making Light of Christ,' 818.

he asked, 'What does your own experience say, and how has God dealt with you in time past? Has not your suffering done you good?'[10] Or, as seen already in 'The Absolute Sovereignty of Christ,' he appealed to them, 'If I speak not the truth and reason, then reject it with disdain, and spare not; but if it be, and thy conscience tell thee so, take heed.'[11] In 'The Fool's Prosperity,' he said, 'Let me, with due submission, propound to your sober consideration these questions, which your consciences are concerned to resolve.'[12]

Next, he would implore and plead with his people. He would work on their consciences, rebuking them for sin, pressing charges against them and urging them to change. In his 'Sermon of Repentance,' for example, he wrote:

> And now I beseech you all, consider, is it not better to remember your sins on earth, than in hell? before your Physician, than before your Judge? for your cure, than for your torment? Give me leave, then, before I go any further, to address myself to you as the messenger of the Lord, with this importunate request, both as you stand here in your private and in your public capacities. In the name of the God of heaven, I charge you, remember the lives that you have led! remember what you have been doing in the world! remember how you have spent your time! and whether, indeed, it is God that you have been serving, and heaven that you have been seeking, and holiness and righteousness that you have been practising in the world till now![13]

In making his appeals he did not let them off the hook lightly. Continuing in the same sermon he closed in on them even more:

> And I beseech you observe here, that it is your own misdoings that you must remember. Had it been only the sins of other men, especially those that differ from you, or have wronged you, or stand against your interest, how easily would the duty have been performed! How little need should I have had to press it with all

[10] Baxter, 'Farewell Sermon,' 1017 (language updated).
[11] Baxter, 'The Absolute Sovereignty of Christ,' 802.
[12] Baxter, 'The Fool's Prosperity,' 521.
[13] Baxter, 'A Sermon of Repentance,' 885.

this importunity! How confident should I be that I could convert the most, if this were the conversion!... But if ever God indeed convert you,... he will teach you to begin at home, and take the beam out of your own eyes, and to cry out, I am the miserable sinner.[14]

At times he would pose a cutting question as he did to Members of the House of Commons: 'Will you sit all day here to find out the remedy of a diseased land; and will you not be entreated by God or man to sit down one hour, and find out the disease of, and remedy for, your own souls?'[15] Questions were very characteristic of all his preaching. By this means he could bring a matter close to them and demand response in their own minds.

Appeal to reason and the conscience were constantly intermingled. They were not really two separate approaches but one. In 'Making Light of Christ,' for example, Baxter wanted to bring conviction of the sin of taking Christ too lightly. He sought to do so firstly by pressing many questions, so that their consciences felt the issues, and then by bringing various reasons before them, so that their minds would have to grapple with it. The transition between these approaches afforded Baxter the opportunity to say exactly what he was doing:

> Thus much I have spoken in order to your conviction. Do not some of your consciences by this time smite you, and say, I am the man that have made light of my salvation? If they do not, it is because you make light of it still, for all that is said to you. But because, if it be the will of the Lord, I would fain have this damning distemper cured, and am loth to leave you in such a desperate condition,... I will give you some considerations, which may move you, if you be men of reason and understanding,...; and I beseech you to weigh them, and make use of them as we go, and lay open your hearts to the work of grace.[16]

In many ways Baxter took the stance of a lawyer presenting his case to the jury. He presented reasons, argued motives, set forth the evidence, informed them of what the law said on the matter, and

[14] Ibid., 886. [15] Ibid.
[16] Baxter, 'Making Light of Christ,' 814.

asked them to consider the case. He appealed to their sense of natural justice and urged them to make a right judgment.

It is worth noting that the New Testament terms used to describe preaching often carry very similar overtones. Luke, in describing the apostolic preaching in Acts, underlines both the rational and persuasive dimensions of preaching. In regard to the former he uses the verbs teach (*didaskein*), argue (*dialegesthai*), dispute (*suzetein*), prove (*paratithemi* and *sumbibazein*), persuade (*peitho*), confound (*sunchunnein*) and confute (*diakataleggkein*).[17] For example, in Acts 19:8 we are told, 'Paul entered the synagogue and *spoke boldly* there for three months, *arguing persuasively* about the kingdom of God.' In Acts 17:2-3 we are told, 'As his custom was, Paul went into the synagogue, and on three Sabbath days he *reasoned* with them from the Scriptures, *explaining* and *proving* that the Christ had to suffer and rise from the dead.' He talked and debated, reasoned and proved, argued and explained the message of Scripture.

This reasoned presentation of truth was combined with a strongly persuasive element. Paul describes his own preaching in 2 Corinthians 5:20-21: 'We are therefore Christ's ambassadors, as though God were making his *appeal* through us. We *implore* you on Christ's behalf: Be reconciled to God.' Such appeal also marked Paul's preaching to the unsaved. He told the Athenian philosophers that God '*commands* all people everywhere to repent' (Acts 17:30). Similarly, speaking of Peter on the day of Pentecost, Luke records that, 'With many other words he *warned* them; and he *pleaded* with them,' and the result was that many were 'cut to the heart' (Acts 2:38).

Such rigorous preaching makes for vigorous preaching. As we open texts of Scripture we have a case to present, an appeal to make, a message to proclaim, a truth to press on the heart, and a response to solicit. Our preaching will be far more vigorous when we work hard to convince, persuade, reason, motivate and convict people of the truth with which we are dealing.

When a child is disciplined for wrongdoing, it is least effective

---

[17] A useful discussion of these terms can be found in John W. Stott, *The Preacher's Portrait* (Grand Rapids: Eerdmans, 1961), 55-58.

when a mother or father blows up, ranting and raving and hurriedly administering physical punishment, while the child remains unconvicted of the offence. The child may appear penitent, but in reality he or she is merely fearful of anger and pain. Discipline is much more effective when a parent calmly but firmly interacts with his or her child: Why did you do that? Was that right? What are you meant to do? What are the consequences of doing that? Do you understand that you must now be punished? Most children will be broken by such loving, earnest appeal to the conscience. If physical discipline follows, it can at the same time be less severe and much more effective. Once the heart is softened, a right response is more readily forthcoming.

The same applies in preaching. Merely ranting and raving, and threatening damnation achieves little. Effective preaching presses eternal realities on the mind and conscience, and seeks a response from a convinced and convicted heart.

Tests for self-examination

God's Word is described in Scripture as a mirror in which a person may see a true reflection of himself (James 1:23-25). The preacher's task is to hold that mirror up and force people to look at themselves. He does not merely hold the mirror up to be admired as a wonderful mirror. He holds it up that people may see themselves for what they are, and change accordingly.

One helpful aid in this task is the provision of tests by which people may examine their own souls. This is fundamental to experimental preaching. The 'experiment' is on the very hearts of the hearers, and is actually undertaken by them as the preacher gives the apparatus by which they may examine their souls. In the *Westminster Directory for Public Worship,* a succinct and cogent statement of the essentials of preaching drawn up by the Westminster Divines in the 1640s (at the very time Baxter was preaching in Kidderminster), the following statement is made about 'tests':

> It is also sometimes requisite to give some notes of trial (which is very profitable, especially when performed by able and experienced ministers, with circumspection and prudence, and the signs clearly grounded on the holy scripture), whereby the hearers may be able

to examine themselves whether they have attained those graces, and performed those duties, to which he exhorteth, or be guilty of the sin reprehended, and in danger of the judgements threatened, or are such to whom the consolations propounded do belong; that accordingly they may be quickened and excited to duty, humbled for their wants and sins, affected with their danger, and strengthened with comfort, as their condition, upon examination, shall require.[18]

This was very common in Baxter's preaching and occurred both in the negative (tests that exposed false experience) and the positive (tests of true spirituality).

The most pressing need was for tests that would distinguish true and false conversion. The Puritans recognised that not every response to the gospel was sound. Not all who say, 'Lord, Lord,' are in fact saved (Matt. 7:21). Not every branch that seems to be in the vine is actually bearing fruit from union with Christ (John 15:1-8). They were not simply trying to notch up as many 'decisions' as possible. They wanted to make clear the nature of true conversion, and give tests and signs of a genuine change of heart.

In *A Call to the Unconverted*, for example, Baxter described the signs of a wicked man as opposed to those of a converted person. He exposed false conversions so that they would be warned against spurious experience, and he taught his readers how to search their own hearts and examine themselves:

> Now, as ever you believe the word of God, and as ever you care for the salvation of your souls, let me beg of you this reasonable request, and I beseech you deny me not: That you...enter into an earnest search of your hearts, and say to yourselves.... What state is my soul in? Am I converted, or am I not? Was ever such a change or work done upon my soul? Have I been illumined by the word and Spirit of the Lord?... Is my heart broken or humbled within me for my former life? Have I thankfully entertained my Saviour and Lord?... Do I hate my former sinful life?... Do I give up myself to a life of holiness and obedience to God?[19]

[18] 'The Directory for the Publick Worship of God,' in *The Confession of Faith* (1646; reprint, Inverness: Free Presbyterian Publications, 1976), 380.

[19] Baxter, *A Call to the Unconverted,* 33-34.

Similarly, in 'Right Rejoicing,' he said, 'If you say, How can it be known to me whether my name be written in heaven or not? I shall briefly but satisfactorily, answer it.' He did so by laying out five tests. First, if you have come to see the vanity of things on earth, and esteem the things of heaven more highly, and have resolved that heaven shall be your happiness whatever it cost you on earth, and you devote yourself to God, then your name is written in heaven. Second, if obtaining heaven is your principal care and business, then your name is written there. Third, if you have found yourself lost in sin and you see your need of Christ, and his sufficiency, and you desire his grace and righteousness and take him as your Saviour and Lord, then your name is written in heaven. Fourth, if you desire to be holy, and long to obey God rather than live in sin, then your name is written in heaven. Finally, your name is written there if you have a special love for the heirs of heaven, that is, for other believers. 'These evidences,' he says, 'are sure. By these you may know, while you sit here in these seats, yea, if you lay in the darkest dungeon, that you are the heirs of heaven, and your names are there.'[20]

We have seen that in 'Making Light of Christ,' he first described reasons why people make light of Christ. Later he held up the plumbline against the lives of his hearers. 'Let me, therefore, by these following questions, try whether none of you are slighters of Christ and your own salvation. And follow me, I beseech you, by putting them close to your own hearts, and faithfully answering them.'[21] He set out eight positive tests. For example, he observed that the things that men highly value will be remembered, and therefore the hearer should consider what he 'daily runneth after'. He noted that things we highly value will be matter of our discourse, so we should consider what things we speak about. The things we highly value we try to secure the possession of, and therefore we should see if we have sought to be certain and sure that we are saved. And the things we highly value deeply affect us, so we should see if we have been affected by the things of Christ.

Later he turned to negative tests, exposing what was no true

[20] Baxter, 'Right Rejoicing,' 899.
[21] Baxter, 'Making Light of Christ,' 813.

experience of the work of the Spirit. He made clear that they may have a notional knowledge of Christ, and the necessity of his blood, and of the excellency of salvation, and yet perish as neglecters of him. They may weep at the history of his passion and yet make light of him, and perish for so doing. They may come desirously to his Word and ordinances, even as Herod gladly heard John preach. Many do who yet perish as neglecters of salvation. They may, because of fear, have strong desires for Christ in order to be saved from God's wrath, and yet perish for making light of Christ. They may obey him in many things so far as it will not ruin their life in the world, and yet neglect him.[22]

While such tests particularly focused on true and false conversion, they could equally be applied to almost any aspect of practical Christianity. We may give tests of true humility, tests of genuineness in prayer, tests of true love, tests of a healthy church and so on. Negatively, we may give tests of hypocrisy, tests of sinful self-love and pride, tests of worldliness. The benefit of this approach is that it brings the spiritual truth being addressed close to the experience of each person.

Such application is inconsistent with any quick-fix, easy-believism gospel. If you are out to notch up converts, or tickle people's ears, such tests will not fit in at all. This is for the preacher who wants to deal plainly and seriously with the hearts and souls of men and women.

Questions are an essential ingredient of such preaching. By asking questions we force people to test their own experience and answer from their own heart. Typically Baxter said something like this:

> And first, let me a little inquire into your subjection to Christ. Do you remember the time when you were the servants of sin, and when Satan led you captive at his will?... Do you remember when the Spirit in the word came powerfully upon your hearts?... Hath Christ now the only sovereignty in your souls?'[23]

With such questions, multiplied one on top of the other, he tested the state of their souls, helping them examine their response to Christ,

[22] Ibid., 817
[23] Baxter, 'The Absolute Sovereignty of Christ,' 800.

their dependence on him and their love for him.

Tests and questions, however, need not always be searching and probing. Sometimes they can serve very pastoral ends, helping true saints overcome self-doubts. In the funeral sermon for Mrs Coxe, having spoken of the gospel as the joy of our hearts, he anticipated the concern of some of his hearers: 'But some may say, I cannot say that it is the rejoicing of my heart.' To which he replied with some gentle pastoral questioning:

> 1. Can you say that you take it for that in which you place and seek your joy, though you cannot yet attain it?
> 2. Cannot you say that it is this word that maketh you hope that there is for man a better life, and that you shall not perish like the beasts? and that your fears and sorrows are somewhat abated by the promises of God?
> 3. Cannot you say that you perceive a pleasing goodness in the word of God, which maketh it welcome and acceptable to you?[24]

He then reasoned on these bases that such a person may have good hope of their own salvation: 'Though your joy be small, you may know that it is of the right kind, when it is chiefly sought in God's love and promises; and you would not let go the word of God, and lose your part in it, for all the vanities of the world.'[25]

If we are prepared to employ such tests and questions we will be greatly aided in preaching directly, forcefully and personally. Of course this requires depth of thinking not only about a particular text but about the spiritual outworking of biblical truth. It requires spiritual experience and observation on the part of the preacher. Indeed, it is most profitable when 'performed by able and experienced ministers, with circumspection and prudence'. We ought to be aiming to become men who can help others to search and examine their own hearts.

---

[24] Baxter, 'A True Believer's Choice,' 985.
[25] Ibid.

Stirring the affections

In considering Baxter's philosophy of preaching we saw that the affections were, in his view, the bottom of the soul. In preaching, he wanted to move people at this deepest level. He was not interested in playing lightly on people's feelings and emotions, and his careful argumentation ensured this was not the case. But he did not want his preaching to be purely intellectual. He wanted to stir their deepest inner affections, drawing them away from the things of the world and toward the things of God.

One common failing among those from the Reformed tradition is a tendency to measure spirituality in terms of the 'intellectual acquisition of biblical and theological knowledge'.[26] The focus falls on how sound a person is in their convictions, irrespective of how much those convictions shape the person's speech, life, faith, actions, attitudes and relationship with God. Too often this leads to preaching that seeks only to inform. Truth is explained, defended and taught, but insufficient emphasis is given to the importance of people being moved and transformed by the truth. The affections are not really stirred.

How can this deficiency be addressed? One means is the use of 'affective' language. The use of imagery, illustration and appropriate words can do much to sharpen and deepen the effect made on a person's soul. This use of strong, moving words and phrases that perhaps shock or delight, help to access inner affections. The use of brief images and analogies may throw fresh light on a truth. The use of personal example and illustration may bring a matter home to the heart. Some of these devices will be demonstrated in the next chapter, but it is important to note here that it is one of the chief means of stirring the affections.

Another means is to present the gospel in terms of its effect on the affections. Believing that a fundamental change took place in the affections when a person was converted, Baxter couched some of his 'tests' in terms of the affections:

[26] Arturo G. Azurdia III, *Spirit Empowered Preaching: The Vitality of the Holy Spirit in Preaching* (Ross-shire, Great Britain: Mentor), 37.

When the gospel doth not affect men, or go to their hearts; but though they seem to attend to what is said, yet men are not awakened by it from their security, nor doth it work in any measure such holy passion in their souls, as matters of such everlasting consequence should do: this is making light of the gospel of salvation. When we tell men what Christ hath done and suffered for their souls, and it scarce moveth them: we tell them of keen and cutting truths, but nothing will pierce them: we can make them hear, but we cannot make them feel...; as if we spake to men that had no hearts or feeling: that is making light of Christ and salvation.[27]

He expected changed affections when the gospel took root in the heart:

O sirs, if men made not light of these things what working would there be in the hearts of all our hearers! What strange affections would it raise in them to hear of the matters of the world to come! How would their hearts melt before the power of the gospel! What sorrow would be wrought in the discovery of their sins! What astonishment at the consideration of their misery! What unspeakable joy at the glad tidings of salvation by the blood of Christ!'[28]

He also sought to move people's affections by setting forth in the plainest terms the eternal realities they faced and the affections they would experience in the light of those realities:

Can you make so light of heaven and hell? Your corpse will shortly lie in the dust, and angels or devils will presently seize upon your souls; and every man or woman of you all will shortly be among other company, and in another case than now you are. You will dwell in these houses but a little longer; you will work in your shops and fields but a little longer; you will sit in these seats and dwell on this earth but a little longer; you will see with these eyes and hear with these ears, and speak with these tongues, but a little longer, till the resurrection-day; and can you make shift to forget this? O what a place you will shortly be in of joy or torment! O what a sight you will shortly see in heaven or hell! O what thoughts will shortly fill your hearts with unspeakable delight or horror! What work will

[27] Baxter, 'Making Light of Christ,' 809.
[28] Ibid., 814.

you be employed in! to praise the Lord with saints and angels, or to cry out in fire unquenchable, with devils; and should all this be forgotten?[29]

Clearly, Baxter was not presenting truth in a purely intellectual way, but seeking to move people by the truth.

Perhaps his greatest means of doing this was by passionate appeal. A preacher needs at times to launch into full flight, and with his own affections deeply stirred, address directly and passionately the affections of his hearers. Leaving aside his notes, abandoning a studied and measured pace, forgetting the opinion of others, he finds himself so engaged by the truth he presents that he communicates heart to heart with his hearers. He speaks of his own heart and his longing and desire for his hearers. He asks questions of his hearers, urging and pleading with them. He offers hope and then warns against hardness of heart. He stings and sings, wounds and heals. He speaks with warmth, passion, pathos, intensity, love.

An extended quotation from 'The Fool's Prosperity' illustrates just this. Toward the end of the sermon Baxter reached a turning point in his message:

> Oh that I were now able to speak such enlightening and awakening words to you as might show you at once your worldly prosperity and the heavenly glory in their proper value! and that God would now open your eyes and hearts accordingly, to esteem and seek them![30]

He continued,

> O sirs, it must surely be a grief to a man with foresight to think about what a change is coming, and what a sad preparation you are making, and what a short time the music, the feast, the cards and dice, and filthy lusts and careless amusements, will continue!... In compassion to those that are passing soon to another world, I beseech you, sometimes withdraw yourselves from sensual distractions, and think about whether you will have this place and

---

[29] Baxter, *A Call to the Unconverted,* 31-32.
[30] Baxter, 'The Fool's Prosperity,' 521.

company forever; how long this merry life will last; and whether
this is the work that the God of heaven sent you to do in the world.
And consider whether it would be more comfortable to review
your life when it is gone, to think of days of sensual delight, or of a
holy, and humble, and heavenly conversation;... Oh then you will
wish that you had never heard those high titles, and never possessed
those sumptuous houses, or tasted those delicious feasts, or worn
that gay attire, or known that deceiving company, or been polluted
and made a brute by those beastly lusts! Then conscience will
force [you] to cry out, Oh that I had been the most despised man
on earth when honour fooled me! Oh that I had lain in medicinal
poverty and rags instead of taking this mortal excess of prosperity!
Oh that I had lain in tears and sorrow, instead of being infatuated
by fleshly mirth and pleasure, and that I had been among the saints
that foresaw and provided for this day, instead of drowning the
voice of Christ and conscience with the laughter of a fool and the
noise of worldly business and delights!... I am ashamed of my heart
that it does not melt with compassion in foreseeing your woe, and
that I beg not with tears and importunity to prevent it, and to have
mercy on yourselves. . . .

I suppose you are afraid of the austerities of religion. The devil
would persuade you that it is but a self-torturing or hypocritical life
that we commend to you under the name of godliness,.. but I must
profess it is sorrow that I call you from, and would prevent. It is no
unnecessary grief that I persuade you to, but to a life of heavenly
peace and joy.... Do you think that I cannot have more solid joy
with my daily bread, in the apprehensions of the love of God, and
the belief of his promises of eternal life, than foolish mirth brings,...
You are for mirth, and we are for mirth, but it is a hearty, solid,
spiritual, grounded, lasting mirth that we invite you to; and it is a
beastly, sensual pleasure that ungodly men desire. For my part, it is
almost half my work to promote the joys of true believers, and to
dissuade them from such causeless despondency and troubles as
would rob them of their comforts, and rob God of their love and
thanks and praise. Had you but tasted once the difference between
this inward feast and yours, I should need no more words with you
to persuade you that godliness is a life of joy. . . .

What pity is it to see men destroy themselves with the mercies
of the Lord! What pity is it to see them so eager for prosperity, and

so regardless of the proper use and benefit of it! O be not like the bee that is drowned in her own honey! And do not so greedily desire a greater burden than you can bear; and to have more to answer for, when you have been so unfaithful in a little. And if you believe Christ, who tells you how difficult it is for rich men to enter heaven, and how few of them are saved, don't long for danger, and don't complain if you don't have these exceeding difficulties to overcome. You would be afraid to dwell in that air where few men escape infection; or to feed on that diet that most are killed by. It is evident by the effects that prosperity fools and undoes the most; we find you on your sick beds in a more tractable frame.[31]

Preaching at such times begins to soar, and it is often at such moments, enabled by the power of the Spirit, that the message finds its way into the hearts and affections of those who hear. Baxter bemoaned the fact that,

Alas! we speak so drowsily and so softly, that sleepy sinners cannot hear. The blow falls so lightly that hard-hearted sinners cannot feel. The most of ministers will not so much as exert their voice, and stir up themselves to an earnest utterance.[32]

He believed that,

It is a kind of contempt of great things, especially of so great things, that we speak of them without much affection and fervency. The manner, as well as the words, must set them forth.[33]

If we are to speak to the affections we must speak with affection. We must feel deeply the things we have opened up. We must press them on the hearts of our people. Specific sins must be named, warnings given, promises held out, personal concern expressed, questions asked, reasons given, images used. These devices must be compressed into a single-minded appeal to the heart and soul. There is neither a playing on the emotions, nor a detached, academic

[31] Ibid., 522-3 (language updated).
[32] Baxter, *The Reformed Pastor,* 147.
[33] Ibid., 148.

informing of the mind. Rather, there is a passionate appeal designed to challenge at the deepest level the hearers' response to the message of the gospel.

Discriminatory application

This term has reference to the preacher's work of bringing appropriate forms of application to particular classes of people in the congregation. Packer regards it as arguably the 'most valuable legacy that Puritan preachers have left to those who would preach the Bible and its gospel effectively today'.[34] It was an approach that was first defined by the father of Puritan preaching, William Perkins. In his work *The Art of Prophesying* he defined seven categories of people with whom the preacher must deal: unbelievers who are ignorant and unteachable; those who are teachable but ignorant; those who have knowledge but have not been humbled; the partially humbled; those who already believe; those who have backslidden; and finally 'a mixed people', a phrase perhaps referring to the variety of conditions of soul that believers may experience.[35]

These categories are a useful catalyst for any preacher as he prepares a message. They prompt such questions as, Who specifically needs to be challenged by the Word that is being brought? What types of people are present, and what are the varying needs of their conditions? What sort of people make up this church or community? What classes of people must I seek to address? What are their spiritual diseases that need to be treated?

It is evident that Baxter thought in these terms. Through his personal catechising he became familiar with the types of people in his parish, and in 1658 he described his constituency in twelve categories. First, there were those who were 'serious professors of religion'; then those 'of competent knowledge and exterior performances'. These two categories together comprised about 600 people who were the communicants of the church.[36] Next, he said, there were some who

[34] Packer, *A Quest For Godliness*, 288.
[35] William Perkins, *The Art of Prophesying* (1592; reprint, Edinburgh: Banner of Truth Trust, 1996), 56-63.
[36] This figure equated to about a third of the town's adults.

were 'tractable and of willing minds, that by their expressions seem to be ignorant of the very essentials of Christianity'. The fourth category were those who were 'of competent understandings and of lives so blameless, that we durst not reject them; but they hold themselves off, because they are taught to disown our administration'.

With his fifth category he moved to unbelievers. There were 'heathens' who mocked the very teachings of Scriptures, followed by those who lived in some scandalous sin. Next came those of a more 'tractable disposition' but who really did not know what Christianity was all about; then those who joined ignorance and wickedness together. The ninth category consisted of those who did not live in any scandalous sin, nor were they ignorant of religion, but nonetheless they lived idle lives and pursued vain things. He then identified those who refused to respond to or strive in spiritual things because of their false understanding of predestination, believing that if God intended to save them he would, without their effort! His final two categories were Anabaptists and Papists, though only a few of each were present in his parish.[37]

This appreciation of the varying classes and categories of people present in his congregation and town gave rise to specific words being addressed to specific groups. In making 'close application' a preacher may begin to divide up his congregation and address particular words to particular groups. He is aware that he cannot give the same application to all present. Indeed, as Baxter once put it, 'that which is spoken to *all*, or to *many*, doth seem to *most* of them as spoken to *none*.'[38]

Some of the sermons we have already considered do exactly this. In 'Making Light of Christ,' after two fairly general uses, he came to a third use for 'closer application' and said that before he inquired after the hearts of his hearers it was right to begin at home, 'and see that we who are preachers of the gospel be not guilty of it ourselves.'[39] He applied specifically to preachers the challenge to

[37] Powicke, *A Life of the Reverend Richard Baxter,* 303-05.
[38] Baxter, 'A Sermon of Repentance,' (1660) quoted in Keeble, 'Richard Baxter's Preaching Ministry,' 550.
[39] Baxter, 'Making Light of Christ,' 812.

examine whether they made light of Christ by way of being negligent in their studies, or by drowsy and dull preaching, or slackness in their private dealings with individuals. Only after that did he address his hearers more generally.

In the funeral sermon for Mrs Coxe he came to particular applications with these words: 'And having described this true copy of the text [the life of Mrs Coxe], I may boldly speak of it to the several sorts.' He then addresses brief comments first to 'quakers and scorners', then to 'unbelievers and Sadducees', then to 'papists' and also to 'the malignant, that call serious godliness hypocrisy'. He challenged each with the realities of godliness exemplified by Mrs Coxe, before coming to those he really wanted to address: 'My most earnest desire is to you the loving husband and beloved children of our departed friend.'[40] Then, beyond addressing the family, he addressed all present, pressing home the matter to each heart.

In 'Right Rejoicing,' he said, 'Give me leave, therefore, to make a little closer application of the several parts of my text to the several sorts of persons whom they do concern. And first to all that yet are not become heirs of heaven.' Having addressed unbelievers he then says, 'My next address must be to them whose names are written in heaven', and so he moves on to speak to believers.[41]

This is a most useful approach to adopt in our own preaching. We may highlight two or three particular groups of people for whom the text may have special relevance. We may address believers and unbelievers; the strong in faith and the weak; those who have long ignored the gospel though they have often heard it; those who are caught up in the affairs of the world; or the tender in conscience, the depressed, the hurting, the grieving. Baxter's categories were not so much social (the old and the young, men and women), as spiritual (the strong and the weak, and all the soul-conditions inbetween). He was conscious that when he sowed the seed, his people's hearts represented different types of soil (Mark 4:1-20).

As application is brought to different categories of people it is obvious that the types of application will vary as well. The

[40] Baxter, 'A True Believer's Choice,' 983-4.
[41] Baxter, 'Right Rejoicing,' 900-01.

Westminster Directory for Public Worship identified six different kinds of application: instruction, confutation of false doctrine, exhortation, admonition, comfort and (as we have already noted above) trial or tests. The preacher is one who must correct, rebuke and encourage. He must teach and instruct, rebuke and admonish, comfort and console, challenge and inspire. There ought never to be a sameness in our preaching, but rather a great variety of moods and matters brought before our people.

It is more apparent in regard to discriminatory application than any other aspect of experimental preaching that the preacher must know his people. To bring application like this we must be pastors at heart. We must know and care about people and have some understanding of their varying needs. Not all people or situations can be met at any one time, but the preacher can discriminate so as to bring particular applications home that will hit the mark.

Directions for implementation
Although Baxter was chiefly concerned to address the mind and heart, he did not shy away from the most practical of directions for his people. His sermons were full of sound advice, and, most commonly toward the end of a message, he would suggest directions for implementation.

Needless to say, his directions were never trite or superficial. This is particularly evident in his evangelistic appeals. There was no simple sinner's prayer. There was no single verse to name and claim. The gospel call was never as easy as inviting people to come to the front, or signing a piece of paper, or raising a hand. His directions were much more searching and were designed to ensure that the whole direction of a person's life had been changed.

In *A Call to the Unconverted,* for example, he closed with ten directions that clarified what it meant to turn to God. First, he described what turning would mean for them: they would immediately be made living members of Christ, renewed in the image of God, adorned with all his graces, saved from the tyranny of Satan and dominion of sin, justified, pardoned all the sins of their whole life, accepted by God, made his sons, given liberty and boldness to call him Father, granted the indwelling of the Holy Spirit, made a part of the brotherhood of the saints, and so on. At death, their souls would go to Christ, and they would enter into their Master's joy where they would experience perfect happiness and would be perfected. They would see their glorified redeemer, take part in the new Jerusalem, and be engaged in glorifying their redeemer and God himself.[42]

Second, he urged seriousness in consideration of these matters:

> Withdraw yourself oft into retired secrecy, and there bethink you of the end why you were made, of the life you have lived, of the time you have lost, the sins you have committed; of the love, and sufferings, and fullness of Christ;... of the nearness of death and judgement; of the necessity and excellency of the joys of heaven;... and of the necessity of conversion and holy life. Absorb your hearts in such considerations as these.[43]

Third, he urged that they attend upon the word of God, and upon the public preaching of the Word. Next, they should give themselves to God in earnest prayer, confessing sins, seeking pardon, and doing so daily. He then counselled them to give over all known and wilful sins, and in the sixth place, to change their company where possible, forsaking unnecessary sinful companions.

His seventh direction was to 'deliver up yourself to the Lord Jesus, as the physician of your souls, that he may pardon you by his blood, and sanctify you by his Spirit, by his word and ministers, the instruments of the Spirit'.[44] They were to study Christ – his person, nature and works. Then in the eighth place, he urged them to do all this speedily; not to delay. In the ninth place, to do it unreservedly, absolutely, universally, so that they do not divide their heart between Christ and the world, parting with some sins but keeping the rest. Finally, he urged them to turn resolvedly, not wavering as if uncertain about whether God is better than the flesh, holiness better than sin, heaven better than hell.

Similar emphases are found at the end of 'Making Light of Christ.' He asked if they would make the things of Christ a matter of their

---

[42] Baxter, *A Call to the Unconverted,* 128-30.
[43] Ibid., 130-31. [44] Ibid., 132.

greatest care and study; if they would set more store on the Word of God; if they would attend to public preaching, and give themselves to daily reading of the Word? He asked if they would give more esteem to the officers of Christ (ministers), and seek out their counsel and advice, and support their ministry? He asked if they would take up seriously and earnestly the duty of prayer each day? Would they also cast away known sins? He told them they could not continue in adultery, swearing, cursing, being proud and contentious etc.[45]

Clearly he wanted people to appreciate the full implications of commitment to Christ. Response to the gospel would mean a changed life and he set out before them some of the critical changes that would be required.

To the saved he also gave clear directions. In the 'Farewell Sermon,' for example, he exhorted his people: 'Learn, then, how to behave yourselves in the absence of your Lord, till his return.' He explained how they were to do that. 'Do not be content and pleased with his absence. You must bear it, but not desire it.... Do not be too indifferent and insensitive to your Lord's departure.... Turn not aside to the creature for content, and seek not to make up the loss of his presence with any of the deceitful comforts of the world. Let him not see you take another in his stead, as if riches, or power, or worldly friends, or fleshly pleasure, would serve you instead of Christ.... Do not be emboldened, by his absence, to sin.... Do not be discouraged by your Lord's delay, but wait for his coming in faith and patience. Can you not wait such a short time for him? Oh! how quickly it will be accomplished. Do not sink into despondency of mind....'[46]

These exhortations and applications are both practical and experimental. They are not merely behavioural; they address heart attitudes. Not that brief practical exhortation is inappropriate. In 'The Fool's Prosperity,' Baxter gave very helpful advice to his hearers arising from his discourse on the reality that prosperity is a great snare to many. He told them not to think that riches themselves were evil; not to cast away their riches or refuse them if offered them by God; not to be tempted to condemn and speak evil of rich governors

[45] Baxter, 'Making Light of Christ,' 817-18.
[46] Baxter, 'Farewell Sermon,' 1023 (language updated).

who had been set over them by God; not to think they would be saved simply for being poor. He counselled them to show compassion to the rich, and not to fear them; to honour with double honour those who are both great and godly, rich and religious, not because of their riches but because of their strength of grace to withstand the temptations of wealth; to offer increased prayer for the rich in view of their temptations and the difficulty of them being saved.[47]

Perhaps the clearest example of the nature of his practical directions to the saints is found in the introduction to *The Saints' Everlasting Rest*. He wrote to his beloved flock, 'I leave you my best advice for your immortal souls, and bequeath you this counsel as the legacy of a dying man, that you may read it and practice it when I am taken from you.' He proceeded to give the following ten instructions:

1. Labour to know and to have sound understanding.... Ignorance is virtually every error, so let the Bible be much in your hands and hearts.... Read much the writings of our old, solid theologians, such as Perkins, Bolton, Dodd, Sibbes, and especially Preston....

2. Do the utmost you can to get a faithful minister when I am taken from you. Be sure you acknowledge him as your teacher, overseer and ruler (see 1 Thess. 5:12-13, Acts 20:28, Heb 13:7,17). Learn from him, obey him, and submit to his doctrine, unless he teaches you anything peculiar, . . .

3. Let all your knowledge turn into feeling and action. Keep open the passage between your heads and your hearts, that every truth may go to the quick.

4. Be conscientious in the great family duties. Teach your children and servants the knowledge and fear of God; do it early and late, in season and out of season. Pray with them daily and fervently.... Read the scripture and good books to them....

5. Beware of extremes in the controversial points of religion. When you avoid one error, take care you do not run into another, especially if you are in the heat of an argument or passion....

6. Follow peace and unity... He who is not a son of peace is not

[47] Baxter, 'The Fool's Prosperity,' 521.

a son of God. All other sins destroy the church as a result, but division and separation demolish it directly.... Do not believe that people are friends of the churches if they try to cure and reform her by cutting her throat....

Mark this: when you feel any sparks of discontent, take them as kindled by the devil from hell, and take heed you do not cherish them....

7. Be sure to get down the pride of your hearts. Do not forget all the sermons I preached to you against this sin. No sin is more natural, more common, or more deadly....

8. Be sure to control your flesh and senses. Few ever fall from God without flesh-pleasing being the cause.... Nothing in the world damns so many people as flesh-pleasing, when people choose it as their happiness instead of God. Remember who has said,... 'Make no provision for the flesh, to satisfy its desires' (see Rom. 8:13, and 13:14). Think of this when you are tempted to drunkenness, gluttony, lustfulness, and worldliness....

9. Conscientiously fulfil the duty of reproving and exhorting those about you. Do not make your souls guilty of the oaths, ignorance, and ungodliness of others, by your silence. Admonish them lovingly and modestly, but be sure you do it, and do it seriously.

10. Maintain a constant delight in God, and a seriousness and spirituality in all his worship. Do not think it is enough to delight in duties, if you do not delight in God.... Do not give way to the dullness of custom in duty: do every duty with all your might.

Especially, do not be slight in secret prayer and meditation. Do not spend the majority of your zeal on external things and opinions, and the smaller things of religion. Let most of your daily work be on your hearts....48

Along these lines, the experimental preacher should be careful to earth his preaching in the practical realities of Christian life. When dealing with issues of the soul there is a danger that the implications remain vague. To be helpful to our people, we must not only impress truth on the heart, but show how that truth should be translated into godly living.

[48] Baxter, *The Saint's Everlasting Rest,* ed. Pipe, 15-24.

Putting it all together

Obviously no one sermon need employ all these devices in order to drive a message home to the heart. Serious thought, however, should be given to which ones are most useful for any given message. It is our task as preachers to think broadly and deeply about the spiritual implications of a text, and how they may best be applied to our hearers.

If we are to preach on Psalm 1, for example, we will need to begin by identifying the main theme (doctrine) of the Psalm and stating it experimentally. It may lead us to a proposition such as this: 'We will experience true blessing when we delight in the things of the Lord, rather than in the ways of sin and the world.' This theme will need to be opened up in terms of a faithful exegesis of the Psalm. We will want to consider the role of the Psalm in the Psalter as a whole, and the way in which it relates to Christ. We will need to study the concepts of blessedness and wickedness, and what is really meant by 'the law'.

But we must do more than that. In order to preach it with spiritual vigour, we need to ask a number of questions of the text. We may begin by asking, 'What *spiritual realities* does it deal with?' Clearly, it addresses such matters as the excellence of delighting in God's Word, the danger of increased entrenchment in sin, the importance of spiritual meditation, the fruitfulness of godliness, the gracious watch of the Lord over his people, the futility of ungodliness, and the certainty of judgement. Some of these realities need explaining. For example, What is spiritual meditation? How does one go about meditating on the Word?

Then we may ask, 'What *motives* for walking in the way of blessedness should be given?' Such things as increased fruitfulness in the service of God, greater refreshment in our own souls, the blessing of being numbered in the assembly of the saints and the need to reckon with the day of judgement may all be used as motives to walking this path.

We may also ask, 'What *spiritual tests* should be given?' It would be useful to provide some tests of whether people really delight in law of the Lord. Do they meditate on it? Do they have a constant habit of spending time with God's Word (day and night)? Do they follow its counsel rather than the counsel of the world? Negatively, we may open some tests of the way of life that the Bible calls 'wicked'. Do they seek to live independently of God? Do they largely ignore his Word in public and private? Do they mostly derive counsel from unbelievers? Wickedness does not mean gross moral evil, so much as life lived outside of fellowship with the Lord.

We may also ask, 'What *affections* are spoken of?' Most obviously the Psalm speaks of the affection of delight, and we would do well to open up what it means to delight in the things of God.

It would also be profitable to ask, 'What *categories of hearer* may be specifically addressed?' There is most obviously a call to speak both to believers and unbelievers. But that may be too general. Among believers we may speak to those who already delight in God's Word, giving them encouragement and comfort. We may also challenge those who have become lax in spiritual disciplines. In addressing unbelievers, we may address the three categories of people indicated in verse 1: those who walk in the counsel of the wicked; those who stand in the way of sinners; and those who sit in the seat of mockers.

These questions open up a great variety and depth of spiritual application. They supply us with an abundance of practical, spiritual applications. It is not hard to see why the Puritans ended up preaching many sermons on one verse! Our challenge will be knowing what to leave out, and how to order the material so as to make the greatest impact on people. With much prayer, we need to press these diverse applications into a message of life and power.

Preachers who work diligently in these ways to apply God's Word to people's lives, may look expectantly to the Holy Spirit to open hearts to the truth.

Chapter 7

Passion and Power

Preach....with plainness and perspicuity, with reverence and
gravity, with convincing evidence and authority, with prudence,
caution, faithfulness, and impartiality, with tender love
and melting compassion, with fervent zeal and unwearied
patience, waiting on God for the success.[1]

The best matter will scarcely move them, if it be not
movingly delivered.... The want of a familiar tone and
expression is a great fault in most of our deliveries, and
that which we should be very careful to amend.[2]

It seldom reacheth the heart of the hearer,
which cometh not from the heart of the speaker.'[3]

Boring! No doubt many a sermon has been written off with that one
devastating word. It is the great dread of almost every preacher. We
know that it is a travesty to preach the powerful, authoritative, life-
giving Word of God boringly. To put people to sleep, to make them
feel that the Word is tedious, to lose them in a tangle of technical
jargon, is to abominate our calling. Of course there will be some
people who find the very best preaching boring. There will be those
who, because of their own dead-heartedness, never find any message
powerful. Some will also come to church so ill-prepared and tired
from the week, that they would sleep through fire from heaven. But
ordinarily, as preachers we ought to bring God's Word with heart-
gripping passion and power.

Baxter urged on people the importance of finding such preachers:
'Live under the most convincing, lively, serious preacher that possibly
you can.'[4] He explained:

---

[1] Baxter, 'The Reformed Liturgy,' in *Practical Works*, 1: 926.

[2] Baxter, *The Reformed Pastor*, 149.

[3] Baxter, *Compassionate Counsel*, 19.

[4] Baxter, *A Christian Directory*, 475.

> There is an unspeakable difference as to the edification of the hearers, between a judicious, clear, distinct, and skilful preacher, and one that is ignorant, confused, general, dry, and only scrapeth together a cento [patchwork] or mingle-mangle of some undigested sayings to fill up the hour with.[5]

This was a distinction he often made. He drew a sharp line between preaching that was clear, distinct and powerful, and that which was weak, dull and muddled. He asked, 'Have you not found the ministry of one sort enlighten, and warm, and quicken, and comfort, and strengthen you, much more than of the other?'[6] Surely, he said, people 'feel the difference between a clear and quickening sermon, and an ignorant, heartless, dead discourse, that is spoken as if a man were talking in his sleep, or of a matter that he never understood, or had experience of.'[7]

His reason for urging people to sit under powerful preaching was not that they might be entertained by a powerful communicator, but that they would be drawn to deeper spiritual experience. There is always the danger that people become sermon connoisseurs. They love good preaching not because their hearts are open and responsive to it, but because they have developed a taste for it. They come to church chiefly to hear sermons, rather than to worship God. They love to evaluate the preacher, assess his skills and abilities, and compare him with others they have heard. They love the sound of great oratory and appreciate good communication. They enjoy the feeling of powerful preaching, but they are sermon-proof. The power is felt in their ears but never in their hearts.

That is always a danger. But it should not deter us from preaching as powerfully as we know how. True power will often break down such defences. Power that is derived from the Spirit of God and his Word, and is not merely the result of human ability, will penetrate, at times, even the hardest hearts.

The church needs powerful preaching. Christians need every help they can have in maintaining spiritual liveliness and vigour:

---

[5] Ibid., 473.   [6] Ibid., 45   [7] Ibid.

Alas, how apt are the best to cool, if they be not kept warm by a powerful ministry! How apt to lose the hatred of sin, the tenderness of conscience, the fervency in prayer, the zeal and fullness in edifying discourse, and the delights and power of heavenly meditations, which before we had! How apt is faith to stagger if it be not powerfully underpropt by the helpers of our faith. How hardly do we keep up the heat of love, the confidence of hope, the resolution and fullness of obedience, without the help of a powerful ministry![8]

No ostentation

Given the importance of powerful preaching, some critical questions arise: What makes for powerful preaching? What helps us to preach powerfully and effectively, in a lively, clear, distinct manner?

This was an issue to which the Puritans gave much attention. Once again, their practice arose from their philosophy of preaching. They were not pragmatists when it came to matters of style and manner. That, sadly, is one of the problems in contemporary preaching. Desperately wanting to be interesting and relevant, many preachers will do almost anything to be popular. They will dress up as clowns. They will tell endless stories and jokes. They will involve puppets, video clips, sports stars – anything that will stop people leaving with feelings of boredom. Yet for all the innovative ploys, there is still little power.

The Puritans faced a very similar issue in their own day. In sixteenth and seventeenth century England the pulpiteers who used gimmicks to gain people's ears were mostly found in the Anglican church.[9] These preachers developed a penchant for flowery, ornate rhetoric. Their sermons were well-crafted speeches that displayed their intelligence and wit. They delighted the sophisticated, learned gatherings that comprised many graduates of Oxford and Cambridge. They quoted extensively from literature, history, poetry, foreign languages and ancient scholars. They were ostentatious and elaborate.

[8] Ibid.

[9] The two most notable Anglican preachers of the early seventeenth century were Bishop Lancelot Andrewes and Dean John Donne. A useful description of their preaching can be found in Davies, *Worship and Theology*, vol. 2, *From Andrewes to Baxter and Fox*, 142-54.

They displayed flair and skill, learning and intelligence, and most of all, great pride. These sermons were carefully designed to establish the preacher's reputation, and truly, they received their reward in full.

It was in opposition to this that the Puritans rethought the art of preaching from the basis of what preaching was all about. They readily concluded that content was more important than form, clarity more important than ostentation, spiritual edification more important than aesthetic beauty, the vast uneducated populace more important than the learned elite, and Christ more important than the preacher. From early in the Puritan period they developed a deep-seated aversion to anything flashy or showy. They resolved to preach plainly and clearly the message of salvation. William Perkins, for example, who was in many regards the father of Puritan preaching, argued that preaching 'must be plain, perspicuous, and evident.... It is a byword among us: *It was a very plain sermon:* And I say again, *the plainer, the better.*'[10]

This became their base conviction regarding style. Preaching was to be plain. Not boring. Not dull. But plain in that it avoided unnecessary displays of learning and all gimmicks that might detract from the message. They would have despised what is taking place in many churches today. The tendency to a predominantly entertaining message with a few spiritual truths scattered here and there; the extensive use of humour; the focus on such universally appealing themes as success, wealth, health and happiness in place of the great biblical themes of regeneration, holiness, redemption and judgement; the use of props and gimmicks to draw crowds and the focus on particular personalities, most notably via TV – these all would have stirred their ire. They saw that such attempts to make preaching effective were entirely self-defeating. Far from generating power, such approaches rob God's Word of its life-giving force.

Baxter was as committed as any to the 'plain style'. He joined the chorus of protest against ostentation:

[10] William Perkins, *Works*, quoted in Ryken, *Worldly Saints*, 104-5, citing Charles H. George and Katherine George, *The Protestant Mind of the English Reformation, 1570-1640* (Princeton: Princeton University Press, 1961), 338.

I feel in myself in reading or hearing, a despising of that wittiness as proud foolery, which savoureth of levity, and tendeth to evaporate weighty truths, and turn them all into very fancies, and keep them from the heart. As a stage-player, or a morris-dancer, differs from a soldier or a king, so do these preachers from the true and faithful ministers of Christ: and as they deal liker to players than preachers in the pulpit, so usually their hearers do rather come to play with a sermon, than to attend a message from the God of heaven about the life or death of their souls.[11]

By contrast he said of his own preaching, 'For my part, I study to speak as plainly and movingly as I can (and next to my study to speak truly, these are my chief studies).'[12]

Plain certainly did not mean boring. For all their aversion to wit, they were extremely good communicators. Haller comments: 'Certainly no group of men ever laboured more earnestly or self-consciously to make themselves understood by their audience as they found it.'[13] Baxter's preaching was passionate and energetic, full of imagery and illustration, easy to understand yet powerful. It was 'plain' though, in that it ignored anything that might be ostentatious, flamboyant or theatrical. In plain language, addressed to the ears of the common man, he found immense power.

Biblical parallels

Before we consider the means by which he sought to preach plainly and movingly, it is important to establish the biblical validity of such preaching. Significantly, two key New Testament preachers made a similar stand against the worldly ostentation of their contemporaries, and preached with a studied plainness that had immense power.

First, this was the mark of our Lord's own preaching. Those who heard him noticed immediately the difference between his preaching and that of the Pharisees and teachers of the law. At the conclusion of the Sermon on the Mount, it was observed that 'the crowds were amazed at his teaching, because he taught as one who had authority,

[11] Baxter, *A Treatise of Conversion*, 399.

[12] Baxter, *The Reformed Pastor*, 196.

[13] Haller, *The Rise of Puritanism*, 131.

and not as their teachers of the law' (Matt. 7:28-29). Several contrasts underlay this observation. One was the contrast between their ostentation and his simplicity. In the Sermon, he had launched some well-aimed attacks on the pride and hypocrisy of the Pharisees. They loved to be noticed, to be regarded as spiritual, to be heard and seen in prayer, in giving, in fasting. Jesus exposed the shallowness and vanity of religion that seeks to impress. By contrast, he cultivated in his followers simple sincerity. He urged prayer in private, as he himself practised, and pleaded for the pursuit of the Father's praise, not that of men.

Another contrast was between their love of learning and his love of ordinary people. He used down-to-earth images and illustrations that appealed to the common people because they were drawn from everyday life: the farm, the economy, the home, the marketplace. His preaching did not go over their heads, nor did it make them feel they were miles below par spiritually. Rather, they saw heaven open before them as he depicted the kingdom of heaven as a place diametrically opposed to the prejudices they laboured under in this world. They came to see that it is blessed to be poor in spirit, to hunger and thirst for righteousness, even to be persecuted. Heaven was not a realm for the spiritually elite; it was for all who would come to the one who was lowly and humble of heart.

A third contrast was in his pointedness. The teachers of the law tended to focus on obscure technicalities of the law, and revelled in quoting and debating the views of earlier rabbis. Sometimes their questions to Jesus were concerned with remarkably insignificant matters: will people marry in heaven, should we pay taxes to Caesar, is it lawful to heal on the Sabbath and so on. At other times, though they asked about the most important matters of life, they did so with ulterior motives rather than a genuine desire to know the truth (see, for example, Luke 10:25). By contrast, Jesus addressed the great issues of life with the greatest urgency and sincerity. He drew sharp distinctions between the broad and narrow roads, life on the rock and life on the sand, trees that bore good fruit and trees that bore bad fruit. He taught about rebirth, judgement and the end of the age. He called people to prayer, to obedience and to self-denial. He trained and equipped men to be witnesses and sent them out with a message of repentance and faith.

This plain preaching drew the crowds. Jesus was an immensely popular preacher. Yet it must be noted that that was not his aim. He did not devise his approach in order to be popular. Frequently, in fact, he tried to get away from the people who pressed all around him, and in the early stages of his ministry he forbid those he healed from saying who had done it. The simple fact was, his ministry, marked as it was by simplicity, earthiness, plainness, directness and selflessness, was also marked by power.

It is not surprising that his greatest successor imitated his studied plainness, similarly opposing the ostentation of his own contemporaries. The apostle Paul provides a second New Testament example of the type of preaching the Puritans promoted. No statement argues his case more clearly than 1 Corinthians 1:18–2:5. He highlights to the Corinthians the threefold foolishness of preaching. First, there is the foolishness of the message itself. The message of salvation through faith in a crucified man was almost impossible for the people of Paul's day to swallow. The Jews were impressed by power. They were won over by miracles, signs and wonders. To proclaim salvation in and through a man they had killed and hung on a cross, was the height of foolishness. The Greeks, by contrast, loved intellectualism. They loved philosophical debates and prized the display of learning. To come with a message of a man from Galilee who was raised as a carpenter, spent three years preaching to a largely peasant audience, and was then rejected by the religious elite in the most ignominious of all deaths, was laughable. Paul, in confining himself to the preaching of the cross, presented a message that was foolishness to both Jew and Gentile.

In every age, there has been the desire to find more impressive ways of proclaiming the gospel. The Greeks would have loved it presented by way of dramas and plays, or clever discourse, witty sayings, poetry and philosophy. The Jews would have loved a signs and wonders movement. Other pagan cultures would have responded to the use of images and idols. But God deliberately shunned those approaches, and adopted the plain proclamation of his Word. Paul's statement could not be clearer: Jews demand miraculous signs, and Greeks look for wisdom, but we preach Christ! The preacher alone has God-given authority. Indeed, to hear faithful preaching is to hear God speak. That is why Paul could commend the Thessalonians by saying that he thanked God continually because 'when you received the word of God, which you heard from us, you accepted it not as the word of men, but as it actually is, the word of God, which is at work in you who believe' (1 Thess. 2:13). Such divine authority is given to no other form of communication.

Next Paul identified the foolishness of the church. He asked the Corinthians to take a look at themselves. How many great philosophers were there among them? How many learned men? How many nobles? How many influential members of society? The reality was, the gospel message was by and large being received by ordinary, down-to-earth people. The composition of the church itself was testimony to the fact that God works in ways contrary to the world.

If we had chosen the first disciples, it is unlikely we would have opted for fishermen, tax collectors and political activists. We would more likely have plundered the ranks of the religious hierarchy, choosing the most eloquent and learned spokesmen for our cause. Yet God's purpose had been that in choosing 'ordinary, unschooled men' his own power would be displayed. Throughout redemptive history this has been God's strategy. He chose a despised nation, a despised Messiah, despised disciples and a despised church, and through them worked his sovereign power. He has deposited his treasure in jars of clay 'to show that this all-surpassing power is from God and not from us' (2 Cor. 4:7).

A pre-occupation with big name stars, status, learning, the wealthy and the impressive is in direct conflict with God's chosen method. Not that the kingdom is closed to the rich and famous, the learned and educated. Although it is hard for a rich man to enter the kingdom, it is by no means impossible with God. But to pitch our preaching at gaining the ear of the sophisticated while ignoring the common person, is to be out of tune with God's revealed purposes. To opt for what is powerful in human eyes is to choose what is weak and contemptible in the sight of God. If we would ever experience true power, we must accept the fundamental paradox of the kingdom: when we are *weak*, then we are strong.

In the third place Paul identified the foolishness of his own preaching. Not only was the content foolish – 'I resolved to know nothing while I was with you except Christ and him crucified' – but the style of delivery was foolish. He did not come with a display of eloquence and superior wisdom. In fact, the report going around was that 'His letters are weighty and forceful, but in person he is unimpressive and his speaking amounts to nothing' (2 Cor. 10:10). Paul had indeed preached with a great measure of fear and weakness. But this had been his deliberate ploy. He had not wanted their faith to rest on his cleverness, his persuasive words, his own wisdom. He wanted, by way of plain preaching, to make way for a demonstration of the Spirit's power.

From a human point of view, Paul was up against it when he preached in cities like Corinth and Athens. Undoubtedly he was up to the challenge from an intellectual point of view, yet he resolved not to compete with their rhetoric and learning, but to preach simply and plainly. He was content to adopt a style that may not win the praise of men, but by God's grace, might win the hearts of sinners. He knew that the only person he needed to please was God himself: 'For we are *to God* the aroma of Christ among those who are being saved and those who are perishing. To one we are the smell of death, to the other the fragrance of life.... Unlike so many, we do not peddle the word of God for profit. On the contrary, in Christ *we speak before God* with sincerity, like men sent from God' (2 Cor. 2:15-17, italics mine).

We must conclude that the Puritans were right in insisting that the manner and style of preaching is as much a biblical issue as the content of preaching. Spiritual work must be undertaken in a spiritual manner. We must be prepared to crucify self if we are ever to experience the power and freedom of the Spirit.

The virtue of simplicity

What in practice does it mean to preach plainly? What style and approach must we adopt in order to allow the Spirit's sovereignty in preaching? In the first place, there must be deliberate simplicity. 'All our teaching must be as plain and simple as possible. This doth best suit a teacher's ends. He that would be understood must speak to the capacity of his hearers. Truth loves the light, and is most beautiful when most naked.'[14]

We must learn to be simple without being simplistic. Simple preaching is clear, incisive, insightful and readily comprehensible. Simplistic preaching is superficial, trite and insignificant. It requires a good mind to be able to grasp complex truth and present it perspicuously. 'It is, at best, a sign that a man hath not well digested the matter himself, if he is not able to deliver it plainly to others.'[15] Our constant concern in sermon preparation ought to be to grasp the truth so clearly in our own minds that we can present it with great clarity to others.

Plain speech touches on several matters. The structure of the message as a whole ought to be logical and progressive. If a sermon is disjointed it will lose clarity. The choice of vocabulary ought to be both fresh and restrained. While the preacher does not want to use language that either seeks to impress others with his own skill, or goes beyond their capacities, neither does he want to be boring. Language that is down-to-earth, colourful and punchy helps hold the attention of hearers. Reference to unknown authorities or the original languages must be minimised, if not eliminated. It is all too easy for preachers to lapse into theological jargon, technicalities and obscurities. If we allow ourselves that luxury, we may as well forget power. It may be impressive; it will seldom be effective.

This was Baxter's deliberate approach. In the preface to one of his works, for example, he wrote, 'You have here presented to you a common subject, handled in a mean and vulgar style, not only without those subtleties and citations, which might suit it to the palates of learned men, but also without that conciseness, sententiousness and quickness, which might make it acceptable to the ingenious and acute.'[16]

[14] Baxter, *The Reformed Pastor*, 115-16.
[15] Ibid., 116.
[16] Baxter, *A Treatise of Conversion*, 399.

Baxter's verbosity and prolixity, far from being contradictory to his insistence on simplicity, actually had its origin in exactly this principle. In the preface to the 1651 edition of *The Saints' Everlasting Rest*, a work that amounts to over 350 pages of fine print, he wrote:

> Some, I hear, blame me for being so tedious, and say, All this might have been in a lesser room.... I considered that I speak to plain, unlearned men, that cannot find our meaning in too narrow a room, and that use to overlook the fullness of significant words. As they must be long in thinking, so we must be long in speaking: or else our words fall short of the mark, and die before they can produce the desired effect, so great is the distance between these men's ears and their brains.... And I confess I never loved affectation, or too much industry about words, nor like the temper of them that do. May I speak pertinently, plainly, piercingly, and somewhat properly, I have enough.[17]

His evaluation of the mental capacities of his hearers was scarcely flattering, but it was realistic. Far from wanting to reach only the learned, he was concerned to speak to the ordinary man on the street. His assessment that this needed to be done by way of many words was one that may have held true in his time, but is unlikely to in our own. The average person today will simply refuse to wade through pages and pages of writing or listen to lengthy sermons. Everything else they receive is in small bites. The evening hour of news, which is probably the heaviest intake of information most people have in the course of a day, is carved into brief items (even briefer if there is no video footage to show), and interspersed by ads, graphics, music and lightweight items. While this ought not to deter us from presenting substantial messages, it does indicate that a concern to be plain and simple will require a different strategy than in seventeenth century England. The ability to be crisp and incisive will carry far greater weight than prolixity.

Baxter's plainness was not only designed to help the simple hearer. It was also in his view the most appropriate style for spiritual matters.

[17] Baxter, *The Saints' Everlasting Rest*, in *Practical Works*, 3: 7

'The plainest words are the profitablest oratory in the weightiest matters. Fineness is for ornament, and delicacy for delight; but they answer not necessity, though sometimes they may modestly attend that which answers it.'[18] Baxter therefore contrasted those who seemed only to play with holy things and 'the plain and pressing downright preacher' who speaks with 'life, and light, and weight'.

Plain language suited plain dealing. In the Dedication to *The Reformed Pastor* he once again defended his manner:

> If it be objected, that I should not have spoken so plainly and sharply against the sins of the ministry, or that I should not have published it to the view of the world; or, at least, that I should have done it in another tongue, and not in the ears of the vulgar.... – I confess I thought the objection very considerable; but that it prevailed not to alter my resolution, is to be ascribed, among others, to the following reasons.[19]

He proceeded to give several reasons, one of which was that, 'If the ministers of England had sinned only in Latin, I would have made shift to admonish them in Latin, or else have said nothing to them. But if they will sin in English, they must hear of it in English.'[20]

Baxter believed that 'If our words be not sharpened, and pierce not as nails, they will hardly be felt by stony hearts.'[21] Consequently his writings contained some surprisingly sharp words. In rebuking men for questioning the ways of God in salvation, he responded, 'O horrid arrogancy of senseless dust! shall ever mole, or clod, or dunghill, accuse the sun of darkness, and undertake to illuminate the world? Where were you when the Almighty made the laws, that he did not call for your counsel?'[22]

Again, when asking why they would not turn to the Lord, he wrote:

> What is it then for a lump of earth, an ignorant sot, that knoweth not himself nor his own soul, that knoweth but little of the things

---

[18] Baxter, *A Treatise of Conversion*, 399.

[19] Baxter, *The Reformed Pastor*, 38.

[20] Ibid., 38-39.   [21] Ibid., 117.

[22] Baxter, *A Call to the Unconverted*, 14.

which he seeth, yea, that is more ignorant than many of his neighbours, to set himself against the wisdom of the Lord! It is one of the fullest discoveries of the horrible wickedness of carnal men, and the stark madness of such as sin, that so silly a mole dare contradict his Maker, and call in question the word of God.[23]

Such language is not particularly user-friendly! We may not dare to address our people in the same manner. It is illustrative, however, of Baxter's concern to present truth strikingly and forcefully rather than flatteringly and elegantly. Occasionally shocking our congregations with strong words may not be altogether a bad thing if it prevents them from being merely entertained, or lulled into complacency.

In developing a plain style of pulpit speech, often what is at stake is our own pride. Baxter knew that to preach plainly he had to lay in the dust his own reputation:

God commandeth us to be as plain as we can, that we may inform the ignorant; and as convincing and serious as we are able, that we may melt and change their hardened hearts. But pride stands by and contradicteth all, and produceth its toys and trifles.... If we have a plain and cutting passage, it taketh off the edge, and dulls the life of our preaching, under the pretence of filing off the roughness, unevenness and superfluity.[24]

To be powerful we must be prepared to crucify all that is proud in our sermons. We ought to scrutinise them and remove not only that which is obscure, but anything that is included chiefly for the display of our own abilities. Purge your sermons of words, phrases and illustrations that are included for cleverness' sake.

Serious, fervent speech

In dealing plainly with people, Baxter felt the overwhelming weight of the message he proclaimed. Just as we would not go to a neighbour's house when it is on fire and sing a little ditty about their house burning down, nor arrive on the scene of a car accident and

[23] Ibid., 79.
[24] Baxter, *The Reformed Pastor*, 137-8.

make some inappropriate joke in order to cheer the poor victims up, neither should we deal lightly and cheaply with people when speaking of heaven and hell, of eternal joy and eternal sorrow. The subject matter of preaching demands seriousness. While we need not be heavy and dour, we must show that we are in good earnest.

Baxter had a particular dislike of frivolity in the pulpit: 'Of all preaching in the world (that speaks not stark lies) I hate that preaching which tends to make the hearers laugh, or to move their minds with tickling levity, and affect them as stage-plays used to do, instead of affecting them with a holy reverence of the name of God.'[25] By contrast what he looked for in a preacher was deep reverence: 'I know not how it is with others, but the most reverent preacher, that speaks as if he saw the face of God, doth more affect my heart, though with common words, than an irreverent man with the most exquisite preparations.'[26]

He defined reverence as 'that affection of the soul which proceedeth from deep apprehensions of God and indicateth a mind that is much conversant with him.'[27] This was the starting point for Baxter. A deep sense of the majesty and glory of God, leading to a sense of the weight and importance of what God says, and therefore a commensurate seriousness in bringing his message to others. 'Oh the gravity, the seriousness, the incessant diligence, which these things require!'[28]

Baxter, appalled by those preachers who but play-acted in the pulpit, versified his grief in these words:

What statues, or what hypocrites are they,
Who between sleep and wake do preach and pray?
As if they feared wakening the dead!
Or were but lighting sinners to their bed!
Who speak of heav'n and hell as on a stage!
And make the pulp't but a parrot's cage?
Who teach as men that care not much who learns;
And preach in jest to men that sin in earns.
Surely God's messenger, if any man
Should speak with all the seriousness he can.[29]

[25] Ibid., 119-20. [26] Ibid., 119. [27] Ibid. [28] Ibid., 203-4.

Baxter was often smitten by his own lack of seriousness in preaching:

> I marvel how I can preach...slightly and coldly.... I seldom come out of the pulpit, but my conscience smiteth me that I have been no more serious and fervent.... It accuseth me not so much for want of ornaments or elegancy, nor for letting fall an unhandsome word; but it asketh me, 'How couldst thou speak of life and death with such a heart? How couldst thou preach of heaven and hell in such a careless, sleepy manner? Dost thou believe what thou sayest? Art thou in earnest or in jest?... Shouldst thou not weep over such a people, and should not thy tears interrupt they words? Shouldst not thou cry aloud, and show them their transgressions, and entreat and beseech them as for life and death?'[30]

It led him to urge his fellow preachers to much greater fervency:

> Methinks we are in nothing so wanting as in this seriousness; yet is there nothing more unsuitable to such a business, than to be slight and dull. What! speak coldly for God, and for men's salvation? Can we believe that our people must be converted or condemned, and yet speak in a drowsy tone? In the name of God, brethren, labour to awaken your own hearts, before you go to the pulpit, that you may be fit to awaken the hearts of sinners.[31]

This is a challenge that needs to be repeatedly impressed on our hearts. Do we feel deeply the truths we are bringing to others? Have we ourselves been convicted by them? Do we believe we have a message of eternal significance? Are we burdened with the word the Lord has laid on our hearts? If not, we are unlikely to preach with great fervour. Passion, pathos and power are the overflow of a heart burdened by the eternal significance of the message we bear. We are 'men sent from God' (2 Cor. 2:17), and must have a manner worthy of the matter.

We must be very wary of being detached and analytical in our

[29] Baxter, *Poetical Fragments*, 40.
[30] Baxter, *The Reformed Pastor*, 203.
[31] Ibid., 148.

handling of truth. True preaching is marked by holy passion. The particular manifestation of passion may vary from one preacher to another. Our personality will profoundly shape the manner of our delivery. Some personalities will be more inclined to tears; some to demonstrative, loud delivery; some to a more low key, but no less intense, style. The preacher must be true to himself. Yet irrespective of our personality, there must be passion for the truths of God's Word and the souls of those to whom we preach. If feeling truth deeply is not innate to us, we must pray for it, and seek to feel what we deliver. When we speak feelingly, it is more likely our hearers will feel the truth also. 'Set these things home with a peculiar earnestness; for if you get not to the heart, you do little or nothing; and that which affecteth not is soon forgotten.'[32]

Given Baxter's concern for seriousness and his aversion to light-heartedness in the pulpit, the question may be raised, Is there a place for humour in preaching? Baxter evidently opposed it, but we need to understand what he was opposing. He opposed anything that either elevated the preacher or undermined the message. When preachers play the role of comedians, seeking to raise a laugh a minute and make light of every serious matter they touch on, they do both. They take centre stage, and the serious issues they deal with are minimised. It may be popular; it is seldom powerful. If we depend chiefly on humour for effect, we leave ourselves and others in doubt as to whether people's response is to our wit, or the Holy Spirit's work. There is undoubtedly a place for preachers to see the humorous side of situations, to share in smiling and laughing with their people, and to portray a joyful sense of humour. There is no place, however, for becoming a stand-up comic.

Baxter's emphasis on seriousness and fervency may be summarised in one more quotation:

Constant experience telleth us undeniably of the different success of the reading or saying of a pulpit-lesson, or of a dull or a mere affected speech, and of the judicious, serious explication and application of well-chosen matter, which the experienced speaker

---

[32] Ibid., 250.

well understandeth, and which he uttereth from the feeling of his soul. And the love of a benefice, no, nor of applause neither, will not make man preach in that manner, as the love of God, and the lively belief of heaven and hell, and as the desire of saving souls will do.[33]

Throwing light on the subject

One great aid to preaching in a lively, clear manner is the use of imagery, illustration and analogy. Yet here again the Puritans proceeded with a carefully reasoned approach. For them it was not simply a matter of using illustrations because people like them. They realised that all too easily illustrations detract from the Word rather than sharpen people's focus on it. By definition an illustration is intended to throw light on a subject. If the light itself draws all the attention, it is self-defeating. When people leave after a message, remembering some great stories and anecdotes, but unable to recall what the stories illustrated, they have effectively looked into a floodlight while failing to see the building that was being lit up.

This, it must be said, is common in contemporary preaching. Many preachers rely on well-told stories to hold the attention of their audience. It is the contemporary equivalent of the Anglican's eloquence, the Greek's love of wisdom, or the Jew's penchant for the miraculous. Taking Jesus' frequent use of stories as a supposedly biblical justification for their approach (forgetting, it seems, that his parables were not intended for entertainment, but for the simultaneous veiling and revealing of truth),[34] many preachers string together one story after another. Often the illustrations are brilliant. Their stories are fascinating and moving. They give an impression of power. But that is where the danger lies. Anyone may be moved by a well-told

[33] Baxter, *Compassionate Counsel*, 19.

[34] See Mark 4:10-12. Jesus' parables deliberately veiled the truth to unbelieving hearts, while opening it to believing hearts. Those with spiritual understanding, who by faith saw that in Jesus the kingdom had come, were instructed in the things of the kingdom by means of the parables; those without faith heard only stories that were but riddles. The parables were appealing as great stories, but Jesus had far greater reason for employing them than sheer entertainment value.

story. Only those indwelt by the Spirit will be moved by biblical truth. In preaching, we must be careful not to confuse our hearers. While we want to bring truth alive for them, we do not want to deceive them.

One revealing test of any message is to remove from it all illustrations, humour, anecdotes and images, and see what is left. If very little remains, the preacher has failed to use these devices appropriately. He has made them the substance of the message, not the spotlight on it.

The Puritans, recognising both the importance and danger of illustrations, adopted a threefold strategy. First, they used biblical illustration wherever possible. If the point they were making could be illustrated from biblical history, or the life of some biblical character, they would opt for that first. In this way, people's attention was not taken away from the Word, but drawn to it. Baxter urged that 'Our evidence and illustrations of divine truth must also be spiritual, being drawn from the Holy Scriptures, rather than from the writings of men. The wisdom of the world must not be magnified against the wisdom of God.'[35]

Next, they drew illustrative material from everyday life. Many of their images and analogies were very homely and familiar. They avoided the temptation to be overly clever. They would no doubt have despised the tendency to use anthologies of professionally devised illustrations. Rather, they wanted peoples' eyes to be opened to the everyday pictures of spiritual truth that surrounded them.

Finally, they opted for brief pictures, rather than detailed stories. More frequently than telling stories, they used simple images and analogies. They didn't want to waste time in telling lengthy stories, but used a multitude of word pictures and images to clarify truth and maintain interest.

Baxter's use of images and word pictures may be illustrated from his 'Farewell Sermon'. He began the sermon, as we have already observed, with an extensive analogy likening his departure from them to a death. He explored this from many angles: death brings a separation of closest friends, it is unwelcome, it signals the end of

[35] Baxter, *The Reformed Pastor*, 120.

earthly comforts, and also earthly labour; it is the effect of painful sickness, and causes in turn grief and mourning; it is also succeeded by judgement. Each analogy was probed to reveal some truth about his departure, though he added that 'the resemblance between death and this our separation, holdeth not in all things'.[36] He noted that he was not the church's soul or life, and the continuance of the church did not depend on any single pastor.

This was his most fully developed analogy in the sermon, but he went on to draw on many spheres of life to illustrate other lessons. He used medical images to illustrate the good suffering may do us and to stress God's sovereign design:

He wounds the body to heal the soul, he lances the sore to let out the corruption, he lets blood to cure our inflammations . . .[37]

If the physician is better than the patient in determining how you are to be treated, and if you are fitter than your infant child, and better qualified than your beast to determine his pasture, work, and usage, surely then you will grant that God is much more fit than we.[38]

He drew on the order and design of nature to illustrate the pattern of suffering preceding joy:

Non-entity was before created entity, the evening before the morning, infancy before maturity of age, weakness before strength, the buried seed before the plant, the flower and the fruit; and infants cry before they laugh.[39]

From nature he also spoke of the joy of Christ's return to his people after a time of his absence spiritually:

How quickly the sun's return recovers the verdure and beauty of the earth, and clothes it in green, and spangles it with the ornaments of odoriferous flowers, and enriches it with sweet and plenteous

[36] Baxter, 'Farewell Sermon,' 1014.
[37] Ibid., 1015-16 (The language in these quotations has been updated).
[38] Ibid., 1017. [39] Ibid., 1016.

fruits: the birds that were either hidden or silent, appear and sing, and the face of all things is changed into joy. So it is with the poor deserted soul, upon the return of Christ.[40]

He turned to the world of agriculture to enforce the idea of suffering producing a harvest:

When the ploughers make furrows on you, it prepares you for the seed; and the showers that water it foretell a plenteous harvest. Think it not strange if he thresh and grind you, if you would be bread for your Master's use. He is not drowning his sheep when he washes them, nor killing them when he is shearing them.[41]

To those who struggled to accept that good often comes from suffering he reminded them that 'there is none of them but would endure the prick of a pin, or the scratch of a briar, or the biting of a flea to gain a kingdom, or the opening of a vein, or the griping of a purge to save their lives'.[42]

Often he used several brief images together to make a point, as he did when explaining that Christ would not bring sorrow on his people forever:

When he hides his face, he does not mean to forsake them; when he takes away any ordinances or mercies, he does not give them a bill of divorce.... When he lets the boar into his vineyard, it is not to make it utterly desolate, or turn it common to the barren wilderness.[43]

At times his images were somewhat graphic, if not brutal:

Fools trust themselves, and wise men trust God: fools tear the tree, by beating down the fruit that is unripe and harsh; and wise men stay till it is ripe and sweet, and will drop into their hands: fools rip up the mother for an untimely birth; but wise men stay till maturity give it them: fools take red-hot iron to be gold, till it burn their fingers to the bone.[44]

In addition to these images and similes, he also used many biblical examples, drawing on the lives of Adam, Noah, Abraham, Cain and

[40] Ibid., 1023. [41] Ibid., 1017. [42] Ibid., 1020. [43] Ibid., 1021. [44] Ibid., 1027.

Abel, Judas, Herod and Ahab. Again, he did not develop these illustrations at length, assuming familiarity with the biblical narrative. They were used simply to provide a deeper insight into the truth he was addressing.

Spirit-dependency

'All our work must be done spiritually, as by men possessed of the Holy Ghost. There is in some men's preaching a spiritual strain, which spiritual hearers can discern and relish; whereas, in other men's, this sacred tincture is so wanting, that, even when they speak of spiritual things, the manner is such as if they were common matters.'[45]

This was Baxter's supreme concern. We must preach spiritually. Everything must be bent to that end. To access the Spirit's power, without which our preaching will be worthless, we must make ourselves submissive to his mode of operation. If he works in and through the Word, then we must be content to confine ourselves to the Word and preach it heartily. If he reveals his power in weakness, then we must be prepared to be weak in the eyes of men, disdaining what they esteem if it is contrary to what the Spirit applauds. If he is pleased to work in the hearts of the humble, then we must be humbled before him, recognising our utter insufficiency for the task, and casting ourselves on his grace. If he ordinarily works in response to earnest prayer, then we must be men of prayer, for 'he preacheth not heartily to his people, that prayeth not earnestly for them'.[46]

If we are to preach with passion and power, we must avoid the temptation of preparing or presenting sermons mechanically.[47] It is possible, once we know the skills of exegesis and sermon

[45] Baxter, *The Reformed Pastor*, 120.

[46] Ibid., 122.

[47] In terms of sermon presentation, it seems Baxter used a variety of methods, ranging from a fully prepared manuscript to an entirely extemporary delivery. On one occasion he was accused by a Quaker of being 'empty of the Spirit' because he prepared his sermons. Baxter replied, 'I pray God forgive me that I Study no more; Do you think that we cannot talk without study as well as you, and I hope a little better.... We do not so despise God, his Word, or our hearers, as to speak before we consider what to say' (Richard Baxter, *The Quakers Catechism*, London: 1655, quoted in Keeble, 'Richard Baxter's

construction, to prepare messages that are sound and faithful, perhaps even insightful and penetrating. But they will be utterly devoid of power if they have not been born in the context of Spirit-dependency. It is not sufficient to prepare a sermon as we want it, and then seek the Spirit's blessing on it.

It is the gracious work of the Spirit to open the Scriptures to us as we use the means for study we have acquired. 'The Holy Spirit assisteth us in our hearing, reading, and studying the Scripture, that we may come, by diligence, to the true understanding of it; but doth not give us that understanding, without hearing, reading or study.'[48] The Holy Spirit alone opens our eyes so that we may know 'piercingly, and effectually, and practically' that which before was only known 'notionally, and ineffectually'.[49]

It is also the Spirit's work to give us delight in the truth:

> The Holy Ghost doth, by sanctifying the heart, possess it with such a love to God, and heaven, and holiness, and truth, as is a wonderful advantage to us.... Experience telleth us, how great a help it is to knowledge, to have a constant love, delight, and desire to the thing which we would know.[50]

And it is the Spirit who makes us spiritually minded:

> There must be some savour of the Spirit in him that will be fit to make us spiritual, and some savour of faith and love in him that would kindle faith and love in us; and he must speak clearly and convincingly that would be understood, and will prevail with such as we; and he must speak feelingly, that would make us feel, and

Preaching Ministry,' 548). Keeble discusses his style of delivery, noting that Baxter disliked the memorisation of a complete sermon, preferring shorthand notes: 'when I take *most pains* for a Sermon, I write *every word*: when I take a *little pains* I write the *heads*; but when business hindereth me from taking *any pains*, I do neither, but speak what is in my mind' (Richard Baxter, *Principles of Love*, quoted in Keeble, 549). This was in line with the Puritan's typical approach. They generally opted for carefully prepared sermons delivered from memory or notes. See Davies, *Worship and Theology*, vol. 2, 141-2.

[48] Baxter, *A Christian Directory*, 41.
[49] Ibid. [50] Ibid.

speak seriously, that would be much regarded by us, and would make us serious.[51]

In preparation, therefore, we must evidence by prayer, meditation and spiritual sensitivity, complete reliance on the Spirit of God. We must be flexible enough to allow for his promptings and leadings, and humble enough to cry out for his aid. This, ultimately, is the key to passion and power.

Avoiding caricatures

One of the greatest mistakes we can make in seeking to follow the example of the Puritans is to imitate their style. If we look and sound as though we were recently transplanted from the seventeenth century, we will completely fail to communicate truth as they did. If we speak in old English, with 'thees' and 'thous'; if we deliver stodgy sermons that can only be digested by the most devout and scholarly hearers; if we use illustrations sparingly and awkwardly, not daring to be in any sense modern lest we undermine our age-old message, then we have settled for but a caricature of Puritanism, not the spirit of it.

The Puritans were not antiquated in their day. They were not dated or irrelevant. Their language was not old-fashioned. Their images and illustrations were not awkward. Their lengthy sermons were not extreme. The Puritans were men of their time who rethought in the most rigorous manner the means of preaching powerfully and effectively to the common man. They rethought the act of preaching not in the light of contemporary culture, but biblical precedent, and then translated that into their own culture. 'Their sermons savoured of close meditation in the closet and no less close observation in the street.'[52] To follow in the spirit of Puritanism is to do the same in our day. Our dress, our vocabulary, the length of our sermons, our choice of images and illustrations and our manner of delivery ought to be appropriate to our own time and culture.

In our speech we need to use the best of contemporary English. We will avoid modern idioms that trivialise great truths, but we will

[51] Ibid., 45
[52] Lewis, *The Genius of Puritanism*, 20.

also avoid archaic language, long, complex sentences and unnecessarily technical vocabulary. Use of biblical theological terms is necessary; use of theological jargon is not. We will have to labour to speak more briefly and concisely.

In our illustration of truth we will want to relate to the world in which our people live. Examples drawn either from the struggles or blessings of our own life, or the realities of the world around us (political, social and economic) help to earth preaching in real life. Frequent, brief images and illustrations will help keep our preaching fresh.

In our manner, we must adopt the principles of seriousness, fervency and humility. It is not that we must all become 'hellfire and brimstone' preachers, but we must be known as men who feel deeply what we say, who are passionate about the truth we preach, and who are authentic practitioners of what we proclaim. Yet we must also be warm and compassionate in our delivery. There ought to be in our manner some reflection of the love of our Saviour.

It is the application of Puritan principles rather than the adoption of their style that will enable us to preach with greater passion and power. Those principles are well summarised in one final quotation from Baxter:

We must be serious, earnest, and zealous in every part of our work. Our work requireth greater skill, and especially greater life and zeal than any of us bring to it. It is no small matter to stand up in the face of a congregation, and to deliver a message of salvation or damnation, as from the living God, in the name of the Redeemer. It is no easy matter to speak so plainly, that the most ignorant may understand us; and so seriously that the deadest hearts may feel us; and so convincingly, that the contradicting cavillers may be silenced. The weight of our matter condemneth coldness and sleepy dullness. We should see that we are well awakened ourselves, and our spirits in such a plight as may make us fit to awaken others.... To speak slightly and coldly of heavenly things is nearly as bad as to say nothing of them at all.[53]

[53] Baxter, *The Reformed Pastor*, 117.

Chapter 8

The Reformed Preacher

If God would but reform the ministry, and set them on their
duties zealously and faithfully, the people would certainly be
reformed. All churches either rise or fall as the ministry doth
rise or fall (not in riches and worldly grandeur),
but in knowledge, zeal and ability for their work.[1]

In the name of God, brethren, labour to awaken your
own hearts, before you go to the pulpit, that you may be
fit to awaken the hearts of sinners.[2]

It is a lamentable case, that in a message from the God of
heaven, of everlasting moment to the souls of men,
we should behave ourselves so weakly, so unhandsomely,
so imprudently, or so slightly, that the whole business should
miscarry in our hands, and God should be dishonoured,
and his work disgraced, and sinners rather hardened
than converted; and all this through our weakness or neglect![3]

Experimental preaching is the Spirit-enabled proclamation of God's
Word, in which truth is held against people's hearts in such a way
that its reality is seen, its excellence felt, its power experienced. Under
such preaching people sense God himself drawing them from the
things of this world into a soul-satisfying relationship with himself.
Such preaching is spiritually nourishing. It is at the same time searching
and satisfying, convicting and convincing, humbling and uplifting. It is
moving, but not manipulative; challenging, but not coercive.

Experimental preaching is more easily recognised than defined. It
is the sort of preaching which you feel instinctively to be very good,
but you are perhaps hard-pressed to state just what it is that is so

[1] Baxter, *Autobiography*, 97.
[2] Baxter, *The Reformed Pastor*, 148.
[3] Ibid., 70.

good about it. What it is, of course, is that God takes hold of you by his Word, just as he has taken hold of the preacher. You do not merely come under the word of man, but the Word of the living God. It moves you, breaks you, thrills you, changes you, as it was meant to do. It uplifts you, and draws you nearer to God.

It is a tragedy that such preaching is so rare. It ought to be the norm in every pulpit. Unfortunately it is not. But we must hope and pray for a better day. If the pulpits of England were once filled with hundreds of 'plain-dealing preachers' at a time when most were against it, we have reason to hope that God may again raise up a generation of preachers who will preach with great spiritual vigour.

Yet such reformation in the church today is not only something we should hope and pray for. It is something we must work for. Baxter challenged his colleagues in that regard. For many years they had prayed and fasted for a time of reformation in the church, when there would be serious discipline and a faithful ministry. 'Oh the earnest prayers which I have heard for a painful [painstaking] ministry, and for discipline! It was as if they had even wrestled for salvation itself.'[4] Yet his grief was that having prayed for it, they were not prepared to work for it. 'We have refused the troublesome and costly part of the reformation that we prayed for.'[5] He warned against being satisfied with superficial changes, when the reformation needed is much more deep-seated:

> Alas! can we think that the reformation is wrought, when we cast out a few ceremonies, and changed some vestures, and gestures, and forms! Oh no, sirs! it is the converting and saving of souls that is our business. That is the chiefest part of reformation, that doth most good, and tendeth to the salvation of the people.[6]

The challenge is one we must not brush aside lightly. There seems to be endless talk of impending revival. Many pray for revival. Some believe they have already experienced it. Some foretell a large and imminent outpouring of the Spirit. Yet for all the talk (and if we are a little more cynical, hype) there seems to be a refusal to lay hold of

[4] Ibid., 209. [5] Ibid., 210. [6] Ibid., 211.

those means by which revival may come. If we refuse to promulgate humble ministries and instead opt for man-centred ones; if we neglect the plain exposition of the Word in favour of more entertaining forms of ministry; if we lecture dryly instead of preaching passionately; if we compromise on issues of personal holiness while accepting every wind of doctrine; if we expend our time on professional marketing and neglect faithful pastoring; if we preach user-friendly messages to the unchurched when we ought to be convicting people of sin, righteousness and judgement; in short, if we adopt strategies that we think might work, that are at variance with what the Scriptures command, we may as well lay to rest our expectations of revival. By these means we may well be able to grow churches, but we will not be one step nearer genuine revival.

The call to an experimental preaching ministry is, at bottom line, a call to run counter to the predominant trends and ethos of the contemporary church.

First things first

To begin in any position other than on our knees would be contrary to the entire spirit of experimental preaching. As Baxter called the pastors of his day to humble themselves and repent of their former coldness and dullness, so must we. We must repent of laziness in our preparation, and dreariness in our presentation. We must repent of our lack of self-discipline, and our desire to finish the job quickly. We must repent of the times we have gone about our preparation without earnestly seeking the power of the Spirit. We must repent of the many times we have failed to think seriously about how to bring truth home to hearts. We must repent of all the sermons we have preached that have not breathed life from God. We must repent of the times we have allowed ourselves to intrude into the message in such a way that Christ has been obscured. We must repent of the pride of our hearts that has sought admiration of our skill, or resented other preachers being more loved or successful than ourselves.

Once we begin to examine our hearts in these regards, we will no doubt be deeply convicted of our lack of skill and grace in the work of preaching. Such humility, expressed in the earnest confession of sin, and the casting of ourselves on God's grace and mercy, is the necessary pre-requisite for true change.

In such a spirit of humility we are made ready to seek the empowerment of the Holy Spirit. We must seek spiritual insight in our study of the Word and spiritual power in our presentation of it to others. Our conviction must be that without the Spirit's presence and aid, our message will be utterly weak and worthless.

In earnestly desiring the Spirit's power, we will also seek the prayers of others. Paul was not above pleading with churches to pray for him, that he would have boldness and freedom in proclaiming the Word.[7] Throughout church history also, preachers have been greatly aided and encouraged by the knowledge that many saints have been upholding them in prayer. It is a plea we should make in our own churches. Confessing our weakness to our congregations, and owning our commitment to the foolishness of preaching, we must urge that they intercede for the ministry of the Word, that it may be clothed with power.

Godly example

We have seen that Baxter was steeped in the early Puritans, and in turn, urged his own followers to read and immerse themselves in the writings of those 'affectionate, practical English writers'. He knew that next to the Scriptures, the most powerful aid to a reformed ministry was the imbibing of true spirituality from other saints.

It is for this reason that we have spent time learning from Baxter. But his preaching is neither the only, nor the perfect, model of spiritual vigour. If we are to grow in our commitment to experimental preaching, we would do well to saturate ourselves in such preaching. There are several benefits to such an approach.

In the first place, preaching, like character, is more caught than taught. Experimental preaching is not so much a method as an ethos; it is therefore not learned by precept as much as by example. While courses in homiletics can impart to us the basic disciplines of exegesis, hermeneutics and the structuring and ordering of sermons, it is the

[7] See, for example, Colossians 4:3-4, Ephesians 6:19-20 and 1 Thessalonians 5:25.

ministry of godly men that imparts to us an awareness of and hunger for true spiritual vigour in preaching. By reading or listening to great preaching, we come to love such plain dealing, and see the power and effectiveness of it. We learn to think more spiritually about the Scriptures. We feel increasingly inspired to preach more powerfully. What preacher has not benefited in this way from the sermons of Spurgeon, or the writings of Ryle; from the godliness of a M'Cheyne, or the prayerfulness of a Muller; from the passion of the Wesleys or the vigour of Whitefield; from the thorough exposition of Lloyd-Jones or the spiritual insight of Tozer?

Secondly, immersing ourselves in the preaching of former giants has the effect of humbling us. If we only compare our preaching with peers who struggle as much as we do, we may well feel quite comfortable with our weaknesses. But when we stand next to those who have preached many times a week, to tens of thousands of people, and have experienced the unction of the Spirit in revival, and opened the Word with immense power that still speaks across the centuries, then we are put in our place. Nothing is more conducive to a right spirit in preaching than a humble hunger for greater preaching.

A third benefit of studying the writings of great preachers from across the centuries is that we gain a broader perspective on contemporary trends in ministry. It is unhealthy to derive principles for preaching exclusively from our own day, especially given the current tendency to undervalue the authority and power of preaching. We must guard ourselves against the largely pragmatic mindset of many church ministry experts today. Church practice is increasingly being driven by what works. It is motivated by what people want, what will grow a church, what has proved successful elsewhere, and what is appropriate to our own culture. If we immerse ourselves in this thinking, without counter-balancing it with insights from other eras in church history, we will most likely develop a distorted view of the preaching ministry. No one period has a monopoly on truth. We must remember that as we study the Puritans, but we must also remember it as we consider the thinking of our own day. Some breadth of input from across the centuries, and especially from times of great blessing in the life of the church, will help us think more clearly about our calling.

Turning to those who have been used of God in times of revival will help stir in our hearts a sense of expectancy that God may renew in our day what he has done in times past. Indeed, he may begin to do so with our next sermon!

Iron sharpening iron

Preachers of the past become, in a sense, our mentors when we turn frequently to their writings. In addition to their input, however, there is much value in interacting with like-minded colleagues. This was a significant part of Baxter's strategy for improving the condition of the church. For many years he held monthly meetings in his own home for other ministers, and then, following one of those meetings in 1652, proposed a scheme for a closer association together.[8] The result was the Worcestershire Association.[9]

The Association was a serious meeting of like-minded ministers. They came together to spur each other on in the work of ministry, edify one another, debate and discuss matters of importance to the churches, and challenge each other to great effectiveness in the pastoral preaching ministry. Baxter's sermon on Acts 20:28, which we now know as *The Reformed Pastor*, was one product of that fellowship. Baxter described the ministers of the Association in these words:

[8] Baxter recalled, 'I stood still some years, as a looker-on, and contented myself to *wish* and *pray* for peace, and only drop now and then a word for it.... I was so conscious of my meanness and inconsiderableness in the Church that I verily thought but very few will regard what I said. But when I once attempted it God convinced me of this error, and, shewed me how little instruments signifie when he will work' (*Reliquiae Baxterianae*, 1696, quoted in Powicke, *The Life of the Reverend Richard Baxter*, 164).

[9] Details of the Association can be found in Powicke, *The Life of the Reverend Richard Baxter*, 165-7. It was really 'a revival of the old Puritan "Exercises," or "Prophesyings"' (Ladell, *Richard Baxter*, 62), and while failing to attract Presbyterians and Anglicans, it nonetheless comprised a significant number of men from throughout the county and beyond. Nuttall says that as many as 70 different ministers participated in the course of the first year alone, though not all concurrently (*Richard Baxter*, 68).

Their preaching was powerful and sober; their spirits peaceable
and meek, disowning the treasons and iniquities of the times as
well as we; they were wholly addicted to the winning of souls;
self-denying, and of most blameless lives; evil spoken of by no
sober men, but greatly beloved by their own people and all that
knew them.... desiring union and loving that which is good in all.[10]

There is a need for ministers of like mind to meet together for
mutual edification and accountability in this way. Often the road to
an experimental preaching ministry is a lonely one. Many will not
share our burdens and concerns. We need, then, to seek out those
who do, so that our attempts to grow in spiritual vigour may be
encouraged and aided by others.

Spiritual preparation
When we have been somewhat humbled, taught, challenged and
encouraged to think differently about ministry, we need to effect
change in our approach to weekly sermon preparation. In the first
place, we must seek to gain deeper spiritual insights into the substance
of our preaching texts. In the context of earnest prayer, our concern
will not merely be to come to a right analysis of the text, but to a
profound understanding of the spiritual issues in a text. We need to
interact not only with the historical, grammatical and literary contexts
of a text, but the spiritual concerns of it. What is the spiritual import
of the passage? What issues of the heart and soul does it address? In
what way does the text deal freshly with our relationship with God?
What aspects of godliness are promoted? What attitudes of the heart
are under consideration?

This prayerful, meditative reflection on the text ought to take
priority in our preparation for preaching. If we *begin* our preparation
with technical concerns (the original languages, grammar, etc.), it is
quite likely we will *end* with a largely technical discourse. If, however,
our preparation is borne in the context of prolonged thought,
meditation and prayer, we are much more likely to deal, throughout
our study of the passage, with the spiritual heart of the text.

Once we have grasped the spiritual meaning of the text in the light

[10] Ibid., 173.

of its original context, we then must consider the relevance of those issues to our lives and the lives of our hearers. We need to begin the hard work of heart application. This may be broken into two stages: the what and the how. We need to consider *what* applications ought to be made – what sins confronted; what difficulties addressed; what attitudes challenged; what needs met. We also need to consider *how* we will bring these applications home. In Baxter's words:

> When you are studying what to say to your people, if you have any concern for their souls, you will oft be thinking with yourself, 'How shall I get within them? and what shall I say, that is most likely to convince them, and convert them, and promote their salvation?'[11]

We have seen that there is a time to use tests, a time to describe realities, a time to reason and persuade, a time to convict the conscience, a time to give practical exhortations, a time to divide the congregation into categories and speak a word to particular groups. Most likely only one or two of these devices can be used in any one sermon. Therefore, much thought should be given as to how best we can make piercing application in the limited time we have.

If the work of application is to comprise, say, 50% of our delivery, it is not unreasonable to take 50% of our preparation time to consider these matters. Instead of spending most of our time in exegetical study and the structuring and writing of the sermon, we would do well to spend far more time reflecting, thinking and meditating on how best to bring the message to bear on human hearts.

Once this work is done, there remains one more vital element in preparation for experimental preaching: we must awaken our own heart. The process of preparation should have done that. But recognising the speed with which the fire may die down, we need to fan the flames again before we preach. The final hours before preaching are most critical. We need a mind that is focused. We need a conscience that is clear before God. We need a heart that is warm. We need a deep familiarity with our message, so that we are not utterly bound to our notes, but open to the prompting of the Spirit as we speak. We need a prayerful, humbled spirit. The

[11] Baxter, *The Reformed Pastor*, 65.

experimental preacher is aware that the preparation of his own heart and soul is just as important as the preparation of his sermon. If we are to communicate heart to heart with our people, we had better ensure our heart is in a state that will be edifying to them.

Baxter explained the dynamics as follows:

> In preaching, there is a communion of souls, and a communication of somewhat from ours to theirs. As we and they have understandings and wills and affections, so must the bent of our endeavours be to communicate the fullest light of evidence from our understandings to theirs, and to warm their hearts, by kindling in them holy affections as by a communication from our own.... We should, therefore, be furnished with all kind of evidence, so that we may come as with a torrent upon their understandings, and with our reasonings and expostulations to pour shame upon all their vain objections, and bear down all before us, that they may be forced to yield to the power of truth.[12]

If the torrent has not come on our understandings, we are unlikely to unleash it on theirs. In order to ready our hearts and minds for the act of preaching, then, we do well to heed this advice:

> A minister should take some special pains with his heart, before he is to go to the congregation: if it be then cold, how is he likely to warm the hearts of his hearers? Therefore, go then specially to God for life: read some rousing, awakening book, or meditate on the weight of the subject of which you are to speak, and on the great necessity of your people's souls, that you may go in the zeal of the Lord into his house. Maintain, in this manner, the life of grace in yourselves, that it may appear in all your sermons from the pulpit, – that every one who comes cold to the assembly, may have some warmth imparted to him before he depart.[13]

This alone will not kindle a mighty fire, but if it is the final act after many days of prayer, study, meditation and preparation, we may look expectantly for God to grant his blessing, and send us among his people with great spiritual vigour.

[12] Ibid., 149-50.   [13] Ibid., 62-3.

Appendix

Baxter's Farewell Sermon[1]

*And ye now, therefore, have sorrow; but I will see you
again, and your heart shall rejoice, and your joy
no man taketh from you (John 16:22).*

My dearly beloved in our dearest Lord,
I consent with your troubled thoughts about this unwelcome day,
confessing that to me, as well as you, it seems to resemble the day of
death.

1. Death is the separation of the closest companions, soul and body.
How close the union between us is, both in our relation, and in our
affection, which this day comes to some kind of dissolution, I will
rather tell to strangers than to you.

2. Death is unwelcome both to soul and body (though it does not
destroy the soul, it does the body). So also, dear companions do not
part willingly. Your hearts and minds are so well aware of this reality,
words can well be spared.

3. Death is the end of human conversation here on earth. We must
see and talk with our friends here no more. And this separation of us
is likely to end the conversation we have had in our duties together.
We must no more go up together, as we used to, to the house of God.
I must no more speak to you publicly in his name, nor comfort my own
soul in opening to you the gospel of salvation, nor in the mention of his
covenant, his grace, or kingdom. Those souls that have not been
convinced and converted, are never likely to hear more from me for
their conviction or conversion. I have finished all the instruction, reproof, exhortation and persuasion, which I can ever use for their
salvation. I must speak no more to inform the ignorant, to reform the
wicked, to reduce the erroneous, to search the hypocrite, to humble
the proud, to bow the obstinate, or to bring the worldly, the impenitent
and the ungodly to the knowledge of the Word, themselves, and God.
I must speak no more to strengthen the weak, to comfort the afflicted,
or to build you up in faith and holiness. Our day is past, our night has

[1]The text of this sermon as presented here has been modernised.

come, when we cannot work as we formerly did! My opportunities here are at an end.

4. Death is the end of earthly comforts, and our separation is likely to be the end of that comfortable communion which God granted us for many years. Our public and private communion has been sweet to us. The Lord has been our pastor, and has not suffered us to want. He made us lie down in his pleasant pastures, and he led us by the silent streams! (Psalm 23:1, 2). He restored our souls, and his very rod and staff comforted us. But his time for smiting and scattering has come. These pleasures are now at an end.

5. Death is the end of human labours – there is no ploughing or sowing, no building or planting in the grave. And so our separation ends the works of our mutual relationship in this place.

6. Death is the effect of painful sickness, and usually of the folly, intemperance or oversight of ourselves. And, though our consciences do not reproach us for gross unfaithfulness, yet our failings are so many and so great as to force us to justify the severity of our Father, and to confess that we deserve this rod. Though we have been censured by the world for being too strict, and doing too much for the saving of our own and others' souls, yet it is another kind of charge that conscience has against us. How earnestly we now wish that we had done much more: that I had preached more fervently, and you had heard more diligently, and we had all obeyed God more strictly, and done more for the souls of the ignorant, careless, hardened sinners that were among us! It is just that God should put to silence so dull a preacher, that could speak without tears and fervency to impenitent sinners, when he knew that it was for no less than the saving of their souls, and foresaw the joys which they would lose, and the torment which they must endure, if they did not repent. With what shame and sorrow I now look back upon the cold and lifeless sermons I preached; and on those years of neglecting the duty of privately instructing your families, before we set on that task in an orderly way. Our destruction is of ourselves! Our failings and negligence have caused us to forfeit our opportunities. As good Melancthon said, 'The arrow that has wounded us, was feathered from our own wings.'

7. Death causes those friends who live on to enter into mourning. Their laments are the chief part of funeral solemnities. And in this also we have our part. The compassion of mourners, however, is greater than we desire because sorrow tends to become unruly and exceed its

bounds, and bring on more sufferings. It also looks too much at the instruments, and to be more offended at them than at our sins.

8. Death is the end of all the living. The mourners must also follow after us, and, alas! how soon! It makes our fall more grievous to us to foresee how many others must soon come down! How many hundred pastors must shortly be separated from their flocks. If there were no epidemic malady to destroy us, our ministry has its mortality. Your fathers, where are they? And the prophets, do they live for ever? (Zech. 1:5). This made us the more importunate with you in our ministry, because we knew that we must preach to you, and pray with you, and instruct you, and watch over you, but a little while. Though we did not know what instrument death would use, we knew our final day was coming, when we must preach, and exhort and pray our last with you! We knew that it behoved us to work while it was day (and, oh, that we had done it better!) because the night was coming when no one could work (John 9:4).

9. And as it is appointed to all men once to die, so after death there follows judgement. And we also have our further judgement to undergo. We must expect our hour of temptation. We must be judged by men, as well as chastened by God. We must prepare to bear the reproach and slander of malicious tongues, and the unrighteous censures of those who do not know us, and those who think it their interest to condemn us. And we must also call ourselves to judgement. We are likely to have unwelcome leisure with which to review the days and duties which are past. It will then be time for us to call ourselves to account for our preaching and studies, and other ministerial works, and to sentence our labours and our lives. And it will be time for you to call yourselves to account for your hearing and profiting, and to ask, 'How have we used the mercies which have been taken from us?' Yes, God himself will judge us according to our works. He will not justify us if we have been unfaithful in little and have been such as Satan and his instruments, the accusers of the brethren, report us to be. But if we have been faithful, we may expect his double justification. 1. By pardon he will justify us from our sins. 2. By plea and righteous sentence he will justify us against the false accusations of our enemies, and that is enough. How small a thing should it seem to us to be judged of men, when we must stand or fall under the final sentence of the Almighty God.

10. The separated soul and body retain their relationship, and the

soul retains its desire to be reunited with its body. And though our present relationship is now dissolved, and our communion with each other is hindered, yet I know we will never forget each other, nor will the bond of love which unites us ever be loosened and made void. Much of our relationship will still continue, as intimated in those texts, 1 Cor. 4:15-16, 12:14; Phil. 4:1, etc.

11. The power of death will not be everlasting. There will, at last, be a resurrection and reunion, but whether in this world, I cannot prophesy. I am inclined to think that most of us must die in the wilderness, and that our night must bear some proportion with our day. But the things not revealed belong only to God. It is sufficient for me to be sure of this, that as our kingdom is not of this world, so our comforts are not of this world. As Christ said, so his servants under him may say, 'Behold I and the children which God hath given me (Heb. 2:13), and that we shall present you as chaste virgins to Christ' (2 Cor. 11:2). 'And therefore we have preached, taught, and warned, that we might present you perfect in Christ Jesus' (Col. 1:28). 'For what is our hope, or joy, or crown of rejoicing, are not even ye in the presence of our Lord Jesus Christ at his coming? For ye are our glory and our joy' (1 Thes. 2:19, 20).

The resemblance between death and our separation, however, does not hold in all things.

1. It is not I, or any pastor, that is the church's soul or life. This is the honour of Christ, the Head. Being planted into him, you may live even if all his ministers were dead or all your teachers driven into a corner (Is. 30:20).

2. The continuation of your church does not depend on the continuation of any one single pastor. God can provide you with others to succeed us, who may do his work for you more successfully than we did. And if I could but hope that they should be as able, and holy, and diligent as I desire, then how little I would share with you in today's sorrows. If I had not given you these exceptions, malicious tongues would have reported that I made myself your life or soul, and take the churches to be all dead when such as I are silenced and cast out. But I remember Psalm 12.

Though what I have said, and what you feel, may make you think that a funeral sermon is most appropriate on such a day, I have chosen instead to preach to you the doctrine of rejoicing, because your sorrow is not as men who have no hope, and because I must consider what will tend most to your strength and steadfastness. That you may see that in this I imitate our Lord, I have chosen his words to his troubled disciples, before his departure from them (John 16:22.)

I do not doubt it will be said with scorn that I make myself as Christ, and that I seditiously encourage you by the expectations of my restitution. But I will not refrain from using my Saviour's consolatory words, but will remember to whom and on what occasion he said, 'Every plant which my heavenly Father hath not planted, shall be rooted up. Let them alone, they be blind leaders of the blind; and if the blind lead the blind, both shall fall into the ditch' (Matt. 15:13, 14).

These words are Christ's comfort to his orphaned, sorrowful disciples, expressing first, their present condition, and that which they were now to taste of, and secondly, their future state. Their present case is a state of sorrow, because Christ must be taken from them. Their future case will be a state of joy, which is expressed, 1. In the future aspect of the cause: 'but I will see you again,' 2. In the promise of the effect, 'and your heart shall rejoice.' 3. In the duration and invincibility of it, 'and your joy no man taketh from you,' or 'shall take from you.'

He had before likened their sorrows on this occasion to the pains of a woman in child-birth, which is but short and ends in joy. And in relation to that simile, the Syriac translates *lupē* 'sickness,' and the Persian translates it 'calamity.' Some expositors limit the cause of their sorrows to the absence of Christ, or that death of his which will for a time both shake their faith and astonish their hopes, and deprive them of their former comforts. And others limit the word 'therefore' to the following crosses or sufferings which they must undergo for the sake of Christ, and accordingly they interpret the cause of their succeeding joy. But I see no reason why both are not included in the text, but principally the first, and the other consequently. It is as if he had said, 'When you see me crucified, your hearts and hopes will begin to fail, and sorrow will overwhelm your minds, and you will be exposed to the fury of the unbelieving world; but it will be but for a moment, for when you see that I am risen again, your joy will be revived, and my Spirit afterwards, and continual encouragements shall greatly increase and perpetuate your joys, which no persecutions or sufferings will deprive you of, but they shall at last be perfected in the heavenly everlasting joys.'

The cause of their sorrow is first his absence, and next their sufferings with him in the world. When the bridegroom is taken from them they must fast, that is, live an afflicted kind of life in various sorrows. The causes of their succeeding joy, are first, his resurrection, and next his Spirit, which is their comforter, and lastly, the presence of his glory when they are received into his glorious kingdom. Their sorrow was to be short, as that of a woman in travail, and it was to have a tendency to their joy. And their joy was to be sure and near, 'I will see you again,' and great, 'your heart shall rejoice,' and everlasting, 'your joy no man taketh from you.'

The sense of the text is contained in these six doctrinal propositions:

Doctrine 1. Sorrow goes before joy for Christ's disciples.

Doctrine 2. Christ's death and departure was the cause of his disciples' sorrows.

Doctrine 3. The sorrows of Christ's disciples are only short. They are but 'now.'

Doctrine 4. Christ will again visit his sorrowful disciples, though at the present he seems to be taken from them.

Doctrine 5. When Christ returns or appears to his disciples, 'their sorrows will be turned into joy.'

Doctrine 6. The joy of Christians in the return or re-appearing of their Lord is such that no Man can take it from them.

With God's assistance, I will speak of these doctrines in order, and therefore only be short on each.

Doctrine 1

Sorrow goes before joy for Christ's disciples. The evening and the morning make their day. They must sow in tears before they reap in joy. They must have trouble in the world, and peace in Christ. God will first dwell in the contrite heart, to prepare it to dwell with him in glory. The pains of labour must go before the joy of birth.

Question: What kind of sorrow is it that goes before our joy ?

Answer 1. There is a sorrow that is positively sinful. It should not go before our joy, though in fact it does. Although this is not the direct meaning of the text, it all too commonly precedes our comforts. It is not the joys of innocence that are our portion, but the joys of restoration. The pains of our disease go before the ease and comfort of our recovery. We have our worldly sorrows, and our passionate and peevish sorrows, like Jonah's sorrow about the gourd when it withered. According to the extent of our remaining corruption, we have our sorrows.

Sometimes we are troubled at the providences of God, and sometimes at the dealings of men; at the words or actions of enemies, of friends, of all about us. We are grieved if we do not have what we want, when we want it. Nothing really pleases us until we are so devoted to pleasing God that we are pleased in the pleasing of him.

2. We have our sorrows in which, because of our sinful weakness and imperfection, and the languishing feebleness of our souls, we are overly troubled by what we may legitimately sorrow for with moderation. Impatience causes us to make a greater issue of our afflictions than we ought. If God tests us with wants or crosses; if we lose our friends, or if they prove unkind, we double the weight of the cross by our impatience.

This comes from the remnants of unmortified selfishness, carnality, and the excessive love of earthly things. If we loved them less, we would sorrow for them less. If we had seen their vanity, and mortification had made them nothing to us, we should then part with them as with vanity and nothing. It is seldom that God or men afflict us, but we therefore afflict ourselves much more. As the destruction of the wicked is of their own making, so largely are the troubles of the godly.

3. There is a mere natural suffering or sorrow, which is neither morally good or bad. Like when we are weary with our labour, or pained with our diseases; or when we feel hunger and thirst, cold and heat; when we are averse to death as death, as Christ himself was, and we at last must undergo it and lie down in the dust. There are many sorrows which are the fruits of sin, which yet, in themselves, are neither sin nor duty.

4. There are castigatory sorrows from the hand of God, which are intended to cure us if we use them according to his appointment. Such are all the natural sufferings just mentioned, when considered as God's means and instruments for our benefit. He wounds the body to heal the soul, he lances the sore to let out the corruption, he lets blood to cure our inflammations and apostemated parts. He chastens all that he loves and receives (Heb. 12:1-14) and we must be subject to a chastening Father if we will live, for he does it for our profit, 'that we may be partakers of his holiness.'

5. There are honourable and profitable sufferings that come from blind, malicious, wicked men. They are for the cause of Christ and righteousness, as the gospel frequently warns believers to expect. These

sorrows have the promises of fullest joy. Not that the mere suffering in itself is acceptable to God, but what is accepted by him is the love for him which is manifested by these sufferings. The sufferings are more or less acceptable to the degree in which they express more or less love to God, and the honour of Christ is more or less intended in them. For to give the body to be burned without love will profit us nothing. But when the cause is Christ's, and the heart intends him as the end of the suffering (1 Cor. 13:3) then 'blessed are they which are persecuted for righteousness' sake, for theirs is the kingdom of heaven,' etc. (Matt. 5:10-12).

6. There are penitential and medicinal sufferings, for the killing of sin and assisting the work of grace. These sufferings are our duty. In the former sorrows mentioned we are to be but submissive patients, but in these we must be obedient agents, and must inflict them on ourselves. Such are the sorrows of contrition and true repentance; the exercises of fasting, abstinence, and humiliation; the grief of the soul for God's displeasure, for the hiding of his face, and the abatement of his graces in us; all the works of mortifying self-denial, and forbearing all forbidden pleasures which God calls his servants to. Though in the primitive and principal part of holiness there is nothing but what is sweet and pleasant to a soul, in so far as it is holy (such as the love of God and the love of others, and worshipping God, and doing good, and joy, and thanks, and praise, and obedience, etc.); yet the medicinal parts of grace or holiness have something in them that is necessarily bitter, such as are contrition, self-denial, mortification, and abstinence, as just stated.

7. There are charitable sorrows in which we sorrow for the dishonour of God, and for the sin, hurt, and miseries of others. These also are our duties, and we must be agents in them as well as patients. As we must first pray for the hallowing of the name of God, and the coming of his kingdom, and the doing of His will on earth as it is done in heaven, so we must grieve most for the abuse and dishonour of God's name, the hindering of His kingdom, and the breaking of his laws.

We grieve that so many nations do not see their peril, and do not know God, and do not have the gospel, or will not receive it, but live in rebellion against their Maker, and in blindness, obstinacy and hardness of heart, and are given to committing uncleanness with greediness (Eph. 4:18, 19). We grieve that so many nations which are called

Christians are captivated in ignorance and superstition, by the blindness, pride, carnality, and covetousness of their usurping, self-obtruding guides; that so many men professing Christianity have so little of the knowledge or power of what they generally and ignorantly profess, and live to the shame of their profession, the great dishonour and displeasure of their Lord, and the grief or hardening of others. We grieve that the church of Christ is broken into so many sects and factions, possessed with such an uncharitable, destroying zeal against each other, and persecuting their brethren as cruelly as Turks and heathens do. We grieve that the best of Christians are so few, and yet so weak and liable to miscarriages. All these are the matter of that sorrow which God has made our duty; and all these sorts of sorrow go before a Christian's fullest joy.

Reason 1. God will have some conformity between the order of nature and of grace. Non-entity was before created entity, the evening before morning, infancy before maturity of age, weakness before strength, the buried seed before the plant, the flower and the fruit, and infants cry before they laugh. No wonder, then, if our sorrows go before our joys.

2. Sin goes before grace, and therefore our sorrows are before our joys. The seed that is sown first bears fruit first. Joy, indeed, has the older parent, *in esse reali et absoluto* [essentially real and absolute], but not *in esse causali et relativo* [essentially causal and relative]. We are the children of the first Adam, before we are children of the second; we are born flesh of flesh, before we are born spiritual of the Spirit. (1 Cor. 15; John 3:6.) And where Satan goes before Christ, it is equal that sorrow go before joy.

3. Our gracious Father and wise Physician sees this to be the best method for our cure. If we are to deny ourselves, we must know how little we are beholden to ourselves, and must smart by the fruit of our sin and folly before we are eased by the fruit of love and grace. It is the property of the flesh to judge by sense, and therefore sense shall help to mortify it. The frowns of the world will be an antidote against its flatteries. The world kills by its pleasures, and therefore it may help our cure to have its displeasure. Loving the world is men's undoing; and its hurting us is the way to keep us from loving it too much.

These wholesome sorrows greatly disable our most dangerous temptations, and preserve us from the pernicious poison of prosperity. They rouse us up when we are lazy and ready to sit down; they wake us up when we are ready to fall asleep; they drive us to God when we are ready to forget him, and dote upon a deceiver; they teach us part of the meaning of the gospel. Without them we do not know well what 'a Saviour,' a 'promise,' a 'pardon,' 'grace,' and many other gospel terms, mean. They teach us to pray, and teach us to hear and read with understanding. They tell us the value of all our mercies, and teach us the use of all the means of grace. They are needful to fix our flashy, light, inconstant minds, which are apt to be gaze on every bait, and touch or taste the forbidden fruit, and to be taken with those things which we had cast behind our backs, till medicinal sorrow awakens our reason, and make us see the folly of our dreams. Yes, if sorrow does not check us, and make us wise, we are ready to lay aside our grace and wit, and follow any goblin in the dark, and, like men bewitched, to be deceived by we know not what, and to go on as a bird to the fowler's snare, as an ox to the slaughter, and as a fool to the correction of the stocks (Prov. 7:22, 23).

4. Moreover, precedent sorrows will raise the price of following joys. They will make us more desirous of the day of our deliverance, and will make it more welcome when it comes. Heaven will be seasonable after a life of so much trouble, and those who come out of great tribulation will joyfully sing the praises of their Redeemer (Rev. 7:14).

5. God wants the members of the body conformed to their Head (Luke 14:28, 33). This was Christ's method, and it must be ours (Rom. 8:17, 18). We must take up the cross, and follow him, if ever we will have the crown. We must suffer with him if we will be glorified with him (2 Tim. 2:12).

Though the will of God alone should satisfy his creatures, yet these reasons show you the equity and goodness of his ways.

Use 1: If sorrow before joy is God's ordinary method of dealing with his most beloved servants, learn to understand, then, the importance of your sorrows! You say as Baruch did, 'Woe is me now; for the Lord has added grief to my sorrow. I fainted in my sighing, and I find no rest' (Jer. 45:3). You are ingenious in recounting and aggravating your afflictions. But are you as ingenious in expounding them correctly? Do you not judge them more by your present senses, than by their use and intent? You do not judge the bitterness of a medicine, or the working of a purge or vomit that way. You like it best when it works in that way which most usually produces a cure. Should you not therefore be glad to find that God works with you in the way that he most usually takes with those that he saves. Surely you do not set light by the love of God. Why, then, do you complain so much against the signs and products of it? Is it not because you have yet much unbelief, and judge of God's love as the flesh directs you, instead of judging by the effects and prognosis which he himself has asked you to judge by?

We acknowledge that to the flesh no discipline seems joyful at the time, but grievous. Yet, if you believe the Spirit, afterward it yields the peaceable fruit of righteousness. Those 'whom the Lord loves, he chastens, and scourges every son whom he receives' (Heb. 12: 6, 11). Do not misunderstand, then, the prognosis of your present sorrows. Think how they will work as well as how they taste. They bode good, though they are unpleasant. If you were bastards and reprobates you might feel less of the rod. When the ploughers make furrows on you, it prepares you for the seed; and the showers that water it precede a plenteous harvest. Think it not strange, then, if the Master thresh and grind you so that you may be bread for his use. He is not drowning his sheep when he washes them, nor killing them when he is shearing them. But by this he shows that they are his own. The newly shorn sheep most visibly bear his name or mark, while on those with longer fleece it is almost worn out and scarcely discernible.

If you love the world and prosperity best, then rejoice most in it, and grieve most for the want of it. But if you love God best, and take him for your part and treasure, then rejoice in him, and in that condition which has the fullest indications of his love, and grieve most for his displeasure, and for that condition which either signifies it, or most entices you to displease him (2 Cor. 4:18; Matt. 6:20, 21). If present things are your portion, then seek them first and rejoice in them, and mourn when they are taken from you (Col. 3:1-4). But if really your portion is above with Christ, let your hearts be there; and let your joys and sorrows and endeavours show that. The sense of brutes judges pain and pleasure only by their present feeling; but the reason of a man and the faith of a Christian evaluates them according to their signification and importance.

I know that it is in vain to think that by reason our flesh and senses may be reconciled to their sufferings. But if I may speak to you as to men, indeed, to Christians, and reason with you, I will not at all despair of success:

Question 1. Tell me, then, who is it that you suffer by? Who principally has the hand in disposing of all this? Is it one that you can reasonably suspect of any lack of power, wisdom, or goodness? Is he not much better equipped to deal with you than you are, or any other mortals? If the physician is better than the patient in determining how you are to be treated, and if you are better than your infant child, and if you are better qualified than your beast to determine his pasture, work, and usage, surely then you will grant that God is much better equipped than we are. And if he would give you the choice and say, 'It will be for you all your days, prosperity or adversity, life or death, as you choose for yourself, or as your dearest friend will choose,' then you would say, 'No, Lord. Let it be as you will. For I and my friend are foolish and have limited understanding, and we do not know what is best for ourselves. Not our wills, but thy will be done.'

Question 2. Do you not see that carnal pleasure is far more dangerous than all your sorrows? Look at the ungodly who prosper in the world, and tell me whether you would choose to be in their condition? If not, why do you long for their temptations? If you would not choose, along with the rich man (Luke 16) to be damned for sensuality, or with the fool (Luke 12:19,20) say, 'Soul, take your ease,' etc. when your souls are about to be taken from you, or with the rich man (Luke 18:22, 23) go away from Christ sorrowful, then do not desire the temptations which brought them to it! If you would not oppress the people of God with Pharaoh, nor persecute the prophets with Ahab and Jezebel, nor resist the gospel and persecute the preachers of it with the Scribes and Pharisees, do not desire the temptations which led them to all this.

Question 3. Would you not rather follow your Saviour and be conformed to him and to his saints, than to the wicked that have their portion in this life ? And do you not want to go to heaven in the way that the saints of old have gone before you? Read the Scripture and all church history, and observe which is the beaten path of life. Observe even among believers and the pastors of the church, whether it was the persecuted or the prosperous that most honoured their profession, and which of them it was that corrupted the church with pride and domination, and kindled in it those flames of contention which are consuming it to this day; and sowed those seeds of divisions whose sour fruit have set their children's teeth on edge. Mark whether it was the suffering or the prospering part that has had the greatest hand all her sufferings.

Question 4. What does your own experience say, and how has God dealt with you in time past? Has not your suffering done you good? If it has not, you may thank yourselves: for I am sure God's rod has a healing virtue, and others have received a cure from it. How much mankind owes to the cross! When David was weeping on mount Olivet, he was in a safer case than when he was gazing on Bathsheba from his battlements. And when Christ was sweating blood on mount Olivet (Luke 22:44) it was a sign that man's redemption was at hand. And when he was bleeding on the cross and drinking vinegar and gall, it was almost finished.

If the cross has borne such happy fruit, what reason have we to be so much against it? If it has proved good for you that you were afflicted, and no part of your lives have been more fruitful, why should your desires so much contradict your own experience? If bitter things have proved the most wholesome, and a full and luscious diet has caused your disease, what else do you need to direct your judgement in these things, if you will judge as men, and not as brutes?

Objection. But, you will say, it is not all sorrow that precedes joy. Some pass from sorrow to greater sorrow. How then will we know whether our sorrows will lead to worse or to better?

Answer. It is true that there are sorrows which have no such promise as those in the text. As, for example, 1. The mere vindictive punishment of the wicked. 2. The sinful sorrows which men keep up in themselves, proceeding from their sinful love of creatures. 3. And the corrections which are not improved by us for our amendment and reformation.

But the promise belongs, 1. To those sorrows which we undergo sincerely for the sake of Christ and righteousness. 2. To those sorrows which we ourselves perform as duties, either for the dishonour of God, or the sins or miseries of others; or our penitential sorrows for our own offences. 3. And to those sorrows of chastisement which we patiently submit to, and use for true change in our hearts and lives. For though sin be the material cause, or the meritorious cause, yet love which makes reformation the effect, will also make the end to be our comfort.

Use 2. If this is God's method, do not condemn the generation of the righteous simply because you see them undermost in the world and suffering more than other men. Do not consider it a dishonour to them to be in poverty, prisons, banishment, or reproach, unless it be for a truly dishonourable cause. Do not call men miserable for that which God makes the token of his love, and the basis of their joy. I think that he who has once read Psalms 37 and 73, and Matt. 5:10-12, and Job 13 and 15, and 2 Thes. 1, and really believes them, should never stray into this old condemned error again.

And yet it is common among carnal men to do as some beasts do: when one of their fellows is wounded they all forsake him. So they stand looking with pity, or fear, or strangeness upon a man that is undergoing sufferings and slander, as if it must be deserved. They think it a great dishonour to a man, no matter how innocent he may be, when they hear that he is treated as offenders and malefactors are. They forget that by this they condemn their Saviour, and all his apostles and martyrs, and the wisest, best, and happiest men that the earth has borne. All this is but the blind and hasty judgement of sense and unbelief, which has neither the wisdom to judge by the word of God, nor the patience to wait to the end and see how the sorrows of the godly will conclude and where the triumph of the hypocrite will leave them.

And yet there are some who are apt to err in the other extreme, and to think that every man is happy if he is afflicted, and that the suffering party is always in the right. Therefore they are ready to take part in any deluded sect which they see to be under reproach and suffering. But the cause must be first known before the suffering can be properly judged.

Doctrine 2

Christ's death and departure was the cause of his disciples' sorrows. This is plain in the words – 'Ye now therefore have sorrow; but I will see you again.' The causes of this sorrow were these three together:

1. Their dear Lord, whom they loved, and whom they had heard, followed, and put their trust in, must now be taken from them. If the parting of friends at death causes us to wear clothes that signify our sad and mournful hearts, and causes us to dwell in the houses of mourning, we must allow Christ's disciples some such affections on their parting with the Lord.

2. The manner of his death no doubt much increased their sorrows. That the most innocent one should suffer as a reputed malefactor – he that more despised the wealth, pleasures and glory of the world than ever man did, and chose a poor, inferior life, and would not have a kingdom of this world, and never failed in any duty to high or low –

that he should yet be hanged ignominiously on a cross, as one that was about to usurp the crown! That deluded sinners should put to death the Lord of life, and spit in the face of such a majesty, and hasten destruction to their nation and themselves; and that all Christ's disciples should be regarded the followers of a crucified usurper. Judge for yourself whether this would have been a matter of sorrow to us, as it was to them.

Was it not enough for Christ to have suffered the pain? But he suffered also the dishonour of the imputation of sin – which no man was further from being guilty of than him – and of that particular sin, the usurpation of dominion, and treason against Caesar, which his heart and life were as contrary to, as light to darkness. And was it not enough for Christians to suffer such great calamities of body for righteousness' sake, but they must also suffer the reproach of being the seditious followers of a crucified malefactor whom they would have made a king? No! Our Lord would stoop to the lowest condition for our sakes, which was consistent with his innocence and perfection! Sin is so much worse than suffering, that we may take this for the greatest part of His condescension; and the strangest expression of his love that he should take not only the nature and the sufferings of a man, but also the nature and the imputation of sinners. Though sin itself was inconsistent with his perfection, yet the false accusation and imputation of it was not. He could not become a sinner for us, but he could be reputed a sinner for us, and die as such. And when our Lord has submitted to this most ignominious kind of suffering, it is not fitting that we should choose our sufferings, and say, Lord, we will suffer anything except the reputation of being offenders, and the false accusations of malicious men. If in this we are to conform to our Head, we must not refuse it, nor repine at his disposal of us.

3. Their sorrow for Christ's departure was greater because they had so little foresight of his resurrection and return. It is strange to see how dark they were in these articles of the faith, despite their long conversations with Christ, and his plainly telling them of his death and resurrection; and also how much of their instruction Christ reserved for the Spirit after his departure from them. 'Then took he unto him the twelve, and said unto them, Behold we go up to Jerusalem, and all things that are written by the prophets concerning the Son of man shall be accomplished: for he shall be delivered unto the Gentiles, and shall be mocked and spitefully entreated, and spit upon, and they shall

scourge him and put him to death, and the third day he shall rise again.'
(John 12:16; Luke 18:31-34). And they understood none of these things,
and this saying was hid from them, and they did not understand the
things which were spoken. Had they known all that would follow, and
clearly foreseen his resurrection and his glory, they would then have
been troubled less about his death. But when they saw him die, and
did not foresee that he would revive and rise, and reign, then their
hearts began to fail them, and they said, 'We trusted that it had been
he which should have redeemed Israel.' (Luke 24:21).

Just as we lament excessively when we lay the bodies of our friends
in the grave, because we do not see where the soul is gone, or in what
triumph and joy it is received by Christ (which if we saw, our griefs
would be more moderate), so we over pity ourselves and our friends
in our temporal sufferings because we do not see where they are
going or what will follow them. We see Job on the dunghill but do not
see his restoration. 'Behold we count them happy which endure: ye
have heard of the patience of Job, and have seen the end of the Lord,
that the Lord is very pitiful and of tender mercy' (Jam. 5:11). There is
no judging by the present, but either by staying to the end or believing
God's predictions of it.

Use. It is allowable for Christ's disciples to grieve (in faith and
moderately) for any departure of his from them. They that have had
the comfort of communion with him in a life of faith and grace, must
lament any loss of that communion. It is sad with such a soul when
Christ seems a stranger, or when they pray and seek and seem not to
be heard! It is sad when a believer must say, 'I once had access to the
Father by the Son; I had helps in prayer, and I had the lively operations
of the Spirit of grace, and some of the joy of the Holy Ghost, but now,
alas, it is not so.' And they that have had experience of the fruit and
comfort of his word, and ordinances, and discipline, and the communion
of saints, may lament the loss of this if he take it from them.

It was no unseemly thing in David when he was driven from the
tabernacle of God, to make that lamentation, 'As the hart panteth
after the water-brooks, so panteth my soul after thee, O God; my soul
thirsteth for God, for the living God; when shall I come and appear
before God? My tears have been my meat day and night, while they
continually say unto me, Where is thy God? O my God, my soul is cast
down within me,' etc. (Pss. 42 and 43). And, 'My soul longeth, yea,
even fainteth for the courts of the Lord; my heart and my flesh crieth

out for the living God; yea, the sparrow hath found a house, and the swallow a nest,' etc. 'Blessed are they that dwell in thy house; they will be still praising thee. For a day in thy courts is better than a thousand; I had rather be a door-keeper in the house of my God, than to dwell in the tents of wickedness' (Psalm 84:2-4).

It speaks ill when men can easily let Christ go, or lose his word, or helps, and ordinances. When sin provokes him to hide his face, and withdraw his mercies, and we senselessly let them go, it is a contempt which provokes him much more. If we are indifferent to what he gives us, it is just if he is indifferent too, and set as little by our helps and happiness as we set by them ourselves. But we little know the misery which such contempt prepares us for: 'Be thou instructed, O Jerusalem, lest my soul depart from thee, lest I make thee desolate; a land not inhabited' (Jer. 6:8). 'Yea, woe also unto them when I depart from them' (Hos. 9:12). When God goes, all goes. Grace and peace, help and hope, and all that is good and comfortable is gone, when God is gone. Do not be surprised, therefore, if holy souls cry after God, and fear the loss of his grace and ordinances.

Doctrine 3

The sorrows of Christ's disciples are but short. It is only for now that they have sorrow, and how quickly this will be gone!

Reason 1. Life itself is but short, and, therefore, the sorrows of this life are but short. Man that is born of a woman is of few days, and full of trouble. He comes forth like a flower, and is cut down; he flees also as a shadow, and does not continue (Job 14: 1, 2). Though our days are evil, they are but few (Gen. 47:9). As our time makes haste so also do our sorrows. As the pleasure of sin is but for a season, so are the sufferings of the godly (Heb. 11:26). 'Now, for a season, if need be, ye are in heaviness through manifold temptations' (1 Pet. 1:6).

The pleasures and the pains of so short a life are but like a pleasant or a frightful dream. How quickly we will wake and all is vanished. If we lived as long as they did before the flood, then worldly interest, prosperity and adversity would be of greater significance to us. And yet they should seem as nothing in comparison with eternity. For where now are all the fleshly pains or pleasures of Adam or Methuselah? Much more are they inconsiderable in a life as short as ours. Happy is the man whose sorrows are of no longer continuance than this short and transitory life!

Reason 2. God's displeasure with his servants is but short, and, therefore, his corrections are but short. 'His anger endureth but for a moment, but in his favour is life' (Psalm 30:5). 'For a small moment have I forsaken thee, but with great mercy will I gather thee. In a little wrath I hid my face from time for a moment, but with everlasting kindness will I have mercy on thee, saith the Lord thy Redeemer' (Is. 54:7, 8). 'Come my people, enter into thy chambers, and shut thy doors about thee, hide thyself as it were for a little moment, until the indignation be overpast' (Is. 26:20). Thus even in judgement he remembers mercy, and does not consume us because his compassions never fail (Lam. 3). 'He will not always chide, nor will he keep his anger for ever; for he knoweth our frame, he remembereth that we are dust' (Psalm 103:9, 14). His short corrections are purposely fitted to prepare us for endless consolations.

Reason 3. Our trial must be short, and, therefore, so must our sorrows be. Though God will not have us receive the crown without the preparation of a conflict and a conquest, yet he will not have us fight and race too long, lest it be too much for our strength, and his grace, and we should be overcome. Though we and our faith must be tried in the fire, yet God will see that the furnace is not too hot, and that we do not stay in it longer than necessary for our dross to be separated from us (1 Pet. 1:7,9). God does not put us into the fire to consume us, but to refine us (Ps. 119: 67, 75), that when we come out (Ps. 129:1-3) we may say, 'It is good for us that we were afflicted,' (Ps. 119:71, Is 49:13). Then he will save the afflicted people (Ps. 18:27).

Reason 4. The power of those that wrongfully afflict God's servants is but short, and therefore, the sorrows of those who are afflicted by them can be but short. Though it is foreign churches of whom I speak, I hope it is to those who take their case to be their own. While they are breathing out threats they are ready to breathe out their guilty souls. If a man in a dropsy or consumption persecutes us, we would not be overly fearful of him, because we see he is a dying man. And so little is the distance between the death of one man and another, that we may well say, 'All men's lives are in a consumption' and we may bear their indignation as we would do the injuries of a dying man.

How short is the day of the power of darkness. Christ calls it but an hour: 'This is your hour, and the power of darkness' (Luke 22:53). How quickly was Herod eaten of worms, and many others cut off in the height of their prosperity, when they have been raging in the heat of persecution. Ahab little thought that he had been so near his woeful day, when he had given the order that Micaiah should be fed with the bread and water of affliction, till he returned in peace. What persecutions have the death of a Licinius, a Julian, a Queen Mary, etc. shortened? While they are raging, they are dying. While they are condemning the just, they are going to be condemned by their most just avenger. How quickly will their corpse be laid in dust, and their condemned souls be put under the chains of darkness, till the judgement of the great and dreadful day? (2 Pet. 2:4). He that cannot see their end (Jude 6) in the greatest of their glory is not only an unbeliever, but irrational or inconsiderate.

How easy is it to see these bubbles vanishing, and to foresee the sad and speedy period of all their cruelties and triumphs! 'Knowest thou not this of old, since man was placed upon earth, that the triumphing of the wicked is short, and the joy of the hypocrite but for a moment? Though his excellency mount up to the heavens, and his head reach unto the clouds, yet he shall perish for ever like his own dung. They which have seen him, shall say, Where is he? He shall fly away as a dream, and shall not be found; yea, he shall be chased away as a vision of the night. The eye also which saw him, shall see him no more, neither shall his place behold him' (Job 20:4-9). Though pride surrounds them like a chain, and violence covers them like a garment, and they are corrupt, and speak oppression, or calumny, wickedly, they speak loftily, or from on high; though they set their mouth against the heavens, and their tongue walks through the earth, yet surely they are set in slippery places. God casts them down into destruction. How they are brought into desolation in a moment. They are utterly consumed with terrors. As a dream that one wakes from, so, O Lord, in awaking, thou shalt despise their image, that is, show them and all the world how despicable that image of greatness and power, and felicity was, of which they were so proud.

If such a bubble of vain-glory, such an image of felicity, such a dream of power and greatness be all that the church of God has to be afraid of, it may well be said, 'Cease ye from man, whose breath is in his nostrils' (Is. 2:2). 'For wherein is he to be accounted of' (Psalm 146:4). His breath goes forth, he returns to his earth, in that very day his thoughts perish. And, 'Behold the Lord God will help me, who is he that shall condemn me? Lo, they all shall wax old as a garment, the moth shall eat them up' (Is. 1:9). And, 'Hearken unto me, ye that know righteousness, the people in whose heart is my law. Fear ye not the reproach of men, neither be ye afraid of their revilings, for the moth shall eat them up like a garment, and the worm shall eat them like wood, but my righteousness shall be for ever, and my salvation from generation to generation' (Is. 51:7, 8).

The sorrows which such short-lived power can inflict, can be but short. You read of their victories and persecutions in the news-books one year, and quickly after of their death.

Use. You may therefore learn how injudicious people are when they think that religion is disparaged by such short and small afflictions of believers. You see how inexcusable it is when they yield to temptation, and venture upon sin, and comply with the ungodly, and forsake the truth, for fear of such short and momentary sorrows, when they would readily endure the prick of a pin, or the scratch of a briar, or the biting of a flea to gain a kingdom, or the opening of a vein, or the griping of a purge to save their lives. Oh! how deservedly ungodly men are forsaken by God when for such short pleasure they forsake him, and the everlasting pleasures. And what short trouble they avoid by running into everlasting trouble.

If sin had not first subdued reason, men would never question whether, in order to escape such small suffering, they should break the laws of the most righteous God. Nor would they put such short pain or pleasure into the balance against endless pain and pleasure. And yet, alas! how much these short concerns prevail throughout the world! Unbelievers are short-sighted. They look only or chiefly to things near and present. They prefer a lease on this empty world for a few years, yes, an uncertain tenure of it, instead of the best security for eternal life. Its present pleasures they must have, and its present sorrows they take care to escape. As Christ has taught us to say about these worldly things, so the devil has taught them to say about everlasting things, 'Care not for tomorrow, for the morrow shall take thought for the things of itself; sufficient to the day is the evil thereof' (Matt. 6:34). Therefore when the day of their calamity comes, a despairing conscience will perpetually torment them, and say, 'This is but the sorrow which you chose to endure, or the misery which you ventured on, in order to escape a present, inconsiderable pain.'

If there are any of you that think present sufferings are considerable things, to be put into the scales against eternity, or that are tempted to murmuring and impatience under such short afflictions, I desire you to consider:

1. Your suffering will be no longer than your sin. And if it endures as long, is that surprising? Can you expect to keep your sickness, and yet to be wholly freed from the pain? Can sin and suffering be perfectly separated? Do you think you can continue ignorant and proud, and selfish, and in so much remaining unbelief, carnality, worldliness, and sloth, and yet never feel the rod or spur, nor suffer any more than if you had been innocent? Don't deceive yourselves! Sin lies at the door (Gen. 4:7), and be sure at last it will find you out (Num. 32:23). 'Behold the righteous shall be recompensed in the earth, much more the ungodly and the sinner' (Prov. 11:31). 'Judgement must begin at the house of God, and the righteous are saved with much ado' (1 Pet. 4:17, 18). God is not reconciled to the sins of any man. As he shows by his dealings that he is reconciled to their persons, so he shows that he is not reconciled to their sins. If God continues your sufferings longer than you continue to sin, and if you can truly say, 'I am afflicted though I am innocent,' then your impatience may have some excuse.

2. Your sorrows will not be longer than you make them necessary, and will you therefore begrudge your own benefit? It is but 'if need be that now for a season you are in heaviness through manifold temptations' (1 Peter 1:6). And who makes the need? Is it God or you? Who makes you dull, and slothful, and sensual? Who turns your hearts to earthly things, and deprives you of the sweetness of things spiritual and heavenly? Who makes you proud, and unbelieving, and uncharitable? Is it he that does this, and that causes the need of your afflictions, and is to be blamed for the bitterness of them? Your physician is to be thanked and praised for fitting them so precisely to your cure.

3. Your sorrows will not be as long as you deserve. It is strange ingratitude for a man to begrudge a short affliction that saves him from everlasting misery, and confesses he deserves the pains of hell. Confess with thankfulness that it is his mercy that you are not consumed and condemned, because his compassions fail not. If God be your portion, hope in him; for the Lord is good to them that wait for him, to the soul that seeks him. It is good that you both hope and quietly wait for the salvation of the Lord; it is good for a man that he bear the yoke in his youth; he sits alone and keeps silence, because he has borne it upon him; he puts his mouth in the dust, if only there may be hope. He gives his cheek to him that smites him, he is filled full with reproach; for the Lord will not cast off forever, but though he cause grief, yet

will he have compassion, according to the multitude of his mercies. (Lam. 3:22-33). All that has come upon us is for our evil deeds and our great trespasses, and God has punished us less than our iniquities (Ezr. 9:13).

4. Your sorrows will not be as long as the sorrows of the ungodly, nor as long as those that you must endure if you choose sin to escape these present sorrows. Abel's sorrow is not as long as Cain's; nor Peter's or Paul's as long as Judas's. If the offering of a more acceptable sacrifice costs a righteous man his life, alas, what is that compared to the punishment that malignant, envious Cainites, or treacherous Judases must endure. What is the worst that man can do, or the most that God will here inflict, to the reprobates' endless, hellish torments? Oh, had you seen what they endure, or had you felt those pains but a day or hour, I hardly think that you would ever again make such an issue of the sufferings of a Christian here for Christ, or that you would fear such sufferings more than hell. It is disingenuous to repine at so gentle a rod, at the same time as millions are in the flames of hell, when these sufferings keep you from there.

5. Your sorrows will not be as long as your following joys, if you are persevering, conquering believers. What is a sickness, or a scorn, or a prison, or banishment, or shame, or death, when it must end in the endless joys of heaven. Oh, believe these things with a lively, sound, effectual faith, and you will make light of all the suffering along the way. The mind that is in heaven, and sees him who is invisible, will easily bear the body's pains. You will reckon that the sufferings of this present time are not worthy to be compared with the glory which shall be revealed in us (Rom. 8:18). 'For our light affliction, which is but for a moment, doth work for us a far more exceeding and eternal weight of glory, while we look not at the things which are seen, but at the things that are not seen; for the things which are seen are temporal, but the things which are not seen are eternal' (2 Cor. 4:17, 18).

Use 2. If it be only for now that you must have sorrows, how reasonable is it that those sorrows are moderated and mixed with joy? How just are those commands, 'Rejoice ever-more.' 'Rejoice and be exceeding glad, for great is your reward in heaven' (1 Thes. 5:16; Matt. 5:10-12). 'Rejoicing in hope, patient in tribulation' (Rom. 12:12). How rational was the joy of those who, being beaten and forbidden to preach, departed from the presence of the council, rejoicing that they were counted worthy to suffer shame for the name of Christ' (Acts

5:42). 'Rejoice inasmuch as ye are partakers in Christ's sufferings. If ye be reproached for the name of Christ, happy are ye; for the Spirit of glory and of God resteth upon you; on their part he is evil spoken of, but on your part he is glorified' (1 Pet. 4:13, 14). It is a shame to be dejected under a short and tolerable pain which is so near to the eternal pleasure, and to suffer as if we believed not the end, and so to sorrow as men that are without hope.

Doctrine 4
Christ will again visit his sorrowful disciples. He does not remove himself from them with the intent to cast them off. When he hides his face, he does not mean to forsake them; when he takes away any ordinances or mercies, he does not give them a bill of divorce. When he seems to yield to the powers of darkness, he is not overcome, nor will he give up his kingdom or interest in the world. When he lets the boar into his vineyard, it is not to make it utterly desolate, or turn it to barren wilderness: for,

1. He has conquered the greatest enemies already and therefore there remains none to conquer him. He has triumphed over Satan, death, and hell. He has conquered sin. What is left to depose him from his dominion?

2. He still retains his relationship to his servants; whether he be corporally present or absent, he knows his own, and it is their care also that whether present or absent, they may be accepted of him (2 Cor. 5:7-9). He is their head while they are suffering on earth, and therefore he feels their sufferings and infirmities (Heb. 4:15). That is why he rebukes a persecuting zealot, 'Saul, Saul, why persecutest thou me?' (Acts 9: 4).

3. He has not set aside the least measure of his love. He loves us in heaven as much as he did on earth. 'Having loved his own which were in the world, to the end he loved them' (John 13:1). And as Joseph's love could not long permit him to conceal himself from his brethren, but broke out more violently after being briefly restrained, so that he fell on their necks and wept; so the more tender love of Christ will not permit him to hide his face for long, or estrange himself from the people of his love. When he returns, it will be with redoubled expressions of endearment.

4. His covenant with his servants is still in force. His promises are sure, and will never be broken, though the performance is not as quick

as we desire. 'Know, therefore that the Lord thy God, he is God, the faithful God, which keepeth covenant and mercy with them that love him and keep his commandments, to a thousand generations; and repayeth them that hate him to their face to destroy them; he will not be slack to him that hateth him, he will repay him to his face.' (Deut.7:9). 'He keepeth covenant and mercy with his servants that walk before him with all their heart' (1 Kings 8:23; Dan. 9:4, Neh. 1:5, and 11:32). And it was the promise of Christ when he departed from his servants, that 'He will come again and take them to himself, that where he is, there they may be also' (John 14:3, and 12:26).

5. His own interest, honour, office and preparations, engage him to return to his disconsolate flock. His jewels and peculiar treasure are his interest (Mal. 3:17; 1 Pet. 2:9; Exod. 24:5). He that has chosen but a little flock (Luke 12:32) and confines his interest and treasure into such a narrow compass, will not forsake that little flock, but secure them to his kingdom. He that has made it his office to redeem and save them, and has so dearly bought them, and gone so far in the work of their salvation, will lose none of all his cost and preparations. For his people, and his blood, and his honour, and his Father's will, and love, he will certainly finish what he has undertaken. And, therefore, his withdrawals will not be everlasting.

6. It is for their sakes that he withdraws for a time. Though the bitter part be for their sin, it is intended as medicine for their benefit. Sometimes he does it to awaken and humble them, and stir them up to seek him, and call after him; to show them what they have done in provoking him to withdraw and hide his face, that renewed repentance may prepare them for the comforts of his return. Sometimes he has such work for them to do, which is not so agreeable to his presence; such as fasting, and mourning, and confessing him in sufferings (Matt. 9:15). And sometimes he has comforts of another kind to give them in his seeming absence. 'I tell you the truth, it is expedient for You that I go away; for if I go not away, the Comforter will not come unto you; but if I depart, I will send him to you' (John 16:7). As there were comforts which the disciples were fittest for in Christ's bodily absence, so when he takes away his ordinances, or our prosperity or friends, there are comforts of another sort, in secret communion with him, and in suffering for him, which his people may expect. Not that any can expect if on that pretence they reject these ordinances and mercies, any more than the disciples could have expected the Comforter if they

had rejected the corporal presence of Christ. But God has such supplies for those that mourn for his departure.

Use 1. Do not misunderstand the departures of your Lord. It is too bad to say with the evil servant, 'My Lord delays his coming,' and worse to say he will never return.

1. He will return at his appointed day to judge the world; to justify his saints, whom the world condemned; to answer the desires, and satisfy all the expectations of believers; and to comfort, and everlastingly reward the faithful that have patiently waited for his return. And when he returns with salvation, then we also will return from our calamities and discern between the righteous and the wicked, between those who served God, and those who did not (Mal. 3:18).

Undoubtedly our 'Redeemer liveth, and shall stand at the latter day upon the earth, and though, after our skin, worms devour these bodies, yet in our flesh we shall see God' (Job 19: 25, 26). 'Behold he cometh with clouds; and every eye shall see him, and they also which pierced him; and all kindreds of the earth shall wail because of him. Even so, Amen.' (Rev. 1:7). Though unbelieving scoffers will say, 'Where is the promise of his coming?' (2 Pet. 3: 4), yet believers consider, 'That a day is with the Lord as a thousand years, and a thousand years but as a day; and that the Lord is not slack of his promise but long-suffering' (verses. 8, 9). 'He will not leave us comfortless, but will come unto us' (John 14:18). 'The patient expectation of the just shall not be forgotten, nor in vain' (Ps. 9:7, 8). 'Seeing it is a righteous thing with God to recompense tribulation to them that trouble you; and to you who are troubled rest with us, when the Lord Jesus shall be revealed from heaven with his mighty angels, in flaming fire taking vengeance on them that know not God, and that obey not the gospel of our Lord Jesus Christ: who shall be punished with everlasting destruction, from the presence of the Lord, and from the glory of his power; when he shall come to be glorified in his saints, and admired in all them that believe in that day' (2 Thes. 1:6-10).

2. He will return also to the seemingly forsaken flocks of his disciples; he has his times of trial, when the shepherds being smitten, the sheep are scattered; and he has his times of gathering the scattered ones together again, and 'giving them pastors after his own heart, that shall feed them with knowledge and understanding' (Jer. 3:14, 15). 'Many pastors have destroyed my vineyard, they have trodden my portion under foot, they have made my pleasant portion a desolate

wilderness: and being desolate it mourneth to me; the whole land is made desolate, because no man layeth it to heart.' (Jer. 12:10, 11). 'But woe be unto the pastors that destroy and scatter the sheep of my pasture, saith the Lord. Therefore, thus saith the Lord, against the pastors that feed my people; ye have scattered my flock, and driven them away, and have not visited them; behold I will visit upon you the evil of your doings, and I will gather the remnant of my flock. And I will set up shepherds over them which shall feed them, and they shall fear no more, nor be dismayed, neither shall they be lacking, saith the Lord.' (Ezek. 34). 'Woe to the shepherds of Israel that feed themselves; should not the shepherds feed the flocks? Ye eat the fat, and clothe you with the wool, ye kill them that are fed, but ye feed not the flocks. The diseased have ye not strengthened, neither have ye healed that which was sick, neither have ye bound up that which was broken, neither have ye brought again that which was driven away, neither have ye sought that which was lost; but with force and with cruelty have ye ruled them. Thus saith the Lord, Behold I am against the shepherds, and I will require my flock at their hands, and cause them to cease from feeding the flock; neither shall the shepherds feed themselves any more; for I will deliver my flock from their mouth. Behold I, even I, will both search my sheep and seek them out, and will deliver them out of all places where they have been scattered in the cloudy and dark day. And as for you, O my flock, Behold I judge between cattle and cattle, between the rams and the he-goats. Is it a small thing to you to have eaten up the good pasture, but ye must tread down with your feet the residue of your pastures? and to have drank of the deep waters, but you must foul the residue with your feet? And as for my flock, they eat that which you have trodden with your feet, and they drink that which ye have fouled with your feet. Therefore, thus saith the Lord God unto them; Behold I, even I will judge between the fat cattle and the lean? Because ye have thrust with side and with shoulder, and pushed all the diseased with your horns, till ye have scattered them abroad,' etc. Read the rest. Particular churches may be scattered to dissolution, but none of the faithful members.

3. Christ has his time for returning to the souls of his servants which seem to be forsaken by him. 'Weeping may endure for a night, but joy cometh in the morning' (Ps. 30:5).

When he seems to be their enemy and writes bitter things against them, he is their surest friend and will justify them himself from their accusers. Though they may be troubled when they remember God, and their spirit is overwhelmed in them, and their souls refuse to be comforted, and they say, 'Will the Lord cast off for ever, and will he be favourable no more? Is his mercy clean gone for ever? Doth his promise fail for evermore? Hath God forgotten to be gracious? Hath he in anger shut up his tender mercies?' Yet must we rebuke this unbelief, and say, 'This is my infirmity; I will remember the works of the Lord; surely I will remember thy wonders of old. I will meditate of thy works, and talk of thy doings' (Ps. 77). The long night that has no day, the long winter that has no summer is the reward of the ungodly. But light arises to the righteous in his darkness, and 'joy to them that are upright in heart' (Ps. 92:4). Light is sown for them, and in season will spring up (Ps. 97:11). The righteousness which was hidden from the world by false accusations, and from ourselves by the terrors and mistakes of darkness, God will bring forth as light, and our judgement as the noon-day (Ps. 37:6). Our eclipse will vanish when the sun returns, and our sins no longer interpose. And though all our inquiries and complainings have not brought us out of the dark, yet 'God is the Lord who showeth us light' (Ps. 118:27), 'and in his light we shall see light.' (Ps. 36:9).

Therefore, say, O distrustful, trembling Christian, 'Why art thou cast down, O my soul! and why art thou thus disquieted within me? Hope thou in God, for I shall yet praise him, who is the health of my countenance and my God' (Pss. 42:5, 11, and 43:5). Though now you 'go mourning because of the oppression of the enemy, God will send out his light and truth, and they shall lead you, and bring you to his holy hill and tabernacle: and then you shall go with praise to the altar of God, even of God your exceeding joy' (Ps. 42:2-4).

Use 2. Learn, then, how to behave yourselves in the absence of your Lord, till his return. If you ask me how:

Answer 1. Do not be content and pleased with his absence. You must bear it, but not desire it. Otherwise you are either enemies, or children that have run themselves into such guilt and fears, that they take their father for their enemy.

2. Do not be too indifferent and insensitive to your Lord's departure. Love is not regardless of the company of our beloved. He may well take it ill when you can let him go and be as merry without him as if his absence were no loss to you. If you care no more for him, he will make you care, before you shall feel the comforts of his presence.

Such contempt is the way to a worse forsaking. Call after him till he return, if he hide his face.

3. Turn not aside to the creature for content, and seek not to make up the loss of his presence with any of the deceitful comforts of the world. Let him not see you take another in his stead, as if riches, or power, or worldly friends, or fleshly pleasure, would serve you instead of Christ. If once you come to this, he may justly leave you to your vain contents, and let them serve you as long as they can, and see how well they will supply his room. Oh, see that no idol is admitted into his place till Christ return.

4. Do not be emboldened, by his absence, to sin. Do not say in your hearts, as the evil servant did, 'My Lord delayeth his coming,' and so begin to smite your fellow-servants, and to eat, and drink with the drunken, lest your 'Lord come in a day when you look not for him, and cut you asunder, and appoint your portion with the hypocrites: there shall be weeping and gnashing of teeth' (Matt. 24:45-51). Because Christ does not come to judge the wicked as soon as they have sinned, they are emboldened to sin more fearlessly. And because sentence against an evil work is not speedily executed, the hearts of the sons of men are fully set in them to do evil (Eccl. 8:11) But, 'behold the Judge is at the door' (James 5:9). 'He that cometh will not tarry; and for all these things you must come to judgement' (Eccl. 11:9, and 12:14).

5. Do not be discouraged by your Lord's delay, but wait for his coming in faith and patience. Can you not wait such a short time for him? Oh! how quickly it will be accomplished. Do not sink into despondency of mind. Do not be dismayed at the duties or sufferings to which you are called. 'Lift up the hands that hang down, and the feeble knees, and make straight paths for your feet, lest that which is lame be turned out of the way, but let it rather be healed' (Heb. 12:12,13). 'Be steadfast, unmoveable, always abounding in the work of the Lord, forasmuch as ye know that your labour is not vain in the Lord' (1 Cor. 15:58). 'Be sober, and hope unto the end' (1 Pet. 1:13). 'Ye are the house of Christ, if ye hold fast the confidence, and the rejoicing of the hope firm unto the end' (Heb. 3:6, 14 and 6:11). 'Ye have need of patience, that having done the will of God, ye may inherit the promise' (Heb. 10:36, 11).

Doctrine 5

When Christ again appears to his disciples, their sorrows will be turned into joy. When Christ returns, joy returns, says David (Ps. 30:7). 'Thou didst hide thy face, and I was troubled.' But (vv. 11, 12) 'Thou has turned for me my mourning into dancing: thou hast put off my sackcloth, and girded me with gladness, to the end that my glory may sing praise to thee, and not be silent: O Lord my God, I will give thanks unto thee for ever.'

When the sun rises it is day and it dispels the winter frosts and revives the almost dying creatures, and calls up the life which was hidden in the seed, or retired into the root, after a sharp and spending winter. How quickly the sun's return restores the verdure and beauty of the earth, and clothes it in green, and spangles it with the ornaments of odoriferous flowers, and enriches it with sweet and plenteous fruits. The birds that were either hidden or silent, appear and sing, and the face of all things is changed into joy.

1. So is it with the poor deserted soul upon the return of Christ. Unbelieving doubts and fears vanish. The garments of sadness are laid aside, and those of gladness are put on. The language of distrust and despair are first turned into words of peace, and then into joyful thankfulness and praise. The soul that was not skilled in spiritual discourse, but complaining of a dead and frozen heart, of dull and cold and lifeless duties, is now taken up in rehearsing the works of infinite love, and searching into the mysteries of redemption, and reciting the great and precious promises, and magnifying the name and grace of its Redeemer, and extolling the praises of the everlasting kingdom, the heavenly glory, the blessed society, and especially of the Lamb, and of the eternal God.

You would not think that this is the same person who recently could scarcely think well of God, or that dwelt in tears, and dust, and darkness, and could think of nothing but sin and hell, and from every text and every providence, concluded nothing but undone, or damned. Would you think this joyful, thankful soul, were the same person who so recently was crying on the cross, 'My God, my God, why hast thou forsaken me?'; that could find nothing written on the tablets of his heart, but forsaken, miserable, and undone; that daily cried out, 'It is too late, there is no hope, I had a day of grace, but it is past and gone.'

When Christ returns, and causes his face to shine upon them, all this is turned into 'Praise and honour and glory unto the Lamb, and to the almighty and most holy God, that lives for ever, and is the everlasting joy and portion of his saints.' And sooner or later, it will be like this with all the upright who wait on God in the day of trial, and do not deal falsely in his covenant. The Son who was brought up with the Father, and was daily his delight, rejoicing always before him, rejoicing also in the habitable parts of the earth whose delights were with the sons of men, blesses the children of wisdom with participation in his delights; for 'blessed are they that keep his ways.' 'Blessed is the man that heareth him, watching daily at his gates, waiting at the posts of his doors: for he that findeth him findeth life, and shall obtain favour of the Lord' (Prov. 8:3-36).

Though Christ had left his disciples under fears and trouble, guilty of deserting him, and seemingly now deserted by him, yet early on the third day, he rose for their consolation, and sent them these joyful words in the first speech he utters, and that by a woman that had been sorrowful and a sinner, 'Go to my brethren, and say unto them, I ascend to my Father and your Father, and to my God and your God' (John 20:17). Those that his ministers have long been comforting in vain, Christ will revive when he returns, and comfort them in a moment, and with a word. The soul that now cries 'Oh, it is impossible, it will never be,' little knows how easy it is with Christ. It is but saying, 'Lazarus, arise' or, 'Let there be light,' and there will be life and light immediately at his command.

2. When he restores his ordinances and order to a forsaken church, and restores their holy opportunities and advantages of grace, what gladness and praising of their Redeemer will there be? As it was with the churches upon the death of Julian, and after the heathen and the Arian persecutions, in the happy reign of Constantine, Theodosius, Marcian, etc. How joyfully did the English exiles return to worship God in their native land after the death of Queen Mary. See the fall of Bonner and Gardiner, that had sacrificed so many holy Christians in the flames! How gladly did they grow in the soil that was manured with the blood and ashes of their faithful brethren, and reap the fruit of their fortitude and sufferings!

When Christ whipped the buyers and sellers out of the temple, and would not let them make the house of prayer a place of merchandise, what hosannas were sounded in Jerusalem (Matt. 21:15, 16). 'When the salvation of Israel cometh out of Zion, and the Lord bringeth back the captivity of his people, Jacob shall rejoice, and Israel shall be glad.'

(Ps. 14:7). 'Blessed are they that dwell in his house, for they will be still praising him. For a day in his courts is better than a thousand' (Ps. 84:4, 10). 'Blessed is the people that know the joyful sound; they shall walk, O Lord, in the light of thy countenance; in thy name shall they rejoice all the day, and in thy righteousness shall they be exalted: for the Lord is our defence, and the Holy One of Israel is our king' (Ps. 89:15-18). What gladness there was at a private meeting of a few Christians that met to pray for Peter when they saw that he had been delivered and had come to them (Acts 12:12 and 14). When the churches had rest, they were edified, and walked in the fear of the Lord, and in the comfort of the Holy Ghost (Acts 9:31).

3. But the great joy will be when Christ returns in his glory at the last day. What a multitude of sorrows will then be ended! And what a multitude of souls will then be comforted! What a multitude of desires and prayers, and expectations will then be answered! How many thousand that have sowed in tears will then reap in everlasting joy! When the creature shall be delivered from the bondage of corruption, into the glorious liberty of the sons of God (Rom. 8:26, 27). When all the faith and labour, and patience of all the saints from the beginning of the world, shall be rewarded with the rivers of celestial pleasure, and the just shall enter into their Master's joy (Matt. 25:21)

That you may the better understand the sweetness of all these sorts of joy, which Christ's return will bring to saints, observe these following ingredients in them.

1. It is Christ himself who is the object of their joy. He who is the dearly beloved of their souls, that for their sakes was made a man of sorrows. It is he who is their hope and help, with whom they are in covenant as their only Saviour, in whom they have trusted, with whom they have deponed their souls!

If he should fail them, all would fail them, and they would, of all men, be most miserable. They would be comfortless if he should not come to them, and were not their comfort. The world cannot help and comfort them, for it is empty, vain, a transient shadow. It will not comfort them, for it is malignant, and our professed enemy. For we know that we are of God, and the whole world is set on wickedness (or as some think, because *ho ponēro s* is put for the devil in the foregoing verse, and the article is used here also), is as it were planted into the devil, or put under the devil, to war against Christ and the holy seed. Indeed

Satan does seem in this war against the church to have something like the success he had against Christ himself. As Christ must be a man of sorrows and scorn, and be crucified as a blasphemer and a traitor, before he rejoiced the hearts of his disciples by his resurrection, so the church was a persecuted, scorned handful of men, for the first three hundred years, and then it rose by Christian emperors to some reputation, till Satan by another game overcame them by Judas' successors, who, for 'what will you give me' by way of pride and worldliness, betrayed them into that deplorable state in which they have continued these 900 years at least, so that the Christian name is confined to a sixth part of the world, and serious sanctified believers are persecuted more by the hypocrites that wear the livery of Christ, than by heathens and infidels themselves. And when the church is so low, almost like Christ on the cross and the grave, will not a resurrection be a joyful change? When it cries out on the cross, 'My God, my God, why hast thou forsaken me?' will not Christ appearing for its deliverance be a welcome sight?

It was when Adam had brought a curse on himself and his posterity and all the earth, that redemption by the holy seed was promised; and when Satan had conquered man, that Christ was promised to conquer him. It was when the world was destroyed by the deluge that its reparation was promised to Noah. It was when Abraham was a sojourner in a strange land, that the peculiar promises were made to him and his seed. It was when the Israelites were enslaved to extremity, that they were delivered. And it was when the sceptre was departing from Judah, and they and the world were gone from God, that Christ the light of the world was sent. And when the Son of Man comes, will he find faith on the earth?

When we see how vast the heathen and infidel kingdoms are, and what a poor despised people those are that set their chief hopes on heaven, and how Satan seems everywhere to prevail against them, and mostly by false and worldly Christians, what a trial is this to our faith and hope? As the disciples said of a crucified Christ, we trusted it had been he that should have redeemed Israel. We are almost ready in the hour of temptation to say, we trusted that God's name should have been hallowed, and his kingdom come, and his will be done on earth as it is in heaven? And oh, how seasonable, and how joyful will the church's resurrection be after such low and sad distress? Many a sad Christian under the sentence of death is going forward in fear and trouble, when in a moment they will be transmitted into the joyful presence of their Lord, and the possession of that which with weakness and fear they did but believe.

2. Christ will not come or be alone. With him will come the New Jerusalem. He will put glory on each member, but much more on the whole. Oh, how many of our old companions are now there! Not under temptation, or any of the tempter's power! Not under the darkness of ignorance, error or unbelief! Not under the pains of a languid, diseased, corruptible body! Not under the fear of sin, or Satan, or wicked men. Not under the terror of death or hell, of an accusing conscience, or the wrath of God. Oh, with what joy we will see and enjoy that glorious society! To be translated there from a world such as this, from such temptations, sins, fears and sorrows, from such perfidious malignant wickedness, what will it be but to be taken as from a gaol unto a kingdom, and from the suburbs of hell unto the communion of blessed saints and angels, and into the joy of our Lord.

Doctrine 6

Your joy no man will take from you. The joy that comes at Christ's return will be a secure and everlasting joy. It will be as impregnable as heaven itself. Christ and his church will be crucified no more. Do not look for Christ and his church in the grave. He is not here; he is risen. Who can we fear will deprive us of that joy?

1. Not ourselves, and therefore we need fear no other. Our folly and sin is our enemies' strength. They can do nothing against us without ourselves. The arrows that wound us are all feathered from our own wings. But our trying time will then be past, and confirmation will be the reward of conquest. He that has kept us in the day of our trial, will keep us in our state of rest and triumph. How the (now) fallen angels came to lose their first innocence and welfare is unknown to us. But we have a promise of being forever with Christ.

2. Nor will devils deprive us of that joy, neither by those malicious temptations with which they now molest and haunt us, nor by the unhappy advantages which we have given them by our sin, to corrupt our imaginations and thoughts, and affections, or to disturb our passions, or pervert our understandings, nor by any terror or violence to molest us.

3. Nor will any men take from us that joy. The blessed will increase in it; their joy will be ours and the wicked will be utterly disabled. They

will be miserable themselves in hell. They will no longer endanger us by flattering temptations, nor terrify us by threats, nor tread us down by their power, nor hurt us in their malice, nor render us odious by false accusations, nor triumph over us with pride and false reproach. They that said of the church, as of Christ, 'He trusted in God, let him deliver him now if he will have him; for he hath said, I am the Son of God' (Matt. 27:43), will see that God has delivered his church, and he will have it.

Use 1. Will not a firm belief in all this cause your soul to rejoice in all disappointments and sufferings on earth? Does not our dejectedness and lack of joy declare the sinful weakness of our faith? O sirs, our sadness, our impatience, our small desire to be with Christ, the little comfort that we fetch from heaven tell us that Christianity, and a life of faith, is a harder work than most imagine. The art and form and words of holiness are much more common than a holy, heavenly mind and life. Christ speaks many words of pity to his servants under sorrows and sinking grief, which some mistake for words of approbation or command. 'Why are ye afraid, O ye of little faith,' were words both of compassion and reproof. I am sure the great unbelief that appears in much of our dejectedness and sorrow deserves more reproof than our sufferings deserve to be entertained with those.

Use 2. I will therefore take my farewell of you, in advising and charging you as from God, that you should not be deceived by a flattering world, nor dejected by a frowning world, but place your hopes on those joys which no man can take from you. If you cannot trust the love of God, and the grace and promises of our Saviour, and the witness of the Holy Spirit, you must despair; for there is no other trust.

So many of you seem to have chosen this good part, the one thing necessary which will never be taken from you, that in the midst of our sorrows I must profess that I part with you with thankfulness and joy. And I will tell you why I am so thankful, that you may know what I would have you be for the time to come.

1. I thank the Lord, who chose for me such a comfortable station, even a people whom he purposed to bless.

2. I thank the Lord that I have not laboured among you in vain, and that he opened the hearts of such a great number of you, to receive his word with a teachable and willing mind.

3. I thank the Lord that he has made so many of you as helpful to your neighbours as I have been, and that you have not been uncharitable

to the souls of others, but have with great success sought the good of all.

4. I rejoice that God has kept you humble, that you have not been addicted to proud ostentation of your gifts or wisdom; nor inclined to invade any part of the sacred office, but to serve God in the capacity where he has placed you.

5. I rejoice that God has made you unanimous, and kept out sects and heresies and schisms, so that you have served him with one mind and mouth; and you have not been addicted to proud wranglings, disputes, and contentions, but have lived in unity, love and peace, and the practice of known and necessary truths.

6. I rejoice that your frequent meetings in your houses, spent only in reading, repeating your teacher's sermons, prayer and praise to God, have had none of those effects which the conventicles of proud opinionators and self-conceited persons use to have, and which have brought needful conversation and godly communication into suspicion, at least with some, that argue against duty from the abuse.

Yea, I rejoice that in this way so much good has been done by you. You have had over forty years' experience of the great benefit of such well ordered Christian conversation, increasing knowledge, quickening holy desires, prevailing with God, for marvellous, if not miraculous answers to your earnest prayers, keeping out errors and sects.

7. I am glad that you have had the great encouragement of so many sober, godly, able, peaceable ministers, in that part of the country round about you, and mostly throughout the neighbouring countries: men that avoided vain and bitter contentions, that engaged themselves in no sects or factions. Their principles and practices were reconciling and pacificatory; they consented to catechise all their parishioners, house by house, and to live in the peaceable practice of so much church discipline, as good Christians of several parties were all agreed in. And you have lived to see what that discipline was, and what were the effects of such agreement.

8. I am glad that you were kept from taking the solemn league and covenant,[2] and the engagement, and all consent to the change of the

[2] This was the 1643 agreement between the Scots and English Parliaments. It was designed to preserve Reformation principles and root out popery and prelacy. The English Parliamentarians stressed the civil rather than the religious side of it, as an aid in the struggle against Royalists. Although it was renewed in 1648 in Scotland, it was a dead letter in England after 1644.

constituted government of this kingdom.[3]

9. I greatly rejoice that family religion is so carefully kept up among you, that your children and apprentices seem to promise us a hopeful continuation of piety among you.

10. And I thank God, that so great a number of persons, eminent for holiness, temperance, humility and charity, have safely gone to heaven already, since I first came among you. Now having escaped from the temptations and troubles of this present evil world, they have left you an example worthy of imitation.

Having all this comfort in you concerning what is past, I will once more leave you some of my counsels and requests, for the time to come, which I earnestly entreat you not to neglect.

1. Spend most of your studies in confirming your belief of the truth of the gospel, the immortality of the soul, and the life to come, and in exercising that belief, and laying up your treasure in heaven. See that you are not merely content with talking of heaven, and speaking for it, but that your hopes, your hearts, and your conversation are there, and that you live for it, as worldlings do for the flesh.

2. Do not flatter yourselves with the hopes of long life on earth, but

---

[3] He continued this point with comments specifically related to the history of the time: 'I took the covenant myself, of which I repent, and I will tell you why: I never gave it except to one man (that I remember) and he professed himself to be a Papist physician newly turned Protestant. He came to me to give it to him. I was persuaded that he took it in false dissimulation, and it troubled me to think what it was to draw multitudes of men by carnal interest so falsely to take it. I kept it and the engagement from being taken in your town and country.... Besides the illegality, there are two things that cause me to be against it: 1. That men should make a mere dividing engine, and pretend it is a means of unity. We all knew at that time when it was imposed, that a great, if not the greatest part, of church and kingdom were of another mind, and that as learned and worthy men as the world had were for prelacy (such as Usher, Morton, Hall, Davenant, Brownrig, &c.) And to make our terms of union to be such that should exclude so many and such men, was but to imitate those church dividers and persecutors,... 2. It was an imposing on the providence of God, to tie ourselves by vows to that as unchangeable, which, for all we knew, God might later change. It was as if we were the masters of his providence. No man then knew but that God might so alter many circumstances, as to make some things sins that were then taken for duty, and some things to be duty, which then passed for sin. And when such changes come, we that should have been content with God's obligations, find ourselves ensnared in our own rash vows.'

make it the sum of all your religion, care and business, to be ready for a safe and comfortable death. Until you can fetch comfort from the life to come, you can have no comfort that true reason can justify.

3. Live as in a constant war against all fleshly lusts, and love not the world, as it cherishes those lusts. Take heed of the love of money, as the root of manifold evils. Think of riches with more fear than desire, since Christ has told us how hard and dangerous it makes our way to heaven. If a man falls deeply in love with riches, he is never to be trusted, but becomes false to God, to all others and to himself.

4. Be furnished beforehand with expectation and patience, for all evils that may befall you. Do not make too much of sufferings, especially poverty, or wrong from men. It is sin and folly in poor men that they overvalue riches and are not thankful for their peculiar blessings. I hope that God will give you more quietness than many others, because none of you are rich. It is a great means of safety to have nothing that tempts another man's desire, or for which he envies you. Despised men live quietly, and he that has an empty purse can sing among the robbers. He who lies on the ground need not fear falling.

When Judea (and similarly when England by Saxons, Danes, etc.) was conquered, the poor were left alone to possess and till the land, and they had more than before. It was the great and rich that were destroyed, or carried or driven away. Is it not a great benefit to have your souls saved from rich men's temptations, and your bodies from the envy, assaults, fears, and miseries that they are under?

5. Take heed of self-conceited, unhumbled understanding, and of hasty and rash conclusions. It is the fool that rages and is confident. Sober men are conscious of so much darkness and weakness that they are suspicious of their apprehensions. Proud self-conceitedness, and rash, hasty conclusions cause most of the mischiefs in the world which might be prevented if men had the humility and patience to wait until things have been thoroughly weighed and tried. Do not be ashamed to profess uncertainty where you are indeed uncertain. Humble doubting is much safer than confident erring.

6. Maintain union and communion with all true Christians on earth. Hold, then, to catholic principles of mere Christianity, without which you will crumble into sects. Love Christians as Christians, but the best most. Locally, do not separate from anyone, unless they separate from Christ or deny you their communion, unless you sin. The zeal of a sect as such, is partial, turbulent, hurtful to dissenters, and makes men like

thorns and thistles. But the zeal of Christianity as such, is pure and peaceable, full of mercy and good fruits; mellow, and sweet, and inclined to the good of all.

If God give you a faithful or a tolerable public minister, be thankful to God, and love, honour, and encourage him. Do not let the imperfections of the Common Prayer make you separate from his communion. Prejudice will make all modes of worship that differ from what we prefer, to seem like some heinous, sinful crime. But humble Christians are most careful about the frame of their own hearts, and conscious of so much faultiness in themselves, and all their service of God, that they are not apt to accuse and aggravate the failings of others, especially in matters which God has left to our own determination. Whether we should pray with a book or without, in diverse short prayers or one long one; whether the people should sing God's praise in tunes or speak it in prose, etc., is left to be determined by the general rules of concord, order, and edification. Yet do not withdraw from the communion of sober, godly non-conformists, though they are falsely called schismatics by others.

7. Be sure that you maintain due honour and subjection to your governors: 'Fear the Lord and the king, and meddle not with them that are given to change' (Prov. 24:21). 'Curse not the king, no not in thy thought, and curse not the rich in thy bed-chamber; for a bird of the air shall carry the voice and that which hath wings shall tell the matter' (Eccl. 10:20).

Obey God with your first and absolute obedience, and do not obey man over and against him. But obey the just commands of magistrates, out of obedience to God, and suffer patiently when you cannot obey. If God should ever cast you under oppressing and persecuting governors, in your patience possess your souls. Trust God and keep your innocence, and abhor all thoughts of rebellion or revenge. He that believes will not be hasty. Do nothing but what God will own, and then commit yourselves and your way to him. Repress wrath, and hate unpeaceable counsels. Our way and our time must be only God's way and time. Self-saying men are usually the destroyers of themselves and others. Peter, who drew his sword for Christ, denied him the same night, with oaths and curses. Fools trust themselves, and wise men trust God. Fools tear the tree by beating down the fruit that is unripe and harsh, and wise men stay till it is ripe and sweet, and will drop into their hands. Fools rip up the mother for an untimely birth, but wise men stay till maturity gives it to them. Fools take red-hot iron to be gold, till it burn their fingers to the bone; they rush into seditions and blood, as if it were a matter of jest. But wise men sow the fruit of righteousness in peace, and as much as it is possible with them, live peaceably with all men. All men are mortal, both oppressors and oppressed. Wait a little, and mortality will change the scene. God's time is best. Martyrdom seldom kills a hundredth of those killed by wars, and he who regards martyrdom to be loss is no true believer. Christ is more interested in his gospel, church, and honour than we. Queen Mary's cruelty, and the bishops' bonfires, caused religion to be received universally more easily once her short reign was ended. We may learn from the fool, who seeing great guns and muskets, asked what they were for, and was answered that they were to kill men. He replied, 'Don't men die here without killing? In our country they die of themselves.'

8. Be sure to keep up family religion, especially in the careful education of youth. Keep them from evil company, and from temptations, especially of idleness, fullness, and baits of lust. Read the Scripture and good books, and call upon God, and sing his praise. Recreate youth with reading the history of the church, and the lives of holy men and martyrs. Instruct them in catechisms and fundamentals.

9. Above all, live in love to God and man. Do not let not selfishness and worldliness prevail against it. Think of God's goodness as equal to his greatness and wisdom. Take yourselves as members of the same body with all true Christians. Blessed are they that faithfully practise those three grand principles which all profess, viz., 1. To love God as God above all (and so to obey him.) 2. To love our neighbours as ourselves. 3. And to do as we would be done by. Love is not envious, malignant, censorious; it does not slander, it does not persecute, it does not oppress, it does not defraud; it does not strive to gain by another's loss. Get men once to love their neighbours as themselves, and you may easily prognosticate peace, quietness, and concord; happiness to the land; and salvation to the people's souls.

Finally, brethren, live in love, and the God of love and peace will be among you. The Lord save you from the evils of which I have here, and often warned you. Remember with thankfulness, the many years of abundant mercy which we have enjoyed (though too much mixed with our sins, and vilified by some). 'Comfort yourselves together, and edify one another, even as also ye do; and I beseech you, brethren, to know them which labour among you, and are over you in the Lord, and admonish you, and to esteem them very highly in love, for their work sake, and be at peace among yourselves.' (1 Thes. 5:11-13). And the Lord deeply write on all our hearts these blessed words, 'We have known and believed the love that God hath to us: God is love, and he that dwelleth in love, dwelleth in God, and God in him' (1 John 4:16). And remember, 'Seeing all these things shall be dissolved, what manner of persons ought ye to be in all holy conversation and godliness, looking for and hasting the coming of the day of God, wherein the heavens being on fire, shall be dissolved and the elements shall melt with fervent heat; nevertheless we, according to his promise, look for new heavens and a new earth, wherein dwelleth righteousness' (2 Peter 3:11-13).

I need not lengthen my counsels further to you now, having been called by the will and providence of God to leave behind me a multitude of books, which may remind you of what you heard and acquaint the world with the doctrine I have taught you. If further studies teach me to retract and amend many failings in the writings or practice of my unripe and less experienced age, I hope it will not seem strange or ungrateful to you. Though we must hold fast the truth we have received, both you and I are much to be blamed if we do not grow in knowledge, both in matter, words, and method. The Lord grant that also we may grow in faith, obedience, patience, in hope, love, and desire to be with Christ.

Now the God of peace, that brought again from the dead our Lord Jesus, that great Shepherd of the sheep, through the blood of the everlasting covenant, make you perfect in every good work, to do his will, working in you that which is well-pleasing in his sight, through Jesus Christ, to whom be glory for ever and ever. Amen. (Heb. 13:20, 21).

Bibliography

1. Works By Richard Baxter

A Call to the Unconverted. 1657; reprint, Grand Rapids: Baker Book House, 1976.

The Autobiography of Richard Baxter (Reliquiae Baxterianae). 1696; abridged by J. M. Lloyd Thomas, London: Dent, 1925; reprint, with an introduction, and edited, by N. H. Keeble. London: Dent, 1974.

Invitation to Live: An Up to Date Version of a Timeless Classic by Richard Baxter. Edited by John Blanchard. Durham: Evangelical Press, 1991.

The Ministry We Need: An Abridged and Re-written Version of 'The Reformed Pastor' by Richard Baxter. Edited by W. Stuart Owen. London: Grace Publications Trust, 1997.

Poetical Fragments. 1681; reprint, Westmead, England: Gregg International Publishers, 1971.

The Practical Works of the Rev. Richard Baxter. Edited by the Rev. William Orme, in 23 Volumes. London: James Duncan, 1830.

The Practical Works of Richard Baxter in Four Volumes. London: George Virtue, 1846; reprint, Ligonier, PA: Soli Deo Gloria Publications, 1990.

The Reformed Pastor. 1656; abridged by William Brown, 1829; reprint, with introduction by J. I. Packer, Edinburgh: Banner of Truth Trust, 1974.

The Saints' Everlasting Rest. 1650; reprint, abridged, London: Religious Tract Society, 19-?.

The Saints' Everlasting Rest. 1650; reprint, edited by Christopher Pipe, London: Hodder and Stoughton, 1994.

2. Secondary Literature

Adam, Peter. *Speaking God's Words: A Practical Theology of Preaching.* Leicester, England: IVP, 1996.

Adams, Jay. *Preaching with Purpose.* Phillipsburg: Presbyterian and Reformed Publishing Company, 1982.

Azurdia, Arturo. G. III. *Spirit Empowered Preaching: The Vitality of the Holy Spirit in Preaching.* Ross-shire, Great Britain: Mentor, 1998.

Boersma, Hans. *A Hot Pepper Corn: Richard Baxter's Doctrine of Justification in its Seventeenth-Century Context of Controversy.* Zoetermeer, Netherlands: Uitgeverij Boekencentrum, 1993.

Caiger, J. A. 'Baxter's Reformed Pastor.' In *Profitable for Doctrine and Reproof.* Papers presented at the Puritan Conference, 1967, pp. 42-53.

Chapell, Bryan. *Christ-Centred Preaching.* Grand Rapids: Baker Books, 1994.

Cook, P. 'The Life and Work of a Minister According to the Puritans.' In *A Goodly Heritage.* Papers presented at the Puritan Studies Conference, 1958, pp. 8-17.

Davies, Horton. *Worship and Theology in England.* Vol. 1, *From Cranmer to Hooker, 1534-1603*; Vol. 2, *From Andrewes to Baxter and Fox, 1534-1690.* Princeton: Princeton University Press, 1961-75. Combined edition, Grand Rapids: William B. Eerdmans Publishing Company, 1996.

Davies, Horton. *The Worship of the English Puritans.* Dacre Press, 1948; reprint, Morgan, PA: Soli Deo Gloria Publications, 1997.

Freer, Brian. 'The Pastor as Preacher in Seventeenth Century England.' In *The Office and Work of the Minister.* Papers presented at the Westminster Conference, 1986, pp. 55-76.

Goldsworthy, Graeme. *Preaching the Whole Bible as Christian Scripture: The Application of Biblical Theology to Expository Preaching.* Grand Rapids: Eerdmans Publishing Company, 2000.

Haller, William. *The Rise of Puritanism.* New York: Columbia University Press, 1938; reprint, New York: Harper and Brothers, 1957.

Hill, Christopher. *The Century of Revolution 1603-1714.* Edinburgh: Thomas Nelson and Sons, 1961.

Howard, Leon. *Essays on Puritans and Puritanism.* Edited by James Barbour and Thomas Quirk. Albquerque: University of New Mexico Press, 1986.

Kaiser, Walter C. Jr. *Toward an Exegetical Theology: Biblical Exegesis for Preaching and Teaching.* Grand Rapids: Baker Book House, 1981.

Keeble, N. H. *Richard Baxter: Puritan Man of Letters.* Oxford: Clarendon Press, 1982.

Keeble, N. H. 'Richard Baxter's Preaching Ministry: its History and Texts.' *Journal of Ecclesiastical History*, vol. 35, no. 4 (October 1984): 539-59.

Ladell, A. R. *Richard Baxter: Puritan and Mystic*. London: SPCK, 1925.

Lewis, Peter. *The Genius of Puritanism*. Heath, Sussex: Carey Publications, 1979.

Lloyd Jones, D. Martyn. *Preaching and Preachers*. Grand Rapids: Zondervan, 1971.

Lloyd Jones, D. Martyn. *The Puritans: Their Origins and Successors*. Edinburgh: Banner of Truth Trust, 1987.

Logan, Samuel T. ed. *The Preacher and Preaching: Reviving the Art in the Twentieth Century*. Phillipsburg, NJ: Presbyterian and Reformed Publishing Company, 1986.

MacArthur, John. *The Glory of Heaven*. Crossway Books, 1996.

Martin, A. N. *What's Wrong with Preaching Today?* Edinburgh: Banner of Truth Trust, 1967.

Martin, Hugh. *Puritanism and Richard Baxter*. London: SCM Press, 1954.

Millar, Perry, and Thomas H. Johnson, ed. *The Puritans: A Sourcebook of Their Writings*. Vol. 1. New York: Harper, 1963.

Morgan, Irvonwy. *The Godly Preachers of the Elizabethan Church*. London: Epworth Press, 1965.

Murray, Iain. *The Puritan Hope*. Edinburgh: Banner of Truth Trust, 1971.

Murray, John. 'The Study of the Bible.' In *Collected Writings of John Murray*. Vol. 1, *The Claims of Truth*. Edinburgh: Banner of Truth Trust, 1976.

New, John, F. H. *Anglican and Puritan: The Basis of Their Opposition, 1558-1640*. London: Adam and Charles Black, 1964.

Nuttall, Geoffrey F. *The Puritan Spirit*. London: Epworth, 195-.

Nuttall, Geoffrey F. *Richard Baxter*. London: Thomas Nelson, 1965.

Packer, J. I. *Knowing God*. London: Hodder and Stoughton, 1973.

Packer, J. I. *A Quest For Godliness: The Puritan Vision of the Christian Life*. Wheaton: Crossway Books, 1990.

Perkins, William. *The Art of Prophesying*. 1592; reprint, Edinburgh: Banner of Truth Trust, 1996.

Pipa, Joseph A. 'William Perkins and the Development of Puritan Preaching.' Ph.D. diss., Westminster Theological Seminary, 1985.

Piper, John. *The Supremacy of God in Preaching*. Grand Rapids: Baker Book House, 1990.

Powicke, Frederick. J. *A Life of the Reverend Richard Baxter,*

1615-1691, London: Jonathan Cape Ltd., 1924.

Powicke, Frederick. J. *The Reverend Richard Baxter Under the Cross (1662-1691)*, London: Jonathan Cape Ltd., 1927.

Rooy, Sidney H. *The Theology of Missions in the Puritan Tradition*. Grand Rapids: William B. Eerdmans Publishing Company, 1965.

Rowell, Ed. *Preaching with Spiritual Passion*. The Pastor's Soul Series. Edited by David L. Goetz. Minneapolis: Bethany House Publishers, 1998.

Ryken, Leland. *Worldly Saints: The Puritans as they Really Were*. Grand Rapids: Zondervan, 1986.

Sarles, Ken. L. 'The English Puritans: A Historical Paradigm of Biblical Counseling.' In John F. MacArthur and Wayne A. Mack, et. al., *Introduction to Biblical Counseling: A Basic Guide to the Principles and Practice of Counseling*, Dallas: Word, 1994, pp. 21-42.

Stitzinger, James F. 'Pastoral Ministry in History.' In John F. MacArthur, et. al., *Rediscovering Pastoral Ministry: Shaping Contemporary Ministry with Biblical Mandates*, Dallas: Word, 1995, pp. 34-63.

Stitzinger, James F. 'The History of Expository Preaching.' In John F. MacArthur, et. al., *Rediscovering Expository Preaching: Balancing the Science and Art of Biblical Exposition*, Dallas: Word, 1992, pp. 36-60.

Stott, John W. *The Preacher's Portrait*. Grand Rapids: Eerdmans Publishing Company, 1961.

Toon, Peter. *Puritans and Calvinism*. Pennsylvania: Reiner Publishers, 1973.

Watkins, Owen C. *The Puritan Experience*. London: Routledge, 1972.

Westminster Confession of Faith. 1646; reprint, Inverness: Free Presbyterian Publications, 1976.

Wooldridge, D. R. 'Richard Baxter's Social and Economic Teaching.' In *A Goodly Heritage*. Papers presented at the Puritan Studies Conference, December 1958.

Subject Index

Scripture Index